YOUR EXAM PREP JOURNEY STARTS NOW

Welcome to the Becker CPA Exam Review course and congratulations on taking the first steps to becoming a CPA! With more than 60 years of experience and a time-tested learning approach, we're here to help you gain the confidence you need to pass the CPA Exam.

GET STARTED ON YOUR PATH TO CPA EXAM SUCCESS WITH THESE STEPS:

1. ACCESS BECKER'S CPA EXAM REVIEW COURSE

- Log in to Becker's CPA Exam Review at **online.becker.com**
- Watch the orientation video
- Download the mobile app to access your course and study on the go; Available for Apple® and Android™ tablets and smartphones

Pick up right where you left off. Your progress will automatically synchronize among all your devices.

2. DEVELOP YOUR STUDY PLAN

- Create your customized study plan using Becker's interactive **Study Planner**

3. START STUDYING

- Follow your study plan and reach out for academic support

4. CONNECT WITH US

- Visit our blog at **beckerpinnacle.com** to stay up-to-date on our latest tips, stories, and advice
- You can also find us on Facebook, Twitter, LinkedIn, YouTube, and Google+
- For more information on getting started, visit **becker.com/cpagettingstarted**

For Exams Scheduled After June 30, 2019

FINAL REVIEW

AUDITING

ACADEMIC HELP
Click on Customer and Academic Support under CPA Resources at
http://www.becker.com/cpa-review.html

CUSTOMER SERVICE AND TECHNICAL SUPPORT
Call 1-877-CPA-EXAM (outside the U.S. +1-630-472-2213)
or click Customer and Academic Support under CPA Resources at
http://www.becker.com/cpa-review.html

This textbook contains information that was current at the time of printing. Your course software will be updated on a regular basis as the content that is tested on the CPA Exam evolves and as we improve our materials. Note the version reference below and click on Replacement Textbooks under CPA Resources at http://www.becker.com/cpa-review.html to learn if a newer version of this book is available to be ordered.

V 3.4

ISBN: 978-1-943628-88-9

Printed in the United States of America.

LICENSE AGREEMENT—TERMS & CONDITIONS

DO NOT DOWNLOAD, ACCESS, AND/OR USE ANY OF THESE MATERIALS (AS THAT TERM IS DEFINED BELOW) UNTIL YOU HAVE READ THIS LICENSE AGREEMENT CAREFULLY. IF YOU DOWNLOAD, ACCESS, AND/OR USE ANY OF THESE MATERIALS, YOU ARE AGREEING AND CONSENTING TO BE BOUND BY AND ARE BECOMING A PARTY TO THIS LICENSE AGREEMENT ("AGREEMENT").

The printed Materials provided to you and/or the Materials provided for download to your computer and/or provided via a web application to which you are granted access are NOT for sale and are not being sold to you. You may NOT transfer these Materials to any other person or permit any other person to use these Materials. You may only acquire a license to use these Materials and only upon the terms and conditions set forth in this Agreement. Read this Agreement carefully before downloading, and/or accessing, and/or using these Materials. Do not download and/or access, and/or use these Materials unless you agree with all terms of this Agreement.

NOTE: You may already be a party to this Agreement if you registered for a Becker Professional Education CPA Final Review program (the "Program") or placed an order for these Materials online or using a printed form that included this License Agreement. Please review the termination section regarding your rights to terminate this License Agreement and receive a refund of your payment.

Grant: Upon your acceptance of the terms of this Agreement, in a manner set forth above, Becker Professional Development Corporation ("Becker") hereby grants to you a non-exclusive, revocable, non-transferable, non-sublicensable, limited license to use (as defined below) the Materials by downloading them onto a computer and/or by accessing them via a web application using a user ID and password (as defined below), and any Materials to which you are granted access as a result of your license to use these Materials and/or in connection with the Program on the following terms:

During the Term (as defined below) of this Agreement, you may:

- use the Materials for preparation for one or more parts of the CPA exam (the "Exam"), and/or for your studies relating to the subject matter covered by the Program and/or the Exam), and/or for your studies relating to the subject matter covered by the Materials and/or the Exam, including taking electronic and/or handwritten notes during the Program, provided that all notes taken that relate to the subject matter of the Materials are and shall remain Materials subject to the terms of this Agreement;
- download the Materials onto any single device;
- download the Materials onto a second device so long as the first device and the second device are not used simultaneously;
- download the Materials onto a third device so long as the first, second, and third device are not used simultaneously; and
- download the Materials onto a fourth device so long as the first, second, third, and fourth device are not used simultaneously.

The number of installations may vary outside of the U.S. Please review your local office policies and procedures to confirm the number of installations granted—your local office's policies and procedures regarding the number of allowable activations of downloads supersedes the limitations contained herein and is controlling.

You may not:

- use the Materials for any purpose other than as expressly permitted above;
- use the downloaded Materials on more than one device, computer terminal, or workstation at the same time;
- make copies of the Materials;
- rent, lease, license, lend, or otherwise transfer or provide (by gift, sale, or otherwise) all or any part of the Materials to anyone;
- permit the use of all or any part of the Materials by anyone other than you;
- share your user ID or password with anyone else; or
- reverse engineer, decompile, disassemble, or create derivate works of the Materials.

Materials: As used in this Agreement, the term "Materials" means and includes any printed materials provided to you by Becker, and/or to which you are granted access by Becker (directly or indirectly) in connection with your license of the Materials and/or the Program, and shall include notes you take (by hand, electronically, digitally, or otherwise) while using the Materials relating to the subject matter of the Materials; any and all electronically-stored/accessed/delivered, and/or digitally-stored/accessed/delivered materials included under this License via download to a computer or via access to a web application, and/or otherwise provided to you and/or to which you are otherwise granted access by Becker (directly or indirectly), including, but not limited to, applications downloadable from a third party, for example Google® or Amazon®, in connection with your license of the Materials.

Title: Becker is and will remain the owner of all title, ownership rights, intellectual property, and all other rights and interests in and to the Materials that are subject to the terms of this Agreement. The Materials are protected by the copyright laws of the United States and international copyright laws and treaties.

Use of Navigator 2.0: If your employer or college/university has instructed Becker to use its Navigator 2.0 to track your studies, the following will occur: a) once you have activated your software (course log-in), you will be asked to set up your study planner. In order to do this, you may be required to provide information about yourself as part of the Program registration process, or as part of your continued use of the Materials. You agree that any registration information you give to Becker will be shared by Becker with your employer or college/university ; and b) once that is done, Navigator 2.0 will automatically track if you are behind in your studies based on your study planner, your office location, your service line within the firm, your college/university course, which course parts were purchased (Audit and Attestation, Financial Accounting and Reporting, Business Environment and Concepts, and Regulation), what format are you using (online, live, self-study), your course progress, study time details (hours/min in course, # of log-ins, last log in), exam progress details including: whether you applied to take the exam, and if so, the state to which you applied; whether you received your NTS (notice to schedule), and if so, its expiration date; whether you scheduled your exam, and if so, the date; whether you received any scores and what they were; and the number of attempts to pass each of the four parts.

Navigator 2.0 Liability Provisions: You hereby waive any claims, causes of action, and damages, and agree to hold harmless and indemnify Becker and its affiliates, officers, agents, and employees from any claim, suit or action arising from or related to your use of the Materials, the sharing of any of your information by Becker with your employer or violation of these terms, including any liability or expense arising from claims, losses, damages, suits, judgments, litigation costs and attorneys' fees.

SUBJECT TO THE OVERALL PROVISION ABOVE, YOU EXPRESSLY UNDERSTAND AND AGREE THAT BECKER, ITS PARENT CORPORATION, SUBSIDIARIES AND AFFILIATES, AND THE OFFICERS, AGENTS AND EMPLOYEES OF THOSE ENTITIES, SHALL NOT BE LIABLE TO YOU FOR ANY LOSS OR DAMAGE THAT MAY BE INCURRED BY YOU, INCLUDING BUT NOT LIMITED TO LOSS OR DAMAGE AS A RESULT BECKER SHARING YOUR INFORMATION WITH YOUR EMPLOYER OR COLLEGE/UNIVERSITY.

THE LIMITATIONS ON BECKER'S LIABILITY TO YOU IN THE PARAGRAPHS ABOVE SHALL APPLY WHETHER OR NOT BECKER HAS BEEN ADVISED OF OR SHOULD HAVE BEEN AWARE OF THE POSSIBILITY OF ANY SUCH LOSSES ARISING.

Term: The license granted under this Agreement commences upon your receipt of these Materials, as further delineated within the Term and Termination sections herein. The duration of the license grant under this Agreement is contingent on the product offering you have selected (referred to individually as, the "Term").

- **<u>4 part CPA</u>:** eighteen (18) months after you log-in to access the Materials, which is the first time you visit the Becker homepage and log-in using your user identification and password; or upon expiration of the twenty-four (24) months period beginning upon your purchase of the Material, whichever of these periods first transpires.
- **<u>Becker Bundle</u>:** for as long as you are using the Materials until you pass the exam. Provided, however, Becker has the right to disable your account if your account is inactive for three years, meaning you have not logged into your account for three years. If we have disabled your account due to inactivity and you have not passed the exam, call Becker at 800-868-3900 and we will reactive your account at no additional charge.

Termination: This license shall terminate upon the earlier of: (i) ten (10) business days after notice to you of non-payment of or default on any payment due Becker which has not been cured within such 10-day period; or (ii) immediately if you fail to comply with any of the limitations set forth in the Grant section above; or (iii) upon expiration of the Term. In addition, upon termination of this license for any reason, you must delete or otherwise remove from your computer and/or other device(s) any Materials you downloaded, including, but not limited to, any archival copies you may have made. The Title, Exclusion of Warranties, Exclusion of Damages, Indemnification and Remedies, Severability of Terms and Governing Law provisions, and any amounts due, shall survive termination of the license granted herein.

Your Limited Right to Terminate this License and Receive a Refund: You may terminate this license for the in-class, online, and self-study Programs in accordance with Becker's refund policy as provided below.

Cancellations and Refunds: To cancel your enrollment and receive a refund, contact Becker Professional Education at 800-868-3900.

Textbooks should be returned within 10 days of notification of withdrawal. Students should contact Becker for a "Return Materials Authorization" number prior to shipping returns. Students should ship materials by certified mail or an alternative traceable method. Flashcards and the material license fees for the Becker Promise are non-refundable. The cost to return materials is the responsibility of the student. Refunds will be made within 30 days from the date of cancellation. Non-receipt of shipment disputes must be made with 90 days of original purchase date.

All returns must be sent to: Becker Professional Education.
Attn: Becker Returns, 200 Finn Ct., Farmingdale NY, 11735

For **Online CPA Exam Review Course and CPA Final Review course students***, a full tuition refund (less any applicable savings and fees) will be issued within 10 days of initial purchase or first login, whichever comes first.

For **Live Format and Cohort Program CPA Review students***, a full tuition refund (minus all applicable savings) will be issued to students who withdraw on or before the 5th business day or if students do not attend any part of the course (no-shows) after the start date of the scheduled section and provided that electronic course materials are not accessed. Thereafter, no refund will be issued as full access to course content has been granted.

Under certain circumstances, a live class may be cancelled up to 5 days in advance of the scheduled start date. Students will be provided with rescheduling options which could include access to self-study materials when live courses are not available. If rescheduling efforts are not successful, a refund for the cancelled course section may be issued and access suspended provided that the section content has not been accessed.

No Shows are students who never attend a live/live online class and do not access any portion of the course software/electronic materials.

For **Atlanta Intensive and Final Review students***, a full tuition refund (minus all applicable savings) will be issued to students who withdraw on or before the 2nd class of the first scheduled part. Thereafter, no refund will be issued as full access to course content has been granted.

For **SkillMaster Workshops**: A full refund will be issued to students who withdraw at least 10 business days before the scheduled workshop. Thereafter, no refund will be issued.

(*Applicable in all states except those noted below.)

The following cancellation policy is applicable for students in Alabama, Arkansas, District of Columbia, Kansas, Kentucky, Louisiana, Nebraska, Nevada, New Hampshire, New Mexico, Oklahoma, West Virginia:

If cancellation occurs within 3 business days of registration, all monies paid by the student will be refunded even if classes have already started.

A full tuition refund (minus all applicable savings and fees) will be issued to students who withdraw on or before the 5th business day after the start date of the first scheduled section; thereafter, students are entitled to a prorated refund (minus all applicable savings and fees) for the unused portion through 60% of the part taken (75% in Arkansas and DC).

For example, the refund for a candidate who withdraws after completing 12 hours (3 sessions) of Audit classes will be calculated as follows:

- Amount Paid $1131.00
- Amount to be Prorated $1131.00
- 8 Hours Cancelled / 20 Hours Scheduled × $1131.00 = $452.00 (Amount Refunded)

Residents are not required to submit written notification of withdrawal.

New Hampshire Students: Any buyer may cancel this transaction by submitting written notification of withdrawal any time prior to midnight of the third business day after the date of this transaction.

Oklahoma Students: Becker Professional Education is licensed by Oklahoma Board of Private Vocational Schools, 700 N. Classen Blvd. #250, Oklahoma City, OK 73118.

Classroom Locations: University of Oklahoma, 307 West Brooks, Room 200, Norman, OK 73019; Oklahoma Christian University, 2501 E Memorial Rd., Edmond, OK 73136; and Oklahoma State University, 108 Gunderson Hall, Stillwater, OK 74078.

Tennessee Students: At a minimum, refunds are calculated as follows:

Date of Withdrawal During:	Percent Refund of Tuition (Less Administrative Fee)
First day of scheduled classes	100%
Balance of week 1	90%
Week 2	75%
Weeks 3 and 4	25%
Weeks 5–8	0%

Refunds are to be prorated as of last day of actual attendance, notification is not required. All monies paid by an applicant will be refunded if requested within three days after signing an enrollment agreement and making an initial payment.

Holder in Due Course Rule: Any holder of this consumer credit contract is subject to all claims and defenses which the debtor could assert against the seller of goods and services obtained pursuant hereto or with the proceeds hereof. Recovery hereunder by the debtor shall not exceed that paid by the debtor. (This Federal TradeCom Regulation became in effect 5/14/75.)

Becker Professional Education is licensed by Oklahoma Board of Private Vocational Schools, 700 N. Classen Blvd. #250, Oklahoma City, OK 73118.

NON-REFUNDABLE ITEMS: Charges for Flashcards, Supplemental Multiple-Choice Questions, 0% APR* Financing Processing Fee and the Becker Promise material license fee are non-refundable.

*Annual Percentage Rating

Attendance:

<u>CPA Exam Review Courses—Live Classroom Non-F1 Students</u>

Attendance is defined as a student physically attending a live classroom on the enrolled/registered dates and times. BPE tracks attendance through rosters at live classes for students who selected and enrolled in this format. Classroom coordinators or student assistants are responsible for collecting attendance information. The faculty member supervises the attendance process at each class.

The purpose of BPE's CPA Exam review course is to prepare students for the CPA Exam. BPE does not issue grades, degrees, licenses or diplomas at course completion. A student may request a live course completion certificate by calling Becker's customer service at 800-868-3900. CPA live course completion certificates are offered for each section of the course (Audit, Business, Financial and Regulation). A student must attend a minimum of 50% of the live lectures for each section to receive the course completion certificate for that section. The student must complete any classes not attended live by viewing the corresponding lecture content (which is similar in length and content as the Live Course) using Becker's e-learning platform.

The student must demonstrate completion of the relevant e-learning lectures by providing the Performance Summary report. Upon confirmation that the student has completed 100% of the lectures with at least 50% of the lectures in the live classroom, the student will receive the course completion certificate.

Students who are tardy or depart early must notify the instructor who will note on the attendance sheet with "T" for tardy (arriving 20 or more minutes late) and/or "ED" at early departure (leaving 20 or more minutes before the end of class). All students are required to sign in upon arrival at the class. Note that receiving a "T" or "ED" means that student may not count that class toward the live attendance requirement to receive a completion certificate.

No Shows are students who never attend a live/live online class and do not access any portion of the course software/electronic materials.

CPA Exam Review Courses—LiveOnline (LiveOnline courses are not I-20 eligible)

Attendance is defined as a student logging in to a LiveOnline webcast on the enrolled/registered dates and times. BPE tracks attendance using the webinar platform's built-in tracking of when registered students log in and log off. LiveOnline webcast registration and attendance tracking are the responsibility of the U.S. Accounting Operations team.

The purpose of BPE's CPA Exam review course is to prepare students for the CPA Exam. BPE does not issue grades, degrees, licenses or diplomas at course completion. A student may request a LiveOnline course completion certificate by calling Becker's customer service at 800-868-3900. CPA LiveOnline course completion certificates are offered for each section of the course (Audit, Business, Financial and Regulation). A student must attend a minimum of 50% of the LiveOnline lectures for each section to receive the course completion certificate for that section. The student must complete any classes not attended via webcast by viewing the corresponding lecture content using Becker's e-learning platform. The student must demonstrate completion of the relevant e-learning lectures by providing the Performance Summary report. Upon confirmation that the student has completed 100% of the lectures with at least 50% of the lectures via LiveOnline webcast, the student will receive the course completion certificate. Students who arrive more than 20 minutes late or leave more than 20 minutes early may not count that class toward the LiveOnline attendance requirement.

No Shows are students who never attend a live/live online class and do not access any portion of the course software/electronic materials.

Course Overview: To review Becker's full live course overview, catalog and policies applicable to live course enrollment, please visit https://www.becker.com/content/dam/bpe/cpa/live/pdf/cpa_exam_review_course_catalog_4-6-18.pdf

Auditing: This course includes 18 hours of live instruction* and prepares students to pass the Auditing and Attestation section of the CPA Exam.

Business: This course includes 18 hours of live instruction* and prepares students to pass the Business Environment and Concepts section of the CPA Exam.

Financial: This course includes 30 hours of live instruction* and prepares students to pass the Financial Accounting and Reporting section of the CPA Exam.

Regulation: This course includes 24 hours of live instruction* and prepares students to pass the Regulation section of the CPA Exam.

*Hours of instruction represent allotted schedule time for live classes. Actual pre□recorded lecture hours may vary.

Exclusion of Warranties: YOU EXPRESSLY ASSUME ALL RISK FOR USE OF THE MATERIALS. YOU AGREE THAT THE MATERIALS ARE PROVIDED TO YOU "AS IS" AND "AS AVAILABLE" AND THAT BECKER MAKES NO WARRANTIES, EXPRESS OR IMPLIED, WITH RESPECT TO THE MATERIALS, THEIR MERCHANTABILITY OR FITNESS FOR A PARTICULAR PURPOSE AND NO WARRANTY OF NONINFRINGEMENT OF THIRD PARTIES' RIGHTS. NO DEALER, AGENT OR EMPLOYEE OF BECKER IS AUTHORIZED TO PROVIDE ANY SUCH WARRANTY TO YOU. BECAUSE SOME JURISDICTIONS DO NOT ALLOW THE EXCLUSION OF IMPLIED WARRANTIES, THE ABOVE EXCLUSION OF IMPLIED WARRANTIES MAY NOT APPLY TO YOU. BECKER DOES NOT WARRANT OR GUARANTEE THAT YOU WILL PASS ANY EXAMINATION.

Exclusion of Damages: UNDER NO CIRCUMSTANCES AND UNDER NO LEGAL THEORY, TORT, CONTRACT, OR OTHERWISE, SHALL BECKER OR ITS DIRECTORS, OFFICERS, EMPLOYEES, OR AGENTS BE LIABLE TO YOU OR ANY OTHER PERSON FOR ANY CONSEQUENTIAL, INCIDENTAL, INDIRECT, PUNITIVE, EXEMPLARY OR SPECIAL DAMAGES OF ANY CHARACTER, INCLUDING, WITHOUT LIMITATION, DAMAGES FOR LOSS OF GOODWILL, WORK STOPPAGE, COMPUTER FAILURE OR MALFUNCTION OR ANY AND ALL OTHER DAMAGES OR LOSSES, OR FOR ANY DAMAGES IN EXCESS OF BECKER'S LIST PRICE FOR A LICENSE TO THE MATERIALS, EVEN IF BECKER SHALL HAVE BEEN INFORMED OF THE POSSIBILITY OF SUCH DAMAGES, OR FOR ANY CLAIM BY ANY OTHER PARTY. Some jurisdictions do not allow the limitation or exclusion of liability for incidental or consequential damages, so the above limitation or exclusion may not apply to you.

Indemnification and Remedies: You agree to indemnify and hold Becker and its employees, representatives, agents, attorneys, affiliates, directors, officers, members, managers, and shareholders harmless from and against any and all claims, demands, losses, damages, penalties, costs or expenses (including reasonable attorneys' and expert witnesses' fees and costs) of any kind or nature, arising from or relating to any violation, breach, or nonfulfillment by you of any provision of this license. If you are obligated to provide indemnification pursuant to this provision, Becker may, in its sole and absolute discretion, control the disposition of any indemnified action at your sole cost and expense. Without limiting the foregoing, you may not settle, compromise, or in any other manner dispose of any indemnified action without the consent of Becker. If you breach any material term of this license, Becker shall be entitled to equitable relief by way of temporary and permanent injunction without the need for a bond and such other and further relief as any court with jurisdiction may deem just and proper.

Confidentiality: The Materials are considered confidential and proprietary to Becker. You shall keep the Materials confidential and you shall not publish or disclose the Materials to any third party without the prior written consent of Becker.

Use of Your Data: You understand that you will be providing personal information if you register for the Program and that the following will occur: (a) once you have registered, logged in, and activated your account, you will be asked to provide information about yourself as part of the registration process, or as part of your continued use of the Materials. You agree that any registration information you give to Becker will be used and stored by Becker. By using the Materials, you hereby consent to Becker retaining your personal information for purposes of the Program and for future purposes in marketing to you regarding other Becker Products.

Waiver of Liability: You hereby waive any claims, causes of action, and damages, and agree to hold harmless and indemnify Becker and its affiliates, officers, agents, and employees from any claim, suit, or action arising from or related to your use of the Materials, the use and storing of any of your information by Becker, or violation of these terms, including any liability or expense arising from claims, losses, damages, suits, judgments, litigation costs, and attorneys' fees.

SUBJECT TO THE OVERALL PROVISION ABOVE, YOU EXPRESSLY UNDERSTAND AND AGREE THAT BECKER, ITS PARENT CORPORATION, SUBSIDIARIES AND AFFILIATES, AND THE OFFICERS, AGENTS, AND EMPLOYEES OF THOSE ENTITIES, SHALL NOT BE LIABLE TO YOU FOR ANY LOSS OR DAMAGE THAT MAY BE INCURRED BY YOU, INCLUDING BUT NOT LIMITED TO LOSS OR DAMAGE AS A RESULT OF BECKER USING OR STORING YOUR INFORMATION WITH YOUR PROFESSOR OR COLLEGE/UNIVERSITY.

THE LIMITATIONS ON BECKER'S LIABILITY TO YOU IN THE PARAGRAPHS ABOVE SHALL APPLY WHETHER OR NOT BECKER HAS BEEN ADVISED OF, OR SHOULD HAVE BEEN AWARE OF, THE POSSIBILITY OF ANY SUCH LOSSES ARISING.

Severability of Terms: If any term or provision of this license is held invalid or unenforceable by a court of competent jurisdiction, such invalidity shall not affect the validity or operation of any other term or provision and such invalid term or provision shall be deemed to be severed from the license. This Agreement may only be modified by written agreement signed by both parties.

Governing Law: This Agreement shall be governed and construed according to the laws of the State of Illinois, United States of America, excepting that State's conflicts of laws rules. The parties agree that the jurisdiction and venue of any dispute subject to litigation is proper in any state or federal court in Chicago, Illinois, USA. The parties hereby agree to waive application of the UN Convention on the Sale of Goods. If the State of Illinois adopts the current proposed Uniform Computer Information Transactions Act (UCITA, formerly proposed Article 2B to the Uniform Commercial Code), or a version of the proposed UCITA, that part of the laws shall not apply to any transaction under this Agreement.

NOTICE TO STUDENTS: ACCET COMPLAINT PROCEDURE

This institution is recognized by the Accrediting Council for Continuing Education & Training (ACCET) as meeting and maintaining certain standards of quality. It is the mutual goal of ACCET and the institution to ensure that educational training programs of quality are provided. When problems arise, students should make every attempt to find a fair and reasonable solution through the institution's internal complaint procedure, which is required of ACCET accredited institutions and frequently requires the submission of a written complaint. Refer to the institution's written complaint procedure which is published in the institution's catalog or otherwise available from the institution, upon request. Note that ACCET will process complaints which involve ACCET standards and policies and, therefore, are within the scope of the accrediting agency.

In the event that a student has exercised the institution's formal student complaint procedure, and the problem(s) have not been resolved, the student has the right and is encouraged to take the following steps:

1. Complaints should be submitted in writing and mailed, or emailed to the ACCET office. Complaints received by phone will be documented, but the complainant will be requested to submit the complaint in writing.
2. The letter of complaint must contain the following:
   a. Name and location of the ACCET institution;
   b. A detailed description of the alleged problem(s);
   c. The approximate date(s) that the problem(s) occurred;
   d. The names and titles/positions of all individual(s) involved in the problem(s), including faculty, staff, and/or other students;
   e. What was previously done to resolve the complaint, along with evidence demonstrating that the institution's complaint procedure was followed prior to contacting ACCET;
   f. The name, email address, telephone number, and mailing address of the complainant. If the complainant specifically requests that anonymity be maintained, ACCET will not reveal his or her name to the institution involved; and
   g. The status of the complainant with the institution (e.g., current student, former student, etc.).
3. In addition to the letter of complaint, copies of any relevant supporting documentation should be forwarded to ACCET (e.g., student's enrollment agreement, syllabus or course outline, correspondence between the student and the institution).
4. **SEND TO:**

   ACCET
   CHAIR, COMPLAINT REVIEW COMMITTEE
   1722 N Street, NW
   Washington, DC 20036
   Telephone: (202) 955-1113
   Fax: (202) 955-1118 or (202) 955-5306
   Email: complaints@accet.org
   Website: accet.org

Note: Complainants will receive an acknowledgement of receipt within 15 days.

ANY HOLDER OF THIS CONSUMER CREDIT CONTRACT IS SUBJECT TO ALL CLAIMS AND DEFENSES WHICH THE DEBTOR COULD ASSERT AGAINST THE SELLER OF GOODS OR SERVICES OBTAINED WITH THE PROCEEDS HEREOF. RECOVERY HEREUNDER BY THE DEBTOR SHALL NOT EXCEED AMOUNTS PAID BY THE DEBTOR HEREUNDER.

Notes

Auditing

Final Review Sections

Auditing Section I | *Ethics, Professional Responsibilities, and General Principles*

A Terms of Engagement: Client Acceptance and Continuance
B Terms of Engagement: Communication With the Predecessor Auditor
C Terms of Engagement: Establishing an Understanding
D Audit Documentation
E Communication With Management and Those Charged With Governance
F Communications Related to Internal Control
G Ethics, Independence, and Professional Conduct
H Quality Control

Auditing Section II | *Assessing Risk and Developing a Planned Response*

A Planning an Engagement
B Understanding an Entity's Internal Control
C Assessing Risks Due to Fraud
D Risk Assessment Procedures
E Assessing the Risk of Material Misstatement
F Responding to Assessed Risk
G Materiality
H Planning for and Using the Work of Others
I Specific Areas of Engagement Risk: Related Parties and Noncompliance
J Specific Areas of Engagement Risk: Accounting Estimates and Fair Value

(continued on next page)

(continued)

Auditing Section III | *Performing Further Procedures and Obtaining Evidence*

A Understanding Sufficient Appropriate Evidence
B Sampling Techniques
C Tests of Controls
D Analytical Procedures
E Substantive Procedures
F Confirmations
G Performing Specific Procedures to Obtain Evidence
H Specific Matters That Require Special Consideration: Inventory and Investments
I Specific Matters That Require Special Consideration: Attorney Letter
J Specific Matters That Require Special Consideration: Going Concern
K Internal Control Deficiencies
L Written Representations
M Subsequent Events
N Subsequent Discovery of Facts

Auditing Section IV | *Forming Conclusions and Reporting*

A Reports on Auditing Engagements
B Integrated Audit Reports
C Reports on Internal Controls
D Reports on Attestation Engagements
E Accounting and Review Service Engagements
F Accounting and Review Service Engagement Reports
G Other Information
H Reports Required by Government Auditing Standards
I Special Reports

Introduction

Final Review is a condensed review that reinforces your understanding of the most heavily tested concepts on the CPA Exam. It is designed to help focus your study time during those final days between your Becker CPA Exam Review course and your exam date.

This Book

Becker's Final Review is arranged based on the AICPA's blueprints. The blueprints outline the technical content to be tested on each of the four parts of the CPA Exam. The blueprints can be found in the back sections of Becker's main CPA textbooks.

The Software

The Final Review software uses an interactive eBook (IEB) format. Watch the introduction video in the Final Review software for a tour of the IEB features.

We recommend progressing through this course in the following order:

- Review the IEB content, including the video introduction to each topic and the lecture audio associated with each page of the IEB.
- Work the embedded multiple-choice questions for each topic as you progress through the content.
- Work the related multiple-choice questions in the question bank for each topic. There are links from the IEB to the question bank.
- Once you have completed all of the IEB sections, topics, and multiple-choice questions, do the practice Simulations in the software.

Becker Customer and Academic Support

You can access Becker's Customer and Academic Support under CPA Resources at:

http://www.becker.com/cpa-review.html

You can also access Academic Support by clicking on the Academic Support button in the Becker software. You can access customer service and technical support from Customer and Academic Support or by calling 1-877-CPA-EXAM (outside the U.S. +1-630-472-2213).

I Ethics, Professional Responsibilities, and General Principles

A Terms of Engagement: Client Acceptance and Continuance

B Terms of Engagement: Communication With the Predecessor Auditor

C Terms of Engagement: Establishing an Understanding

D Audit Documentation

E Communication With Management and Those Charged With Governance

F Communications Related to Internal Control

G Ethics, Independence, and Professional Conduct

H Quality Control

Terms of Engagement: Client Acceptance and Continuance

Topic **A**

1 Client Acceptance and Continuance Policies

The auditor should consider the firm's client acceptance and continuance policies, including:

- The firm's ability to meet reporting deadlines.
- The firm's ability to staff the engagement.
- Independence.
- Integrity of client management.

2 Preconditions for an Audit

Before accepting an audit engagement, the auditor should establish that the preconditions for an audit are present.

2.1 Financial Reporting Framework

The auditor should determine whether the financial reporting framework used by the client is acceptable.

2.2 Management Responsibilities

The auditor should obtain the agreement of management that it acknowledges and understands its responsibility:

- For the preparation and fair presentation of the financial statements
- For the design, implementation, and maintenance of internal control
- To provide the auditor with:
  - access to all information of which management is aware that is relevant to the preparation and fair presentation of the financial statements;
  - additional information that the auditor may request from management for the purpose of the audit; and
  - unrestricted access to persons within the entity from whom the auditor determines it is necessary to obtain audit evidence.

A Terms of Engagement: Client Acceptance and Continuance

Question 2-1 FR-00891

Which of the following auditor concerns most likely would be so serious that the auditor would conclude that a financial statement audit *cannot* be performed?

1. The CPA lacks experience in the client's operations and industry.
2. A portion of supporting evidence stored at an offsite storage facility was destroyed by a hurricane.
3. Management has imposed a restriction that the auditor believes will result in a qualified opinion.
4. There is substantial risk of management intentionally manipulating accounting records.

Related Questions

For related questions, go to the online question bank:

➤ FR-00098

Terms of Engagement: Communication With the Predecessor Auditor

Topic **B**

1 Communication Before Engagement Acceptance

Contact with the predecessor auditor before engagement acceptance is mandatory, but client permission is required. Inquiries can be oral or written. Inquiries should be made regarding:

- management integrity.
- disagreements with the predecessor auditor (principles, procedures, etc).
- reason for the change in auditors.
- any fraud, noncompliance with laws and regulations, or internal control matters and their communication to management, the audit committee, and those charged with governance.
- fee payment problems.

2 Communication During the Audit

- The auditor should obtain sufficient appropriate audit evidence about whether:
  - opening balances contain misstatements that could materially affect the current period financial statements; and
  - accounting policies reflected in the opening balances have been consistently applied.
- In order to do this, the auditor should request that management authorize the predecessor auditor to allow a review of the predecessor's audit documentation related to the most recently completed audit. The predecessor ordinarily allows a review of:
  - Planning documentation
  - Risk assessment procedures
  - Further audit procedures
  - Audit results
  - Matters of continuing accounting and audit significance

B Terms of Engagement: Communication With the Predecessor Audit

Question 2-1 FR-00892

A successor auditor's inquiries of the predecessor auditor should include questions regarding:

1. The number of engagement personnel the predecessor assigned to the engagement.
2. The assessment of the objectivity of the client's internal audit function.
3. Communications to management and those charged with governance regarding significant deficiencies in internal control.
4. The response rate for confirmations of accounts receivable.

Terms of Engagement: Establishing an Understanding

Topic C

1 Agree to the Terms of the Engagement

Establishing an agreement with the client is required to reduce the risk of misinterpretation. The agreement with the client should be documented through a written engagement letter. The agreement should include:

- The objective of the audit
- Management's responsibilities
- The auditor's responsibilities
- Limitations of the engagement
- Identification of the applicable financial reporting framework
- Reference to the expected form and content of any reports to be issued

On recurring audits, the auditor should assess whether circumstances require the terms of the engagement to be revised.

Question 1-1 FR-00895

An auditor's engagement letter most likely would include a statement regarding:

1. The advantages of statistical sampling.
2. The inherent limitations of an audit.
3. Billings to be paid in the form of stock of the entity.
4. The assessment of risk of material misstatement.

Related Questions

For related questions, go to the online question bank:

- FR-00002
- FR-00041

Audit Documentation

1 Audit Documentation (Working Papers)

Audit documentation is a written record of the work performed, evidence obtained, and conclusions reached. Audit documentation:

- is divided into permanent and current files.
- supports the auditor's report/opinion.
- aids in training and in the conduct/supervision of the audit.
- provides a record of accumulated evidence.
- must indicate that the accounting records reconcile with the financial statement.
- must contain enough information to allow an experienced auditor with no previous connection to the audit to understand the work that was performed.

2 Assembly and Retention

Audit documentation is required to be:

- assembled within 45 days (public company audits) or 60 days (other audits) following the report release date.
- kept for seven years (public company audits) or five years (other audits).

Question 2-1 FR-00907

According to PCAOB standards, audit documentation must be retained for:

1. One year.
2. Three years.
3. Five years.
4. Seven years.

Related Questions

For related questions, go to the online question bank:

➤ FR-00908

3 Ownership and Confidentiality

Audit documentation is the independent auditor's property. It is confidential, but can be disclosed without client permission as part of:

- a quality review program.
- the subpoena process.
- an investigation conducted by the AICPA, state CPA society, or under state statute.

Question 3-1 FR-00940

According to professional standards, audit documentation should:

1. Be prepared in enough detail so that a new staff auditor who has no previous connection with the audit can understand the conclusions reached and any significant judgments made to reach those conclusions.
2. Monitor the effectiveness of the CPA firm's quality control activities.
3. Show who performed the work and the date the work was completed.
4. Include a flowchart to show the design and implementation of internal control.

? Related Questions

For related questions, go to the online question bank:

- FR-00080

4 Tickmarks

Auditors often use tickmarks, or symbols indicating the work that has been performed.

American Manufacturers Inc.
LONG-TERM DEBT
October 31, 20X7

Lender	*Interest Rate*	*Payment Terms*	*Collateral*	*Balance 10/31/X6*	*Current Year Borrowings*	*Current Year Reductions*	*Balance 10/31/X7*	*Interest Paid To*	*Accrued Interest Payable 10/31/X7*	*Comments*
▲First National Bank	10%	Interest only on last day of each quarter; principal due in full on 9/30/X9.	Manufacturing equipment	500,000 ■	200,000 ◆ 3/31/X7	(100,000) O 6/30/X7	600,000 ✓	9/30/X7	5,000 ◤	First National confirms that interest payments are current and agrees with account balance.
▲Second State Bank	9%	$10,000 principal plus interest due on the 1st of each month; due in full on 1/1/X0.	First mortgage on production facilities	380,000 ■	0	(110,000) ✚	270,000 ✓★	9/30/X7	2,025 ◤	Monthly payment for $12,025 was mailed on 11/3/X7; Second State agrees with account balance.
▲Third Savings & Loan	12%	$5,000 principal plus interest due on the 15th of each month; due in full on 10/15/X9.	Second mortgage on production facilities	180,000 ■	0	(60,000)	120,000 ✱★	10/15/X7	600	Third Savings & Loan claims 10/15/X7 payment wasn't received as of 11/5/X7; adjusting entry proposed to increase balance $5,000 and increase accrued interest payable.
▲A. Clark, majority stockholder	0%	Due in full 10/31/X9.	Unsecured	700,000 ■	0	(200,000) 10/28/X7	500,000 ✓		0	Borrowed additional $200,000 from Clark on 11/5/X7; need to investigate reborrowing just after year-end and consider imputed interest on 0% stockholder loan.
				1,760,000	200,000	(470,000)	1,490,000 ●		7,625 ●	

Tickmark Legend

▲	Agreed interest rate, terms, and collateral to note & loan agreement.	✓	Confirmed, without exception.
■	Traced amount to prior year's audit documentation	★	Reclassification entry proposed for current portion of long-term debt.
◆	Agreed to loan agreement, validated bank deposit ticket, and board of director's authorization.	✱	Confirmed, with exception.
O	Agreed to canceled check and board of director's authorization.	●	Traced amount to current year's trial balance and general ledger.
✚	Agreed to canceled checks and lender's monthly statements.	◤	Tested reasonableness of calculations.

Communication With Management and Those Charged With Governance

Topic **E**

1 Those Charged With Governance

Those charged with governance are those who bear responsibility to oversee the obligations and strategic direction of an entity, including the board of directors and the audit committee.

1.1 Audit Committee

An audit committee is a subgroup of those charged with governance. An audit committee consists of members of the board of directors, usually three to five "outside" directors, who are neither employees nor part of management and who do not have a material financial interest in the company. Audit committees are meant to strengthen the public's sense of the independence of the public accountant. Audit committee functions include:

- establishing the control environment.
- selecting and appointing the independent auditor.
- reviewing of the quality of the auditor's work.
- reviewing of the scope of the audit.
- responding to any auditor recommendations.
- helping to resolve disagreements related to the accounting treatment of material items.
- providing a bridge between the board of directors and the auditor.

2 Required Communications

The following items should be communicated to those charged with governance:

2.1 Matters Related to the Auditor's Responsibility

- The auditor is responsible for expressing an opinion on the financial statement, following GAAS, and communicating significant matters related to the financial statement audit.
- Internal control is considered as part of planning the audit, not as a means of expressing an opinion on the effectiveness of internal control (nonissuers).
- An audit does not relieve management or those charged with governance of their responsibilities.

2.2 An Overview of the Planned Scope and Timing of the Audit

- The auditor may communicate how significant risks of material misstatement will be addressed, the planned approach toward internal control, factors affecting materiality, and any potential use of internal audit staff.
- The auditor may also solicit information from those charged with governance, such as the entity's objectives, strategies, and risks, or matters to which the auditor should pay particular attention.
- The communication may also include discussion of the attitudes, awareness, and actions of those charged with governance.

2.3 Significant Audit Findings

- The auditor should communicate:
  - The auditor's views about qualitative aspects of the entity's accounting practices.
  - Significant difficulties encountered in performing the audit, or disagreements with management, whether or not resolved.
  - Uncorrected, nontrivial misstatements.
  - Other issues that the auditor judges to be significant.
- If those charged with governance are not involved with managing the entity, the auditor should also communicate material, corrected misstatements resulting from the audit, management representations requested by the auditor, management's consultation with other accountants, and significant issues arising from the audit that were discussed with management.
- The auditor may also request additional information from those charged with governance.

2.4 Additional Requirements for Issuers

Auditors of issuers are required to report to the audit committee all critical accounting policies, all material alternative GAAP accounting treatments, and other material communications between the auditor and management (e.g., management letters, schedules of unadjusted differences, etc.).
In addition, auditors of issuers should discuss and provide a draft of the auditor's report to the audit committee. If no formal audit committee exists, communications should be made to the full board of directors.

Question 2-1 FR-00108

Which of the following statements is correct about an auditor's required communication with those charged with governance?

1. Any matters communicated to those charged with governance also are required to be communicated to the entity's management.
2. The auditor is required to inform those charged with governance about significant misstatements discovered by the auditor and subsequently corrected by management.
3. Disagreements with management about the application of accounting principles must be communicated in writing to those charged with governance.
4. The auditor should not communicate frequently recurring misstatements unless they are material.

3 Form and Timing of Communication

In general, communications may be oral or in writing. Significant audit findings should be communicated in writing when, in the auditor's judgment, oral communication would be inadequate.

- Written communications should include a limitation on the use of the communication.
- Oral communications should be documented; copies of written communications should be retained.
- For nonissuers, timing of the communications should occur in a manner that allows appropriate action to be taken.
- For issuers, communications should be made before the issuance of the auditor's report.

Question 3-1

FR-00100

Which of the following items are included in the auditor's communication to those charged with governance and in management's representation letter to the auditor?

I. The auditor's responsibility under generally accepted auditing standards.

II. Management's responsibility for fair presentation of the financial statements in conformity with generally accepted accounting principles.

III. Uncorrected, nontrivial misstatements identified by the auditor.

	Auditor's Communication to Those Charged with Governance	*Management Representation Letter*
1.	I and III, only	II and III, only
2.	I, II, and III	I and II, only
3.	I and II, only	I, II, and III
4.	I, only	II, only

? Related Questions

For related questions, go to the online question bank:

➤ FR-00927

Communications Related to Internal Control

Topic **F**

1 Responsibility of the Auditor in a Financial Statement Audit Only

The auditor is not required to search for deficiencies that are less severe than a material weakness, or to express an opinion on internal control The auditor may, however, become aware of control deficiencies while performing the audit.

- Both significant deficiencies and material weaknesses must be communicated, in writing, to management and those charged with governance within 60 days of the report release date.
- Previously communicated significant deficiencies and material weaknesses that have not been corrected should be communicated again, in writing, during the current audit.
- The auditor should communicate to management only, in writing or orally, other deficiencies identified during the audit that are of sufficient importance to merit management's attention but that are not significant deficiencies or material weaknesses.
- The auditor may not report the absence of significant deficiencies, but may report on the absence of material weaknesses.

Question 1-1 FR-00107

Jefferson, CPA, has identified five significant deficiencies in internal control during the audit of Portico Industries, a nonissuer. Two of these conditions are considered to be material weaknesses. Which best describes Jefferson's communication requirements?

1. Communicate the two material weaknesses to Portico's management and those charged with governance, but not the three significant deficiencies that are not material weaknesses.
2. Communicate all five significant deficiencies to Portico's management and those charged with governance, distinguishing between significant deficiencies and material weaknesses.
3. Communicate all five significant deficiencies to Portico's management and those charged with governance, but only require a management response with respect to the two material weaknesses.
4. Communicate all five significant deficiencies to Portico's management and those charged with governance, without distinction among the deficiencies.

? Related Questions

For related questions, go to the online question bank:

➤ FR-00958

2 Internal Control Communication (Nonissuers)

Independent Auditor's Report

To Management and [*identify the body or individuals charged with governance*] of ABC Company:

In planning and performing our audit of the financial statements of ABC Company (the "Company") as of and for the year ended December 31, 20XX, in accordance with auditing standards generally accepted in the United States of America, we considered the Company's internal control over financial reporting (internal control) as a basis for designing audit procedures that are appropriate in the circumstances for the purpose of expressing our opinion on the financial statements, but not for the purpose of expressing an opinion on the effectiveness of the Company's internal control. Accordingly, we do not express an opinion on the effectiveness of the Company's internal control.

Our consideration of internal control was for the limited purpose described in the preceding paragraph and was not designed to identify all deficiencies in internal control that might be material weaknesses or significant deficiencies and therefore, material weaknesses or significant deficiencies may exist that were not identified. However, as discussed below, we identified certain deficiencies in internal control that we consider to be material weaknesses and significant deficiencies.

A deficiency in internal control exists when the design or operation of a control does not allow management or employees, in the normal course of performing their assigned functions, to prevent, or detect and correct, misstatements on a timely basis. A material weakness is a deficiency, or a combination of deficiencies, in internal control, such that there is a reasonable possibility that a material misstatement of the entity's financial statements will not be prevented, or detected and corrected on a timely basis. We consider the following deficiencies in the Company's internal control to be material weaknesses:

[*Describe the material weaknesses that were identified and an explanation of their potential effects.*]

A significant deficiency is a deficiency, or combination of deficiencies, in internal control that is less severe than a material weakness, yet important enough to merit attention by those charged with governance. We consider the following deficiencies in the Company's internal control to be significant deficiencies:

[*Describe the significant deficiencies that were identified and an explanation of their potential effects.*]

[*If the auditor is communicating significant deficiencies and did not identify any material weaknesses, the auditor may state that none of the identified deficiencies are considered to be material weaknesses.*]

This communication is intended solely for the information and use of management, [*identify the body or individuals charged with governance*], others within the organization, and [*identify any specified governmental authorities to which the auditor is required to report*] and is not intended to be, and should not be, used by anyone other than these specified parties.

[*Auditor's Signature*]

[*Date*]

1 AICPA Code of Professional Conduct

1.1 Independence Rule

1.1.1 Independence Requirement

- Independence is required for audits and attestation services.
- It is not required for compilations, consulting services or tax work.

1.1.2 Independence Is Impaired in the Following Cases

- Independence is impaired if the CPA has a direct financial interest, regardless of materiality or a material indirect interest.
- Independence is impaired if audit fees remain unpaid for more than one year prior to the issuance of the current audit report. It is considered a loan.
- Independence is impaired if a CPA has a management position with a client or is an employee. The spouse of a CPA can be an employee, but cannot hold a management position.
- Independence is impaired if a CPA makes hiring decisions for a client. The CPA may recommend a job description, screen candidates for the position, and advise the client on hiring.
- Litigation can impair independence, but not for immaterial dollar amounts unrelated to the audit.

1.1.3 Independence Is Not Impaired in the Following Cases

- Independence is not impaired with a bank client by a checking account that is fully insured.
- Independence is not impaired by a fully collateralized auto loan.

1.2 Integrity and Objectivity Rule

- All engagements must be performed with objectivity and integrity.
- The CPA should be free of conflict of interests, although services may still be performed if a conflict is disclosed to the client and the client consents to the CPA performing the engagement.

1.3 General Standards Rule

The general standards apply to all engagements.

1.3.1 Professional Competence

Requires proper education and training. The CPA need not be an expert or attain specialty accreditation. The CPA can consult with or hire experts.

1.3.2 Due Professional Care

The CPA must exercise the same skill a reasonably prudent accountant would. The CPA must critically review the work done by others.

1.3.3 Adequate Planning and Supervision

All engagements must be adequately planned and supervised.

1.3.4 Sufficient Relevant Data

All decisions must be based on sufficient relevant data.

1.4 Compliance With Standards Rule and Accounting Principles Rule

- A CPA performing an engagement must comply with applicable standards.
- A CPA cannot state that financial statements or other data comply with GAAP if there are departures that would have a material effect on the financial statements.
- Unusual circumstances may justify a departure from GAAP if compliance would cause the financial statements to be misleading (e.g., new legislation or new form of business practice). The departure from GAAP must be described and explained.

1.5 Confidential Client Information Rule

Confidential client information cannot be revealed to others without the client's consent. Confidential information can be revealed in a lawsuit and it can be revealed to a state CPA society voluntary quality control review panel. It also can be revealed when subpoenaed and confidential audit documentation can be reviewed by a prospective purchaser of a CPA's practice if confidentiality is assured (but audit documentation may not be turned over to a purchaser without the client's consent).

1.6 Contingent Fees Rule

A contingent fee is a fee dependent upon attaining a specified result. It is not permitted for audits, reviews and most tax work. Contingent fees are permitted for compilations if the CPA discloses the lack of independence. It is also permitted if a CPA represents a client in an examination of a tax return by the IRS.

1.7 Acts Discreditable Rule

The following acts are considered discreditable to the profession:

- Retaining a client's records after the client has demanded that the records be returned or after the employment relationship has been terminated.
- Discrimination in employment.
- Failure to follow standards in audits or government audits.
- Negligently making false or misleading journal entries.

- Failure to timely file tax returns or remit payroll taxes.
- Soliciting or disclosing CPA exam questions or answers.
- Makes false, misleading, or deceptive claims about the member's abilities to provide professional services.
- Disclosure of confidential information, obtained from a prospective client or non-client without consent.

Question 1-1 FR-00664

Smith and Company, CPAs, has been hired to perform the audit of Warehouse Company's Year 10 financial statements. Warehouse Company is an issuer. Under the ethical standards of the profession, which of the following employment relationships would not impair Smith and Company's independence?

1. The lead partner on the audit serves on Warehouse Company's board of directors.
2. The Warehouse Company's former controller, who left the company during Year 10, is assigned to the engagement team that will perform the Warehouse Company audit.
3. The wife of an audit engagement team member works in Warehouse Company's customer service department.
4. The former manager of the Warehouse engagement was hired as Warehouse Company's CFO during Year 10.

Question 1-2 FR-00525

The concept of materiality would be *least* important to an auditor when considering the:

1. Adequacy of disclosure of a client's illegal act.
2. Discovery of weaknesses in a client's internal control structure.
3. Effects of a direct financial interest in the client on the CPA's independence.
4. Decision whether to use positive or negative confirmations of accounts receivable.

? Related Questions

For related questions, go to the online question bank:

- FR-00509
- FR-00541
- FR-00557
- FR-00573
- FR-00589
- FR-00605
- FR-00621
- FR-00941

2 AICPA Conceptual Framework Approach

The rules and interpretations of the AICPA Code of Professional Conduct (discussed above) seek to address many situations; however, they cannot address all relationships or circumstances that may arise. In the absence of an interpretation that addresses a particular relationship or circumstance, a member should apply the appropriate conceptual framework approach.

The conceptual framework approach requires entities to identify threats to compliance with the fundamental principles, evaluate the significance of the threat, and apply safeguards to eliminate threats or reduce threats to an acceptable level, whenever possible.

2.1 Threats to Compliance

Threats to compliance may fall into one or more of the following categories:

2.1.1 Adverse Interest Threat

The threat that a member will not act with objectivity because the member's interests are opposed to the interests of the client or employing organization.

2.1.2 Advocacy Threat

The threat that a member will promote the interests of the client or employing organization to the point that his or her objectivity or independence, as applicable, is compromised.

2.1.3 Familiarity Threat

The threat that, due to a long or close relationship with the client or employing organization, a member will become too accepting of the product or service and/or too sympathetic to the client's or employing organization's interests.

2.1.4 Management Participation Threat

The threat that a member will take on the role of client management or otherwise assume management responsibilities. This threat exits for members engaged in attest engagements.

2.1.5 Self-Interest Threat

The threat that a member could benefit financially or otherwise from an interest in, or relationship with, a client or employing organization, or persons associated with the client or employing organization.

2.1.6 Self-Review Threat

The threat that a member will not appropriately evaluate the results of a previous judgment made, or service performed or supervised, by the member or an individual in the member's firm or employing organization, and that the member will rely on that service in forming a judgment as part of another service.

2.1.7 Undue Influence Threat

The threat that a member will subordinate his or her judgment to an individual associated with a client or employing organization or any relevant third party due to that individual's reputation or expertise, aggressive or dominant personality, or attempts to coerce or exercise excessive influence over the member.

2.2 Safeguards

Safeguards may include those created by the profession, legislation, or regulation, implemented by the client or employing organization, and/or implemented by the firm (if applicable).

3 Sarbanes-Oxley Act of 2002

The Sarbanes-Oxley Act of 2002 created the Public Company Accounting Oversight Board (PCAOB) and outlined the following key standards and independence rules that apply to audits of issuers:

3.1 Records Retention

Audit workpapers and supporting documentation must be maintained for seven years.

3.2 Concurring Partner Review

A concurring or second partner review is required for each audit report.

3.3 Prohibited Services

A registered public accounting firm may not provide the following services for issuers:

- Bookkeeping
- Financial information systems design and implementation
- Appraisal and valuation services
- Actuarial services
- Management functions or human resources services
- Internal audit outsourcing services
- Services as a broker, dealer, investment advisor, or investment banker
- Legal services
- Expert services unrelated to the audit

Tax services may be performed if preapproved by the audit committee.

3.4 Audit Committee Preapproval and Reporting

All audit services and permitted non-audit services must be preapproved by the audit committee. Additionally, the auditor must report the following to the audit committees of audited corporations:

- Critical accounting policies and practices used
- Alternative accounting treatments discussed with management and the treatment preferred by the auditors
- Material written communications between the auditor and management

3.5 Audit Partner Rotation

The lead and reviewing partner must rotate off the audit every five years.

3.6 Conflicts of Interest

The audit firm cannot have employed the issuer's CEO, CFO, controller, or chief accounting officer, or equivalent, for a one-year period preceding the audit (the "cooling off" period).

Question 3-1 FR-00637

Which of the following is not a provision of the Sarbanes-Oxley Act of 2002?

1. The auditor of an issuer may not provide internal audit outsourcing services for the issuer.
2. Audit documentation must be maintained for five years.
3. The lead and reviewing partners must rotate off the audit after five years.
4. Tax services must be preapproved by the audit committee.

? Related Questions

For related questions, go to the online question bank:

➤ FR-00814

4 Public Company Accounting Oversight Board (PCAOB)

4.1 Interim Standards

The PCAOB has adopted the Independence Rule and Integrity and Objectivity Rule from the AICPA Code of Professional Conduct on an interim basis.

4.2 Independence Standards

The PCAOB enforces the provisions of SOX described above and has issued the following additional independence standards that apply to audits of issuers by registered firms:

4.2.1 Contingent Fees

A registered firm may not provide services or products for a contingent fee or commission.

4.2.2 Tax Services

A registered firm may not provide to audit clients any tax services related to certain confidential or aggressive tax transactions and may not provide tax services to corporate officers of audit clients, or the immediate family members of corporate officers.

Proposed tax services and related fees must be communicated to the audit committee in writing and the potential effects of the tax services on audit independence must be discussed with the audit committee and documented.

4.2.3 Non-audit Services Related to Internal Control Over Financial Reporting

Non-audit services related to internal control over financial reporting must be communicated to the audit committee in writing and the potential effects of the tax services on audit independence must be discussed with the audit committee and documented.

4.2.4 Communication With the Audit Committee Concerning Independence

Before accepting an initial engagement with an issuer, and at least annually for each issuer audit client, a registered firm must describe in writing to the audit committee all relationships that might affect independence and the effects of those relationships. As part of the annual communication, the firm must affirm its independence in writing as of the date of the communication.

5 U.S. Securities and Exchange Commission (SEC)

Rule 2-01 of SEC Regulation S-X outlines the independence rules that apply to the auditors of SEC registrants. The SOX independence rules have been incorporated into these rules. According to Regulation S-X, the following circumstances impair auditor independence:

5.1 Financial Relationships

Similar to the AICPA Code of Professional Conduct, the SEC prohibits any direct or material indirect financial interest in an audit client, as well as loans to or from an audit client (other than loans from financial institutions under normal lending circumstances). Additionally, the audit client may not invest in the accounting firm or engage the accounting firm to provide investments services.

5.2 Employment Relationships

Independence is impaired by employment relationships between the accounting firm, covered members of the accounting firm, and the audit client, including:

- Employment of a covered person by the audit client or service on the audit client board of directors.
- Employment of a close family member of a covered person in an accounting or financial reporting role at an audit client.
- Employment at the audit client of a former member of the audit engagement team in an accounting or financial oversight role, unless the individual no longer influences the accounting firms operations, and has no capital balances or financial arrangements with the accounting firm.
- Employment at the audit client of a former member of the audit engagement team in a financial oversight role during the one-year preceding the commencement of audit procedures.
- Employment at the accounting firm of former employees of the audit client, unless the individual does not participate in or influence any audit related to the period in which the individual was employed by the client.

5.3 Performance of Non-audit Services

The prohibited non-audit services outlined under SOX (see above) are also prohibited by the SEC.

5.4 Contingent Fees

Independence is impaired by contingent fee or commission arrangements between the auditor and the audit client.

5.5 Failure to Rotate Partners

The SEC has enhanced the SOX partner rotation rules. The SEC requires the lead and concurring partner to rotate off the audit engagement after five years and requires other audit partners to rotate off the audit engagement after seven years. Lead and concurring partners are subject to a five-year time out period before returning to an engagement and other audit partners are subject to a two-year time out period.

5.6 Failure of the Audit Committee to Administer the Engagement

The audit committee must preapprove all audit, review, and attestation engagements and all permissible non-audit services. Consistent with SOX, the auditor must report the following to the audit committees of audited corporations:

- Critical accounting policies and practices used.
- Alternative accounting treatments discussed with management and the treatment preferred by the auditors.
- Material written communications between the auditor and management.

5.7 Certain Compensation Arrangements

An audit partner cannot earn or receive compensation based on selling engagements to audit clients for services other than audit, review or attest services.

6 U.S. Department of Labor

The U.S. Department of Labor (DOL) has established guidelines for determining when a qualified public accountant is independent for the purpose of rendering an opinion on an employee benefit plan under the Employee Retirement Income Security Act of 1974 (ERISA).

6.1 Independence Required

Auditor independence is required when auditing and rendering an opinion on the financial information required to be submitted to the Employee Benefits Security Administration of the DOL.

6.2 Impairment of Independence

The following situations impair independence with respect to an employee benefit plan:

- Any direct financial interest or a material indirect financial interest in the plan or the plan sponsor.
- Connection to the plan or the plan sponsor as a promoter, underwriter, investment advisor, voting trustee, director, officer, or employee.
- An accountant or a member of the accounting firm maintains financial records for the employee benefit plan.

6.3 Independence Not Impaired

An accountant's independence is not impaired when:

- A former officer or employee of the plan or plan sponsor is employed by the firm, the individual has completely disassociated for the plan or plan sponsor, and the individual does not participate in auditing the financial statements of the plan covering any period of his or her employment by the plan or plan sponsor.
- The accountant or the accountant's firm was engaged by the plan sponsor during the period of the professional engagement with the employee benefit plan.
- An actuary associated with the accountant or the accountant's firm rendered services to the plan.

Question 6-1 FR-00651

Which of the following will not impair independence under the U.S. Department of Labor's independence rules for audits of employee benefit plans?

1. An actuary employed by the audit firm performs services for the employee benefit plan.
2. The audit firm has a material indirect financial interest in the sponsor of the employee benefit plan.
3. A member of the audit firm maintains the financial records of the employee benefit plan.
4. A partner on the engagement team serves on the board of directors of the plan sponsor.

7 GAGAS Conceptual Framework for Independence

7.1 Requirements

The GAGAS independence conceptual framework steps require that an auditor:

- Identify threats to independence;
- Evaluate the significance of the threats identified, both individually and in the aggregate; and
- Apply safeguards as necessary to eliminate the threats or reduce them to an acceptable level.

If no safeguards are available to eliminate an unacceptable threat or reduce it to an acceptable level, independence would be considered to be impaired.

7.2 Threats to Independence

- Self-interest threat is the threat that a financial or other interest will inappropriately influence an auditor's judgment or behavior.
- Self-review threat is the threat that an auditor providing non-audit services will not appropriately evaluate the results of previous judgments made or services when significant to an audit.
- Bias threat is the threat that the auditor's position is not objective.
- Familiarity threat is the threat that aspects of a relationship, such as a close or long relationship, will lead an auditor to take a position that is not objective.
- Undue influence threat is the threat that external influences or pressures will impact an auditor's ability to make independent and objective judgments.
- Management participation threat is the threat that results from an auditor's taking on the role of management or otherwise performing management functions on behalf of the entity undergoing an audit.
- Structural threat is the threat that occurs when an audit organization's placement within a government entity might impact the audit organization's ability to perform work and report results objectively.

7.3 Safeguards

- Safeguards are controls designed to eliminate or reduce to an acceptable level threats to independence.
- Under the conceptual framework, the auditor applies safeguards that address the specific facts and circumstances under which threats to independence exist.

7.4 Evaluation of Non-audit Services

- The auditor should determine whether providing a non-audit service would create a threat to independence.
- A critical component of this determination is consideration of management's ability to effectively oversee the non-audit service to be performed.

Quality Control

1 Quality Control Standards

1.1 System of Quality Control

CPA firms are required to adopt a system of quality control for their auditing, attestation, and accounting and review services.

1.1.1 Human Resources

A firm should have criteria for recruitment and hiring, determining capabilities and competencies, assigning personnel to engagements, professional development, and performance evaluation, compensation and advancement.

1.1.2 Engagement/Client Acceptance and Continuance

Policies and procedures should ensure that the firm minimizes the likelihood of association with a client whose management lacks integrity, undertakes only those engagements that the firm expects to complete with reasonable competence, and complies with legal and ethical requirements.

1.1.3 Leadership Responsibilities

The firm's leadership bears the ultimate responsibility for the firm's quality control system and should create a culture that emphasizes quality.

1.1.4 Engagement Performance

Policies and procedures should be established to ensure that the firm consistently achieves a high level of performance, that engagements are properly supervised, that confidentiality, safe custody, integrity, accessibility, retrievability, and retention of engagement documentation is maintained, that differences of opinion can be resolved, and that guidelines exist to determine when an engagement quality control review should be performed.

1.1.5 Monitoring

The firm should have reasonable assurance that its quality control system is relevant, adequate, operating effectively, and complied with in practice.

1.1.6 Ethical Requirements

Personnel should maintain independence in fact and appearance in all required circumstances, perform all professional responsibilities with integrity, and maintain objectivity in discharging professional responsibilities.

1.2 Deficiencies or Noncompliance

Deficiencies in, or noncompliance with, a firm's quality control standards do not necessarily imply that a specific engagement was not performed in accordance with appropriate standards.

H Quality Control

Question 1-1 FR-00101

A CPA firm should adopt a system of quality control:

1. For all audit and attest services, but not necessarily for accounting and review services.
2. That encompasses human resource policies and practices.
3. Because it maximizes audit efficiency.
4. Because it ensures that all audit engagements will be conducted in accordance with generally accepted auditing standards.

? Related Questions

For related questions, go to the online question bank:

- FR-00055

II Assessing Risk and Developing a Planned Response

Planning an Engagement

Topic **A**

1 Obtain Knowledge of Industry and Business

The auditor is not required to have prior experience with the client's business or industry before accepting the engagement, but must obtain an understanding of the business and industry once the engagement has been accepted.

1.1 Industry Knowledge

Industry knowledge can be obtained from:

- AICPA accounting and auditing guides
- Trade publications and professional trade associations
- Government publications
- GAAP Financial Statements - Best Practices in Presentation and Disclosure

1.2 Business Knowledge

Knowledge of the client's business can be obtained by:

- Touring client facilities
- Reviewing the client's financial history
- Obtaining an understanding of the client's accounting system
- Asking questions of client personnel

Question 1-1 **FR-00900**

Which of the following procedures would a CPA *least likely* perform during the planning stage of the audit?

1. Determine the timing of testing.
2. Take a tour of the client's facilities.
3. Perform inquiries of outside legal counsel regarding pending litigation.
4. Determine the effect of information technology on the audit.

Related Questions

For related questions, go to the online question bank:

➤ FR-00901

2 Audit Strategy and Audit Plan

2.1 Audit Strategy

The auditor should establish an overall audit strategy, including preliminary assessments of materiality. The audit strategy outlines the scope of the audit engagement, the reporting objectives, timing of the audit, required communications, and the factors that determine the focus of the audit.

2.2 Audit Plan

The auditor is required to develop a written audit plan that outlines the nature, extent, and timing of the procedures to be performed during the audit, including:

- Risk assessment procedures
- Further audit procedures (tests of controls and substantive procedures)
- Other audit procedures

The audit strategy and audit plan can be modified as the audit progresses in response to new information or to the results of other procedures.

Question 2-1 FR-00118

Which of the following is required documentation in an audit in accordance with generally accepted auditing standards?

1. A flowchart or narrative of the information system relevant to financial reporting describing the recording and classification of transactions for financial reporting.
2. An audit plan setting forth in detail the procedures necessary to accomplish the engagement's objectives.
3. A planning memorandum establishing the timing of the audit procedures and coordinating the assistance of entity personnel.
4. An internal control questionnaire identifying controls that assure specific objectives will be achieved.

Understanding an Entity's Internal Control

Topic **B**

1 Overview of Internal Control

1.1 Definition

Internal control is a process designed to provide assurance that an entity's objectives will be achieved. Objectives include:

- Reliability of financial reporting
- Effectiveness and efficiency of operations
- Compliance with applicable laws and regulations

1.2 Inherent Limitations

- Human error
- Collusion, deliberate circumvention, fraud
- Management override

Question 1-1 FR-00117

Which of the following situations is *not* an example of an inherent limitation of internal control?

1. A programming error in the design of an automated control allows an employee to give himself an unauthorized pay increase.
2. A lack of physical controls over the safeguarding of assets allows an employee to steal company assets.
3. Management's failure to enforce control policies surrounding access to inventory allows employees to steal assets.
4. A fraud scheme whereby an employee orders personal goods and his supervisor, who is in on the scheme, signs the checks to pay for those goods.

2 Five Components of Internal Control

Mnemonic = **CRIME**

2.1 Control Environment

Sets the tone of an organization and its policies and procedures. Key points include:

- Integrity
- Competence
- Participation of those charged with governance
- Management philosophy
- Organizational structure
- Role assignment
- Promotion and training

2.2 Risk Assessment

Management identifies, analyzes, and manages risks that affect the entity's ability to accomplish its major objectives. Once risks are identified, management considers their significance, likelihood of occurrence, and how they should be managed. Key points include:

- New products
- Rapid growth
- Other changes

2.3 Information and Communication Systems

Methods and records used to identify, capture, and exchange information. Key points include:

- All transactions are recorded and complete
- Detailed enough to provide for adequate financial reporting disclosure
- Communication among management, employees, those charged with governance, and external parties

2.4 Monitoring

Procedures established to assess the quality of the internal control structure, and to make necessary corrections. Key points include:

- Internal audit
- Review and independent checks
- Other procedures such as mailing customer statements

2.5 (Existing) Control Activities

Policies and procedures established to ensure that management objectives are carried out. Key points include:

Mnemonic = **PAID TIPS**

- **P**renumbering of documents
- **A**uthorization of transactions
- **I**ndependent checks to maintain asset accountability
- **D**ocumentation
- **T**imely and appropriate performance reviews
- **I**nformation processing controls
- **P**hysical controls for safeguarding assets
- **S**egregation of duties

3 Audit Requirements

The auditor should:

- understand the five components of internal control.
- evaluate the design of relevant controls and determine whether they have been implemented.
- assess risk.
- design appropriate audit procedures, based on assessed risk.

Question 3-1 FR-00099

Which of the following is true regarding performance of the following audit tasks while obtaining an understanding of internal control?

Audit Tasks:

I. Obtain an understanding of the design of controls.

II. Determine whether internal controls have been implemented.

III. Evaluate the operating effectiveness of controls.

1. The auditor must perform I and II, and is allowed, but not required, to perform III.
2. The auditor must perform I, II, and III.
3. The auditor must perform I and II, but may not perform III.
4. The auditor may, but is not required to, perform I, II, and III.

Related Questions

For related questions, go to the online question bank:

- FR-00012
- FR-00090

4 Service Organizations

4.1 Effect on Internal Control

A service organization's services are considered to be part of a user entity's information system when such services affect the initiation, execution, processing, or reporting of the user's transactions.

4.2 Service Organization Reports

The service organization may issue one of two types of reports:

- **Report on Controls Placed in Operation (Type 1 Report):** Helps the auditor understand controls.
- **Report on Controls Placed in Operation and Tests of Operating Effectiveness (Type 2 Report):** Helps the auditor understand controls and may provide evidence supporting a reduction in the assessed level of control risk.

Question 4-1 FR-00020

Payroll Data Co. (PDC) processes payroll transactions for a retailer. Cook, CPA, is engaged to express an opinion on a description of PDC's internal controls placed in operation as of a specific date. These controls are relevant to the retailer's internal control, so Cook's report may be useful in providing the retailer's independent auditor with information necessary to plan a financial statement audit. Cook's report should:

1. Contain a disclaimer of opinion on the operating effectiveness of PDC's controls.
2. State whether PDC's controls were suitably designed to achieve the retailer's objectives.
3. Identify PDC's controls relevant to specific financial statement assertions.
4. Disclose Cook's assessed level of control risk for PDC.

? Related Questions

For related questions, go to the online question bank:

- FR-00919

5 The Effect of Information Technology (IT) on the Audit

A client's use of information technology affects both the evaluation of internal control and the gathering of evidence, but the audit objectives remain the same.

5.1 Evidence Gathering in an Automated Environment

An auditor can use manual audit procedures, e.g., "auditing around the computer," computer-assisted audit techniques (CAAT), e.g., "auditing through the computer," or a combination of the two.

5.1.1 Auditing Around the Computer

An auditor tests input data, processes data independently, and then compares the independent results to program results.

- This is appropriate for simple batch systems with good audit trails.
- The risks include insufficient paper-based evidence and insufficient audit procedures.

5.1.2 Auditing Through the Computer

- **Transaction Tagging:** Electronically marks a transaction and allows the auditor to follow it through the client's system.
- **Embedded Audit Modules:** An application program collects transaction data for the auditor. The auditor must be involved with the program design.
- **Test Deck (Test Data):** Uses application program to process test data, the results of which are already known (client system, offline).
- **Integrated Test Facility (ITF):** Test data is commingled with live data (client system, auditor's data, online).
- **Parallel Simulation (Reperformance Test):** The auditor reprocesses some or all of the client's live data and compares the results with client files (auditor's system, client data).
- **Generalized Audit Software Packages (GASP):** Allow the auditor to perform tests of controls and substantive tests directly on the client's system.

5.2 The Effect of Information Technology on Internal Control

Information technology use often affects an entity's internal control. IT brings increased risks but may also provide additional benefits.

5.2.1 IT Risks

- Potential reliance on inaccurate systems
- Loss of data and/or data inaccuracies from unauthorized data access
- Unauthorized changes to data, systems, or programs
- Failure to make required changes/updates to systems or programs

5.2.2 IT Benefits

- Accurate and consistent processing of large data/transaction volume
- Improved timeliness and availability of information
- Facilitation of data analysis and performance monitoring
- Reduction in the risk that controls will be circumvented
- Effective implementation of security controls enhances segregation of duties

Note

The accuracy of the IT system is crucial, because even manual controls may be dependent to some extent on the effective functioning of IT.

5.3 Assessing Control Risk

When assessing internal control, the auditor should consider the effects of both risks and benefits. Control risk assessment procedures in a computerized environment are the same as in manual systems (inquiry, inspection, observation, and reperformance).

5.4 The Effect of Information Technology on Audit Testing

- To select appropriate audit procedures, the auditor should consider the extent and complexity of the entity's computer operations, and the availability of an audit trail.
- Substantive tests alone may not suffice. Tests of controls should be performed to assess control risk in entities with significant computerized operations.
- The auditor needs to identify and test both specific application controls, and relevant general controls on which the application controls depend.
- The auditor should obtain an understanding of the internal control in effect throughout the period. Testing for operational integrity at a single point in time is generally not a reliable test of program controls. Although the auditor may make an initial assessment that a control is functioning as planned, subsequent testing is needed to ensure that the control continues to function effectively.

Question 5-1 FR-00005

An auditor most likely would introduce test data into a computerized payroll system to test internal controls related to the:

1. Existence of unclaimed payroll checks held by supervisors.
2. Early cashing of payroll checks by employees.
3. Discovery of invalid employee I.D. numbers.
4. Proper approval of overtime by supervisors.

Question 5-2 FR-00035

When an auditor tests a computerized accounting system, which of the following is true of the test data approach?

1. Several transactions of each type must be tested.
2. Test data are processed by the client's computer programs under the auditor's control.
3. Test data must consist of all possible valid and invalid conditions.
4. The program tested is different from the program used throughout the year by the client.

Related Questions

For related questions, go to the online question bank:

- FR-00015
- FR-00025
- FR-00045
- FR-00083
- FR-00092

B Understanding an Entity's Internal Control

Task-Based Simulations

Task-Based Simulation: Control Procedures

Scroll down to complete all parts of this task.

A CPA firm uses an audit checklist to consider potential misstatements and identify controls which might prevent or detect such errors. The engagement supervisor has instructed the audit assistant to use this checklist to evaluate a client's internal controls. For each of the following potential errors, identify a control procedure that would most likely be effective in preventing or detecting the problem by clicking in the associated cell and selecting the appropriate option from the list provided. Control procedures may be selected once, more than once, or not at all.

	A	B
1	Credit sales are made to individuals with unsatisfactory credit ratings.	
2	Employees receive unauthorized rate increases.	
3	Vendor invoices are paid for more goods than were received.	
4	Fictitious employees are added to payroll.	
5	Sales invoices for goods are posted to incorrect customer accounts.	
6	Goods shipped to customers do not agree with goods ordered by customers.	
7	Customer checks are misappropriated before being forwarded to the cashier for deposit.	
8	The receiving clerk fails to count the goods received.	
9	Customer checks are received for less than the customers' full account balances, but the customers' full account balances are credited.	
10	Terminated employees remain on the payroll.	

Select an option below

- Approved sales orders are required for goods to be released from the warehouse
- Monthly statements are mailed to all customers with outstanding balances
- Shipping clerks compare goods received from the warehouse with approved sales orders
- Customer orders are compared with the approved customer list
- Supervisors approve time cards
- The personnel department authorizes all new hires
- The personnel supervisor's password is required to make rate changes
- Exit interviews are required by the personnel department, which forwards documents to payroll
- The vendor invoice, receiving report, and purchase order are matched before the voucher is approved for payment
- The voucher package and supporting documents are cancelled when checks are signed
- The purchasing department sends a blind copy of the purchase order (i.e., without the quantity) to the receiving clerk
- Total amounts posted to the accounts receivable ledger from remittance advices are compared with the validated bank deposit slip

RESET CANCEL ACCEPT

Explanation

Row 1: Customer orders are compared with the approved customer list
Credit approval should be received before sales are made, to ensure that customers are on an approved list. This should reduce the risk of sales to customers with unsatisfactory credit.

Row 2: The personnel supervisor's password is required to make rate changes
Using password controls reduces the likelihood of unauthorized rate increases. As long as the password is not shared, only the personnel supervisor would have the ability to make such changes.

Row 3: The vendor invoice, receiving report, and purchase order are matched before the voucher is approved for payment
Matching these documents ensures that payment is only made for goods that were ordered and received.

Row 4: The personnel department authorizes all new hires
Requiring authorization for new hires helps prevent the addition of fictitious employees to the payroll.

Row 5: Monthly statements are mailed to all customers with outstanding balances
If sales invoices are posted to incorrect customer accounts, customers who are erroneously billed are likely to make inquiries regarding these invoices.

Row 6: Shipping clerks compare goods received from the warehouse with approved sales orders
Requiring shipping clerks to compare both the amount and the type of goods received from the warehouse with approved sales orders assures that goods shipped agree with goods ordered by customers.

Row 7: Monthly statements are mailed to all customers with outstanding balances
Checks misappropriated prior to forwarding to the cashier are not posted to customer accounts (assuming that the remittance advices were stolen as well). A customer would likely question why his or her account hasn't been appropriately credited.

Row 8: The purchasing department sends a blind copy of the purchase order (i.e., without the quantity) to the receiving clerk
When the receiving clerk only receives a blind copy of the purchase order, he or she is forced to actually count the goods received.

Row 9: Total amounts posted to the accounts receivable ledger from remittance advices are compared with the validated bank deposit slip
The total receipts credited to customer accounts in the subsidiary ledger should equal the total receipts deposited, given that daily receipts are deposited intact.

Row 10: Exit interviews are required by the personnel department, which forwards documents to payroll
Requiring exit interviews and forwarding the related documents to payroll minimizes the risk that departing employees will remain on the payroll.

Assessing Risks Due to Fraud

Topic C

1 Auditor Responsibility

The auditor must obtain reasonable assurance about whether the financial statements are free of material misstatements, whether caused by error or fraud.

1.1 Error

Error is an unintentional misstatement or omission.

1.2 Fraud

Fraud is an intentional misstatement or omission in the financial statements. Fraud often involves management because management is in a position to manipulate, directly or indirectly, accounting records. Management also can override established controls.

Question 1-1 FR-00072

The auditor's responsibility regarding material misstatements caused by *fraud* is:

1. Less than the auditor's responsibility regarding material misstatements caused by *error*.
2. Greater than the auditor's responsibility regarding material misstatements caused by *error*.
3. The same as the auditor's responsibility regarding material misstatements caused by *error*.
4. Either less than or greater than the auditor's responsibility regarding material misstatements caused by *error*, depending on the specific circumstances.

2 Categories of Fraud

Fraud is divided into two categories:

2.1 Fraudulent Financial Reporting

Intentional misstatements or omissions of amounts/disclosures in the financial statements; committed by management with the intent to deceive.

2.2 Misappropriation of Assets (Defalcation)

Theft of an entity's assets; committed by management, employees, or third parties.

3 Presumed Fraud Risk

There is a presumption in every audit that the following two risks exist:

- Improper revenue recognition
- Management override of controls

4 Fraud Risk Factors

Three conditions generally are present when fraud occurs:

- **Incentives/Pressures:** A reason to commit fraud.
- **Opportunity:** Ineffective controls or override of controls.
- **Rationalization/Attitude:** Justification of fraudulent behavior.

Question 4-1 FR-00081

Which of the following is *not* true regarding fraud risk factors?

1. They include incentives/pressures, opportunity, and rationalization.
2. Lack of observation of the three fraud risk factors implies that there is no fraud risk.
3. The existence of all three fraud risk factors is not an absolute indication that fraud has occurred.
4. Fraud risk factors are often present in circumstances where fraud has occurred.

5 Audit Procedures to Address Fraud Risk

The auditor must exercise professional skepticism throughout the audit process.

- Discuss fraud risk with engagement personnel.
- Obtain information to identify specific fraud risks.
- Assess fraud risk and develop an appropriate response.
- Evaluate audit evidence regarding fraud.
- Make appropriate communications about fraud.
- Document the auditor's consideration of fraud.

Question 5-1 FR-00914

Which of the following items is *not* required to be documented about the required fraud brainstorming session?

1. The auditor's responsibility to provide absolute assurance to uncover fraud.
2. The audit team members who participated.
3. How and when the discussion occurred.
4. Significant decisions reached.

6 Communication of Fraud

6.1 To Management and Those Charged With Governance

Fraud that causes a material financial statement misstatement should always be reported directly to management and those charged with governance.

- Obtain sufficient evidence of fraud and its effects on the financial statements.
- Discuss with an appropriate level of management at least one level higher than where fraud occurred.
- Suggest that client consult with legal counsel.

6.2 To Third Parties

Ordinarily, the auditor does not disclose fraud to third parties. However, in certain circumstances a duty to disclose to outsiders may exist:

- to the SEC in order to comply with certain legal and regulatory requirements, such as on Form 8-K and other required reports.
- to a successor auditor when they make inquiries.
- in a response to subpoena.
- to a funding agency that receives governmental financial assistance.

Task-Based Simulations

Task-Based Simulation 1: Fraud Communication

Scroll down to complete all parts of this task.

During the audit, an auditor discovers the following four situations. The auditor is required to communicate any indication of fraud to appropriate parties. For each of these situations, identify the appropriate party/parties by clicking in the associated cells and selecting from the list provided.

	A	B
1	An accounting clerk has stolen $50 from the petty cash fund.	
2	The entity does not have appropriate access controls in place to limit access to company financial records. The auditor believes that this is a significant deficiency in the design of the entity's internal control. This weakness allowed an employee to access the payroll system and give himself an unauthorized pay increase. The auditor concludes that this will not have a material effect on the entity's financial statements.	
3	A clerk in the accounts payable department generated several checks to pay large personal debts. This had a material effect on the current period financial statements.	
4	The CEO deliberately overstates current year revenue by including several key sales that did not occur until the next accounting period.	

Select an option below

- An appropriate level of management at least one level above those involved
- Senior management
- Those charged with governance
- The senior partner of Durham's CPA firm
- Both senior management and those charged with governance
- Both the senior partner of Durham's CPA firm and those charged with governance
- The senior partner of Durham's CPA firm, senior management, and those charged with governance

RESET CANCEL ACCEPT

C Assessing Risks Due to Fraud

Explanation

Row 1: An appropriate level of management, at least one level above those involved
Generally, any indication of fraud (even immaterial fraud) should be discussed with an appropriate level of management at least one level above those involved.

Row 2: Both senior management and those charged with governance
Although the effect of this fraud is immaterial, it represents a significant deficiency, which should be communicated to senior management and those charged with governance.

Row 3: Both senior management and those charged with governance
Fraud that causes a material misstatement of the financial statements should be discussed with senior management and reported directly to those charged with governance.

Row 4: Those charged with governance
Fraud involving senior management should be reported directly to those charged with governance.

Task-Based Simulation 2: Research

What guidance is provided by AICPA Professional Standards about the procedures that should be taken by the auditor if, as a result of identified fraud or suspected fraud, the auditor encounters circumstances that bring into question the auditor's ability to continue performing the audit?

Enter your response in the answer fields below. Guidance on correctly structuring your response appears above and below the answer fields.

Choose a title from the list

Explanation

Source of answer for this question:

AU-C 240.38

Keyword: identified fraud or suspected fraud

Risk Assessment Procedures

1 Audit Risk (AR)

AR is the risk that the auditor may unknowingly fail to modify appropriately the opinion on materially misstated financial statements. The auditor should plan the audit so that overall audit risk is limited to a low level. AR includes:

1.1 Risk of Material Misstatement (RMM)

The risk that the financial statements are materially misstated. It can be subdivided into:

1.1.1 Inherent Risk (IR)

Susceptibility of an assertion to a material misstatement assuming that there are no related controls.

- IR exists independently of the audit.
- The auditor cannot change this risk.

1.1.2 Control Risk (CR)

The risk that a material misstatement could occur in an assertion and not be prevented or detected on a timely basis by an entity's internal control.

- CR exists independently of the audit.
- The auditor cannot change this risk, but can change his/her assessment of the risk based on evidence gathered during the audit.
- The stronger the system of controls, the greater the reliance that may be placed on it, and the fewer the substantive tests (or the lower the quality) required.

1.2 Detection Risk (DR)

The risk that the auditor will not detect a material misstatement that exists in an assertion. DR relates to the auditor's procedures.

- The auditor can change this risk by varying the nature, extent, or timing of audit procedures.
- As the acceptable level of DR decreases, the assurance provided from substantive tests should increase.

1.3 The Audit Risk Model

Audit risk (AR) = Risk of material misstatement (RMM) (assessed by auditor) x Detection risk (DR) (controlled by auditor)

Risk of Material Misstatement	Acceptable Level of Detection Risk	Determine "NET" of Substantive Tests
High ↑ (Bad)	Lower ↓	High ↑
Low ↓ (Good)	Higher ↑	Low ↓

Question 1-1 FR-00062

After making a preliminary assessment of the risk of material misstatement during planning and beginning to apply audit procedures, an auditor determines that this risk is actually higher than anticipated. Which would be the *most likely* effect of this finding on the auditor's desired level of detection risk and the overall level of audit risk, as compared to the levels originally planned?

	Auditor's Desired Level of Detection Risk	*Overall Level of Audit Risk*
1.	Decrease	Same
2.	Increase	Same
3.	Same	Higher
4.	Decrease	Lower

Question 1-2 FR-00911

As the acceptable level of detection risk increases, an auditor may:

1. Change the nature of substantive tests from a less effective to a more effective procedure.
2. Postpone the planned timing of substantive tests from interim dates to year-end.
3. Lower the assessed level of inherent risk.
4. Select a smaller sample size.

? Related Questions

For related questions, go to the online question bank:

- FR-00061
- FR-00116
- FR-00909
- FR-00912
- FR-00922
- FR-00923
- FR-00924

2 Procedures

2.1 Overview

The auditor must perform the following procedures in order to assess and respond to risk:

- Obtain an understanding of the entity and its environment, including its internal control.
- Assess the risk of material misstatement.
- Respond to the assessed level of risk by performing further audit procedures (tests of controls and substantive tests).
- Evaluate audit evidence.

2.2 Obtaining an Understanding

The auditor should understand:

- Industry, regulatory, and other external factors.
- The nature of the entity.
- The entity's objectives, strategies, and business risks.
- The entity's financial performance.
- The entity's internal control:
  - includes evaluating the design of controls and determining whether they have been implemented.
  - does not require an evaluation of the operating effectiveness of controls (but the auditor may purposefully or incidentally obtain evidence about operating effectiveness at this time).
- Under PCAOB standards, the auditor of an issuer must also obtain an understanding of the company's selection and application of accounting principles.

2.3 Risk Assessment Procedures

The understanding is obtained by performing the following risk assessment procedures:

- Inquiry
- Analytical procedures
- Audit data analytics
- Observation and inspection
- Audit team discussion

D Risk Assessment Procedures

Question 2-1 FR-00071

Analytical procedures used in planning an audit should focus on:

1. Reducing the scope of tests of controls and substantive tests.
2. Providing assurance that potential material misstatements will be identified.
3. Enhancing the auditor's understanding of the client's business.
4. Assessing the adequacy of the available audit evidence.

Question 2-2 FR-00913

Which one of the following is a true statement about the required risk assessment discussion?

1. The discussion about the susceptibility of the entity's financial statements to material misstatement must be held separately from the discussion about the susceptibility of the entity's financial statements to fraud.
2. The discussion should involve all members who participate on the audit team, including the engagement partner.
3. The discussion should include consideration of the risk of management override of controls.
4. The risk assessment discussion should occur during the overall review stage of the audit.

? Related Questions

For related questions, go to the online question bank:

- FR-00113
- FR-00910
- FR-00915
- FR-00916

Task-Based Simulations

Task-Based Simulation: Components

Scroll down to complete all parts of this task.

Brown, CPA, is evaluating the risk of material misstatement on an engagement.

For each of the following, identify the risk component most directly affected by clicking in the associated cell in the Risk Component column and selecting the appropriate option from the list provided. Then indicate what effect the situation described would have on this risk by clicking in the associated cell in the Effect on Risk column and selecting the appropriate option from the list provided.

	A	B	C
1		**Risk Component**	**Effect on Risk**
2	The entity's purchasing agent is required to obtain approval from senior management for purchases in excess of $2,000.		
3	A good portion of the entity's fixed asset base consists of capitalized leasehold items.		
4	Brown plans to perform extensive tests of details surrounding the payroll function.		
5	The entity keeps a large quantity of cash on hand.		
6	Brown plans to perform all of its testing related to cash at year-end.		
7	The entity's computer applications are not protected by password controls.		
8	Employees report the hours worked each week without supervisory oversight.		
9	Brown will obtain evidence primarily from external sources in testing the entity's receivables.		
10	The entity's financial statements do not require use of significant estimates.		
11	Brown plans to perform only limited tests of details related to the purchasing function.		

Select an option below

- Inherent risk
- Control risk
- Detection risk

RESET CANCEL ACCEPT

Select an option below

- Increase risk
- Decrease risk

RESET CANCEL ACCEPT

D Risk Assessment Procedures

Explanation

Row 2: Control risk | Decrease risk
Requiring approval for large purchases is a good control that would reduce control risk.

Row 3: Inherent risk | Increase risk
Assertions involving complex calculations (such as lease calculations) have relatively high inherent risk.

Row 4: Detection risk | Decrease risk
Extensive testing reduces detection risk.

Row 5: Inherent risk | Increase risk
Cash is inherently risky as it is easily stolen and not easily identified as to owner.

Row 6: Detection risk | Decrease risk
Testing at year-end (as opposed to during an interim period) reduces detection risk.

Row 7: Control risk | Increase risk
Failure to appropriately limit access to computer applications increases control risk.

Row 8: Control risk | Increase risk
Failure to require supervisory approval of hours worked increases control risk (e.g., the risk that employees may deliberately overstate hours worked).

Row 9: Detection risk | Decrease risk
Use of external evidence reduces detection risk.

Row 10: Inherent risk | Decrease risk
Not having to rely on estimates, which often have a subjective component, reduces inherent risk.

Row 11: Detection risk | Increase risk
Performing limited tests of details increases detection risk.

1 Management Assertions (**COVERU**)

Management makes assertions about transactions and events, account balances, and presentation and disclosure.

1.1 Main Assertions

There are six main financial statement assertions (Note that under PCAOB standards, the main financial statement assertions are completeness; valuation or allocation; existence and occurrence; rights and obligations; and presentation and disclosure):

1.1.1 Completeness

All account balances, transactions, and disclosures that should have been recorded have been recorded and included in the financial statements.

1.1.2 Cutoff

Transactions have been recorded in the correct (proper) accounting period.

1.1.3 Valuation, Allocation, and Accuracy

Account balances, transactions, and disclosures are recorded fairly and at appropriate amounts, and any resulting valuation or allocation adjustments are appropriately recorded.

1.1.4 Existence and Occurrence

Account balances exist and transactions that have been recorded and disclosed have occurred and pertain to the entity.

1.1.5 Rights and Obligations

The entity holds or controls the rights to assets, and liabilities are the obligations of the entity.

1.1.6 Understandability and Classification

Transactions have been recorded in the proper accounts. Financial information is appropriately presented and described and disclosures are clearly expressed.

1.2 Relevant Assertions

Relevant assertions are assertions that have a meaningful bearing on whether an account, transaction, or disclosure is fairly stated.

E Assessing the Risk of Material Misstatement

1.2.1 Transactions and Events

For transactions and events, relevant assertions include completeness, cutoff, accuracy, classification, and occurrence.

1.2.2 Account Balances

For account balances, relevant assertions include completeness, allocation and valuation, rights and obligations, and existence.

1.2.3 Presentation and Disclosure

For presentation and disclosure, relevant assertions include completeness, understandability and classification, rights and obligations, and valuation and accuracy.

Question 1-1 FR-00032

In assessing control risk for purchases, an auditor vouches a sample of entries in the voucher register to the supporting documents. Which assertion would this test of controls most likely support?

1. Completeness.
2. Occurrence.
3. Allocation and valuation.
4. Rights and obligations.

Question 1-2 FR-00112

An auditor wishes to test the completeness assertion for sales. Which of the following audit tests would most likely accomplish this objective?

1. Select a sample of shipments occurring during the year and trace each one to inclusion in the sales journal.
2. Compare accounts receivable turnover (net credit sales / average gross receivables) in the current year to that achieved in the prior year.
3. Use common size analysis to compare recorded sales to sales recorded by other companies in the same industry.
4. Select large individual sales recorded during the year and review supporting documentation.

2 Assessing Risk

The auditor should:

- Identify and assess specific risks at the assertion level and at the financial statement level.
- Give special consideration to significant risks.
- Identify relevant controls.
- Document the following:
  - Key elements of the understanding of the entity and its environment, including the components of internal control
  - Identified risks and related controls
  - Risk assessment procedures performed
  - The auditor's risk assessment and the basis for this assessment

Question 2-1 FR-00902

Which of the following documentation is *not* required for an audit in accordance with generally accepted auditing standards?

1. A written audit plan setting forth the procedures necessary to accomplish the audit objectives.
2. The basis for the auditor's decision to perform tests of controls concurrently with obtaining an understanding of internal control.
3. The auditor's understanding of the entity's control activities that help ensure achievement of management's objectives.
4. The assessment of the risks of material misstatement at both the financial statement and relevant assertion levels.

Related Questions

For related questions, go to the online question bank:

- FR-00031
- FR-00042
- FR-00903
- FR-00904
- FR-00905

E Assessing the Risk of Material Misstatement

Task-Based Simulations

Task-Based Simulation 1: Risk of Material Misstatements

Scroll down to complete all parts of this task.

Durham, CPA, is considering audit risk at the financial statement level in planning the audit of DML Company's financial statements for the year ended December 31, Year 1. DML is a privately-owned entity that contracts with outside companies to provide facilities management services for professional offices.

Based on only the information below, indicate whether each of the following factors would most likely "increase," "decrease," or have "no effect" on the risk of material misstatement (RMM). For each of the items in the table below, identify the effect on audit risk by clicking in the associated cell and selecting the appropriate option from the list provided.

	A	B
1	This was the first time in five years DML operated at a profit because one of its current clients relocated its corporate headquarters to a large local facility, providing a significant increase in revenue.	
2	The internal auditor reports to the controller and the controller reports to Morris, the majority stockholder, who also acts as a chief executive officer.	
3	The accounting department has experienced a high rate of turnover of key personnel.	
4	During Year 1, DML changed its method of preparing its financial statements from the cash basis to the accrual basis, in order to conform with generally accepted accounting principles.	
5	During Year 1, DML sold one half of its controlling interest in Lawrence Equipment Leasing (LEL). DML retained a significant interest in LEL.	
6	During December Year 1, DML signed a contract to lease office equipment from a company owned by Morris' sister. This related party transaction is not disclosed in DML's notes to its Year 1 financial statements.	
7	During December Year 1, DML completed a barter transaction with David's Plumbing Services. DML provided David with a redesigned floor plan for his office, and in exchange, David repaired a major leak in DML's corporate offices.	
8	Inquiries about a substantial increase in revenue recorded by DML in the fourth quarter of Year 1 disclosed a new policy. In an effort to increase its client base, DML began providing an unconditional money back guarantee to clients who are not satisfied with the services provided. Clients may request this refund for up to three months after the completion of the job.	
9	An initial public offering of DML's stock is planned for late Year 2.	

Select an option below

- Increase in RMM
- Decrease in RMM
- No effect on RMM

RESET CANCEL ACCEPT

Explanation

Row 1: Decrease in RMM
Since DML returned to profitable operation, its healthier financial condition leads to a decrease in the risk of material misstatement.

Row 2: Increase in RMM
The risk of material misstatement increases when the internal auditor reports to top management rather than to the audit committee, because it is less likely that the internal auditor will be able to objectively perform his or her duties.

Row 3: Increase in RMM
The risk of material misstatement increases when key management positions (particularly senior accounting personnel) encounter turnover.

Row 4: Increase in RMM
A change to generally accepted accounting principles will increase the risk of material misstatement because the change in basis requires management to prepare a number of entries that have not been made in the past. These entries may be made improperly. Also, difficulty in determining beginning accrual basis balances may increase the risk of misstatement.

Row 5: Increase in RMM
The sale of one half of the company's controlling interest in Lawrence Equipment Leasing is a transaction that is outside the ordinary course of business, and accordingly, increases the risk of material misstatement.

Row 6: Increase in RMM
The risk of material misstatement increases when significant related party transactions occur, as the substance of a transaction may differ somewhat from its form.

Row 7: Increase in RMM
The risk of material misstatement increases where there are unusual and difficult accounting issues present. The barter transaction would be considered to be an unusual transaction.

Row 8: Increase in RMM
Th e risk of material misstatement increases, as it appears that management has taken an aggressive attitude toward reporting this transaction. In addition, this appears to be an unusual and difficult accounting issue involving revenue recognition.

Row 9: Increase in RMM
Entities may have an incentive to intentionally misstate reported financial condition and operating results in situations in which a public (or private) placement of securities is planned. Accordingly, an initial public offering of stock increases the risk of material misstatement.

E Assessing the Risk of Material Misstatement

Task-Based Simulation 2: Audit Testing

Scroll down to complete all parts of this task.

An engagement supervisor has asked the audit assistant to perform the following procedures related to an engagement. For each procedure listed, identify the financial statement assertion being tested by clicking in the associated cell and selecting the appropriate option from the list provided.

	A	B
1	Examine consignment agreements.	
2	Examine check register for the month following year-end for disbursements relating to the current period.	
3	Review bond indenture agreement and ascertain that the client has complied with any restrictive covenants.	
4	Inspect major new additions to furniture and fixtures during the current period.	
5	Ascertain that the financial statements comply with GAAP requirements surrounding the classification of investment securities as current or noncurrent assets.	
6	Test the aging of accounts receivable, discussing long-overdue accounts with the client's credit manager.	
7	Observe procedures, including segregation of duties, for approving sales orders.	
8	Trace shipping documents to sales invoices.	
9	Reperform check on accuracy of vendor invoice pricing.	
10	Trace beginning balance for inventory to prior year's audit documentation.	

Select an option below

- Completeness (account balances)
- Completeness (transactions and events)
- Completeness (presentation and disclosure)
- Existence
- Occurrence
- Allocation and valuation
- Rights and obligations
- Understandability and classification

RESET CANCEL ACCEPT

Explanation

Row 1: Rights and obligations
The audit assistant would examine consignment agreements to ensure that the client has legal title or similar rights of ownership to inventory, and that inventory excludes items owned by others.

Row 2: Completeness (account balances)
The audit assistant would examine subsequent cash disbursements to determine whether any such disbursements relate to liabilities that should have been included in the current period financial statements.

Row 3: Completeness (presentation and disclosure)
GAAP requires disclosure of noncompliance with restrictive debt covenants.

Row 4: Existence
The auditor's direct personal observation of assets provides reliable evidence corroborating management's assertion about the existence of those assets.

Row 5: Understandability and classification
GAAP requires that investment securities be classified into one of three categories, and as current or noncurrent assets, depending on the intent of the company.

Row 6: Allocation and valuation
Overdue accounts should be considered for write-downs or write-offs.

Row 7: Occurrence
The auditor's direct personal observation regarding the approval of sales orders provides evidence that sales really occurred.

Row 8: Completeness (transactions and events)
Tracing from shipping documents to sales invoices tests whether all shipments have been properly recorded in the client's Year 2 financial statements.

Row 9: Allocation and valuation
Reperforming mathematical computations verifies that inventory is properly valued.

Row 10: Allocation and valuation
Agreeing the opening balance of inventory to the prior year's (audited) ending balance provides evidence regarding valuation of the opening balance.

E Assessing the Risk of Material Misstatement

Task-Based Simulation 3: Errors

Scroll down to complete all parts of this task.

An audit assistant encountered the following errors during an audit. Identify the financial statement assertion affected by each error by clicking in the associated cell and selecting the appropriate option from the list provided.

	A	B
1	The assistant noted on a cash confirmation from a bank that there was an outstanding short-term loan at December 31, which was not recorded by the client.	
2	The current portion of long-term debt was excluded from the current liabilities section of the balance sheet, and was included with long term liabilities instead.	
3	The assistant found a number of shipping documents for which there were no related sales invoices.	
4	During the year the client purchased a truck from a private individual, but legal title was not obtained.	
5	During her observation of the client's inventory, the assistant noted a few items in the back of the storeroom that appeared to be rather old. Upon further investigation, the items were deemed to be obsolete and worthless.	
6	The assistant selected several older assets from the client's asset ledger, but was unable to locate those assets for physical inspection. The accounting manager indicated that the assets had been disposed of during the year.	
7	The client bought a piece of property five years ago for investment purposes. The property has quadrupled in value since that time, so the client has written up the investment to more closely reflect its current market value. The client uses U.S. GAAP.	
8	The assistant noted that the accounts receivable subsidiary ledger does not reconcile with the control account due to a transposition error. In posting to the subsidiary ledger, $4,293 was inadvertently posted as $4,239.	

Select an option below

- Completeness (account balances)
- Completeness (transactions and events)
- Completeness (presentation and disclosure)
- Existence
- Occurrence
- Allocation and valuation
- Rights and obligations
- Proper period (cutoff)
- Accuracy
- Understandability and classification

RESET CANCEL ACCEPT

Explanation

Row 1: Completeness (account balances)
Failure to record a loan means that payables are incomplete.

Row 2: Understandability and classification
GAAP requires that the current portion of long-term debt be included in the current liabilities section of the balance sheet.

Row 3: Completeness (transactions and events)
Shipping documents that lack corresponding sales invoices may be indicative of a situation where goods were shipped but not billed. Sales would therefore be incomplete.

Row 4: Rights and obligations
If legal title for the truck was not transferred to the client, then the client does not technically have ownership rights to that asset.

Row 5: Allocation and valuation
Obsolete or worthless assets should be written down to net realizable value or written off, as appropriate.

Row 6: Existence
Assets which are included in the client's books and records, but which have actually been retired, are not considered to "exist" for financial statement purposes as of year-end.

Row 7: Allocation and valuation
GAAP requires that land held for investment purposes be shown at historical cost.

Row 8: Accuracy
The transposition error means that the amount posted to the subsidiary ledger was not recorded appropriately.

Responding to Assessed Risk

1 Levels of Response

1.1 Overall Response

Overall responses to an assessed high risk of material misstatement include:

- Communicate to the audit team an increased need for professional skepticism.
- Assign staff with more experience or specialized skills.
- Increase the level of supervision.
- Incorporate a greater level of unpredictability into the audit.
- Make changes to the nature, extent, and timing of tests.

1.2 Assertion Level Response

There should be a clear linkage between the assessed level of risk at the relevant assertion level and the nature, extent, and timing of further audit procedures, including tests of controls and substantive procedures.

1.3 Response to Significant Risks

If relying on the operating effectiveness of internal controls intended to mitigate significant risk, tests of controls must be performed in the current period. Substantive procedures can consist of tests of details only, or tests of details and substantive analytical procedures.

Question 1-1 FR-00961

Which of the following represents an appropriate overall response to an increase in financial statement level risk?

1. Providing management with more specific details about audit sampling procedures.
2. Changing the general approach of the audit to ensure control testing of all significant accounts.
3. Shifting substantive procedures to interim.
4. Increasing the level of supervision.

Related Questions

For related questions, go to the online question bank:

➤ FR-00920

2 Further Audit Procedures

Based on assessed risk at the relevant assertion level, the auditor designs the nature, extent, and timing of further audit procedures.

- **Nature:** the purpose and type of test.
- **Extent:** the quantity of testing.
- **Timing:** interim or period end.

3 Audit Approaches

3.1 Substantive Approach

Under a substantive approach, only substantive procedures are performed.

3.2 Combined Approach

Under a combined approach, tests of the operating effectiveness of controls and substantive procedures (perhaps at a reduced level) are both performed. In a combined approach, the nature, extent, and timing of substantive testing is affected by the operating effectiveness of controls:

- The more effective a control, the lower the assessed level of control risk (CR). As CR decreases, the acceptable level of detection risk (DR) increases and the assurance required from substantive tests decreases.
- Conversely, as the acceptable level of DR decreases, the assurance that must be obtained from substantive tests increases.
- The stronger a control, the more it can be relied upon, and the fewer the required substantive tests (or the lower the quality).

When Do We Test Controls?

Status of Controls	*Risk Level*	*Audit Work*
No controls	Maximum Risk	Do not test controls*
Weak controls	High Risk	Do not test controls*
Some controls	Moderate Risk	Test the controls
Strong controls	Low Risk	Test the controls

* Exception: If significant electronic processing is used, controls should be tested.

Question 3-1 FR-00052

Using a combined approach most likely would involve:

1. Performing more extensive substantive tests with larger sample sizes than originally planned.
2. Reducing inherent risk for most of the assertions relevant to significant account balances.
3. Changing the timing of substantive tests by omitting interim-date testing and performing the tests at year-end.
4. Identifying specific internal controls relevant to specific assertions.

Related Questions

For related questions, go to the online question bank:

- FR-00921

1 Materiality

Materiality is the amount of error or omission that would affect the judgment of a reasonable person. The auditor should make preliminary assessments of materiality and should revise those assessments as appropriate throughout the audit.

1.1 Materiality for the Financial Statements as a Whole

Materiality for the financial statements as a whole needs to be expressed as a specific amount.

- Materiality should be based on the smallest level of misstatement that could be material to any one of the financial statements.
- Both qualitative and quantitative factors should be used to assess materiality, including:
  - The application of a percentage to an appropriate financial statement benchmark
  - Prior period and current period financial results
  - Known or expected changes in the entity's circumstances, the industry, or the economy

1.2 Performance Materiality

Performance materiality consists of the amount(s) set at less than materiality for the financial statements as a whole in order to reduce to an appropriately low level the probability that the aggregate of uncorrected and undetected misstatements exceeds the materiality for the financial statements as a whole.

1.3 Tolerable Misstatement

Tolerable misstatement is the application of performance materiality to a particular sampling procedure.

1.4 Materiality for Classes of Transactions, Account Balances, or Disclosures

A separate materiality level should be set for a particular class of transactions, account balances, or disclosures when misstatements of an amount less than materiality for the financial statements as a whole could influence the economic decisions of users.

G Materiality

Question 1-1 FR-00896

In which of the following circumstances would an auditor of an issuer be *least likely* to reevaluate established materiality levels?

1. The materiality level was established based on preliminary financial statement amounts that differ significantly from actual amounts.
2. The client disposed a major portion of the client's business.
3. The client released third-quarter results before the SEC-prescribed deadline.
4. Significant new contractual arrangements draw attention to a particular aspect of a client's business that is separately disclosed in the financial statements.

Planning for and Using the Work of Others

Topic **H**

1 Internal Audit Function

Independent auditors cannot share responsibility for audit decisions, assessments, or for issuing the report with a client's internal auditor. However, the internal auditor may assist with routine tasks.

1.1 Critical Factors

An auditor wishing to make use of an internal auditor's work must consider critical factors, including:

- The competence of the internal audit function, as evidenced by education, professional certification, and the quality of internal audit documentation.
- The objectivity of the internal auditors, based on the organizational level to which the internal audit function reports.
- The application of a systematic and disciplined approach, as evidenced by the use of documented internal audit procedures and quality control policies.

Question 1-1 FR-00051

In assessing the competence and objectivity of an entity's internal auditor, an independent auditor would *least likely* consider information obtained from:

1. Discussions with management personnel.
2. External quality reviews of the internal auditor's work.
3. Previous experience with the internal auditor.
4. The results of analytical procedures.

? Related Questions

For related questions, go to the online question bank:

➤ FR-00894

2 Use of Specialists

Actuaries, appraisers, attorneys, and engineers (specialists) may be used to assist the auditor in considering valuation or complex transactions. The auditor should understand the specialist's field of expertise, competence, capabilities, and objectivity to determine the possibility of using the specialist's work.

2.1 Impact on Audit Report

If, as a result of the work performed by the specialist, the auditor decides to add explanatory language or depart from an unqualified opinion, the auditor may refer to the specialist in the report and should indicate that the reference to the specialist does not reduce the auditor's responsibility for the audit opinion. In addition, an auditor of an issuer may reference the specialist if it helps the users understand a critical audit matter. The auditor may need the permission of the specialist before making reference to the specialist.

Question 2-1 FR-00898

Which of the following procedures is the auditor *least likely* to perform when an auditor decides to use the work of an auditor's specialist as audit evidence?

1. Obtain knowledge of the specialist's qualifications.
2. Refer to the auditor's specialist in the audit report to indicate a division of responsibility.
3. Inquire of the entity and the auditor's specialist about any known interests that the entity has with the auditor's external specialist that may affect that specialist's objectivity.
4. Review the working papers of the auditor's specialist.

? Related Questions

For related questions, go to the online question bank:

- FR-00089
- FR-00106
- FR-00897
- FR-00899

Task-Based Simulations

Task-Based Simulation: Research

An auditor may decide to make use of a specialist in obtaining sufficient appropriate audit evidence in certain circumstances that are material to the fair presentation of the financial statements. What guidance is provided by AICPA Professional Standards regarding the types of matters that the auditor may decide require him or her to consider using the work of a specialist?

Enter your response in the answer fields below. Guidance on correctly structuring your response appears above and below the answer fields.

Choose a title from the list

Explanation

Source of answer for this question:

AU-C 620.A1

Keyword: Specialist

Specific Areas of Engagement Risk: Related Parties and Noncompliance

Topic I

1 Related Party Transactions

1.1 Auditor Responsibility

Throughout the audit process, the auditor must be alert for the existence of transactions with related parties, such as entity affiliates, principal owners, management, and members of their immediate families. The auditor's primary concern with respect to related party transactions is their proper disclosure in accordance with GAAP.

1.2 Audit Procedures

Specific procedures regarding material transactions with related parties may include:

- Evaluation of the company's procedures to identify and account for related party transactions.
- Inquiry of management regarding the names of all related parties.
- Review of the reporting entity's filings with the SEC and other regulatory agencies concerning the names of officers and directors who occupy management or directorship positions in other businesses.
- Review of material transactions for related party evidence.

Question 1-1 FR-00120

Which of the following auditing procedures most likely would assist an auditor in identifying related party transactions?

1. Inspecting correspondence with lawyers for evidence of unreported contingent liabilities.
2. Vouching accounting records for recurring transactions recorded just after the balance sheet date.
3. Reviewing confirmations of loans receivable and payable for indications of guarantees.
4. Performing analytical procedures for indications of possible financial difficulties.

? Related Questions

For related questions, go to the online question bank:

➤ FR-00906

2 Noncompliance With Laws and Regulations

2.1 Noncompliance

Noncompliance is an act of omission or commission by an entity, whether intentional or unintentional, which is contrary to prevailing laws and regulations.

2.2 Management's Responsibility

Management and those charged with governance are responsible for ensuring that the entity's operations are conducted in accordance with applicable laws and regulations.

2.3 Auditor's Responsibility

The auditor is responsible for obtaining reasonable assurance that the financial statements are free of material misstatement due to noncompliance with laws and regulations.

- The auditor is not responsible for preventing noncompliance and cannot be expected to detect noncompliance with all laws and regulations.
- The further removed noncompliance is from the financial statements, the less likely the auditor is to recognize the noncompliance.

2.4 Procedures When Noncompliance Is Identified or Suspected

If the auditor suspects that noncompliance may exist, the auditor should discuss the matter with management at least one level above those suspected of noncompliance and, when appropriate, those charged with governance.

2.5 Reporting Noncompliance in the Auditor's Report

2.5.1 Material Effect on the Financial Statements

If the noncompliance has a material effect on the financial statements and has not been adequately reflected in the financial statements, a qualified opinion or adverse opinion should be issued.

2.5.2 Insufficient Evidence

If the auditor is unable to obtain sufficient appropriate audit evidence about the noncompliance or suspected noncompliance, a qualified opinion or a disclaimer of opinion should be expressed.

2.5.3 Client Response

If the client refuses to accept the auditor's report as modified, the auditor should withdraw from the engagement and notify those charged with governance in writing.

Question 2-1 FR-00918

Which of the following information discovered during an audit most likely would raise a question concerning possible noncompliance with laws and regulations?

1. A piece of obsolete office equipment was not retired.
2. Material internal control weaknesses previously reported to management were not corrected.
3. The client receives financial assistance from a federal government agency.
4. There was an illegal payment to a foreign official.

Related Questions

For related questions, go to the online question bank:

- FR-00917

Specific Areas of Engagement Risk: Accounting Estimates and Fair Value

Topic **J**

1 Fair Value Measurements

- Management is responsible for making fair value measurements and disclosures in accordance with GAAP.
- The auditor tests such measurements and disclosures to provide reasonable assurance that they are in conformity with GAAP.

2 Accounting Estimates

The auditor should verify that:

- Appropriate practices are used to develop estimates.
- All material estimates are reasonable.
- Estimates are presented in conformity with GAAP.
- Estimates are properly disclosed.

Question 2-1 FR-00030

Which of the following best describes the auditor's responsibility with respect to fair values?

1. The auditor should determine whether management has the intent and ability to carry out courses of action that may affect fair values.
2. The auditor should assess the risk of material misstatement of fair value measurements.
3. The auditor should obtain sufficient competent audit evidence to provide reasonable assurance that fair value measurements and disclosures are in conformity with GAAP.
4. The auditor should make fair value measurements and disclosures in accordance with GAAP and should identify and support any significant assumptions used.

Question 2-2 FR-00111

With respect to accounting estimates, an auditor:

1. Is not responsible for auditing estimated amounts, since they may be based on subjective determinations made by management.
2. Should verify that all material estimates required by generally accepted accounting principles have been developed.
3. Should focus on assumptions that are objective, insensitive to variation, and don't deviate from historical patterns.
4. Bears responsibility for making reasonable estimates and including them in the financial statements.

Related Questions

For related questions, go to the online question bank:

- FR-00948
- FR-00949
- FR-00950
- FR-00951

III Performing Further Procedures and Obtaining Evidence

A Understanding Sufficient Appropriate Evidence

B Sampling Techniques

C Tests of Controls

D Analytical Procedures

E Substantive Procedures

F Confirmations

G Performing Specific Procedures to Obtain Evidence

H Specific Matters That Require Special Consideration: Inventory and Investments

I Specific Matters That Require Special Consideration: Attorney Letter

J Specific Matters That Require Special Consideration: Going Concern

K Internal Control Deficiencies

L Written Representations

M Subsequent Events

N Subsequent Discovery of Facts

Notes

1 Audit Evidence

Evidence consists of underlying accounting data and corroborating evidence. Evidence must be sufficient and appropriate to afford a reasonable basis for an opinion regarding the assertions in the financial statements.

1.1 Sufficient Audit Evidence

The auditor must use professional judgment to determine the amounts and kinds of evidence sufficient to support an opinion. Sufficiency is influenced by:

- The risk of material misstatement (More risk = More evidence)
- The quality of the audit evidence (Low quality = More evidence)

1.2 Appropriate Audit Evidence

Appropriate audit evidence must be both reliable and relevant. Appropriateness depends on being pertinent, objective, timely, and corroborated.

1.2.1 Reliability

Reliability is dependent on the circumstances under which evidence is gathered. From most reliable to least reliable:

- Auditor's direct personal knowledge and observation
- External evidence
- Internal evidence
- Oral evidence

1.2.2 Relevance

Relevance means the evidence is related to (i.e., tells something about) the assertion under consideration. PCAOB standards state that the relevance of evidence depends on the design of the audit procedure (whether it is designed to test the assertion directly or whether it is designed to test for overstatement or understatement) and the timing of the audit procedure.

A Understanding Sufficient Appropriate Evidence

Question 1-1 FR-00954

Which of the following circumstances most likely would cause an auditor to suspect that there are material misstatements in an entity's financial statements?

1. The entity's management strictly enforces its integrity and ethical values.
2. Monthly bank reconciliations ordinarily include several outstanding checks.
3. Management outsources the internal audit function to another CPA firm.
4. The auditor identifies an inappropriate valuation method that is widely applied by the entity.

? Related Questions

For related questions, go to the online question bank:

- FR-00004
- FR-00932
- FR-00933
- FR-00938
- FR-00939
- FR-00953
- FR-00955
- FR-00956

Sampling Techniques

1 Statistical and Nonstatistical Sampling

Sampling can be statistical (mathematical) or nonstatistical. Both can provide sufficient audit evidence and are acceptable under GAAS; both require professional judgment. Only statistical sampling enables the auditor to measure the sufficiency of the evidence, design an efficient sample, and quantify sampling risk.

2 Types of Statistical Sampling

2.1 Attribute Sampling

Attributes sampling is used to estimate a rate of occurrence (whether or not an attribute is present); primarily used to test internal controls. Methods include:

- Discovery sampling
- Stop and go sampling
- Acceptance sampling

2.2 Variables Sampling

Variables sampling is used to estimate numerical value; typically used in substantive testing. The auditor estimates a population's true value by computing a point estimate of the population and a precision interval around the estimate. Methods include:

- Mean-per-unit estimation (MPU)
- Ratio estimation
- Difference estimation

2.2.1 PPS Sampling

Probability-proportional-to-size (PPS) sampling is a hybrid method that uses attribute sampling theory to express a conclusion in dollar amounts.

B Sampling Techniques

Question 2-1 FR-00046

An advantage of using statistical over nonstatistical sampling methods in tests of controls is that the statistical methods:

1. Can more easily convert the sample into a dual-purpose test useful for substantive testing.
2. Eliminate the need to use judgment in determining appropriate sample sizes.
3. Afford greater assurance than a nonstatistical sample of equal size.
4. Provide an objective basis for quantitatively evaluating sample risk.

Question 2-2 FR-00066

An auditor is likely using attribute sampling when he or she selects a sample of:

1. Receivables and sends confirmations to client customers.
2. Purchase orders and examines them for indication of proper approval.
3. Invoices to verify proper extensions and footings.
4. Cash receipts and traces them to the accounts receivable subsidiary ledger.

? Related Questions

For related questions, go to the online question bank:

- FR-00093

3 Sampling Risk

Sampling risk is the risk that the sample is not representative, and that the auditor's conclusion would be different from the conclusion if the auditor had examined 100 percent of the population.

3.1 Confidence Interval

Numerically, sampling risk is the complement of reliability, or confidence level (e.g., a 5 percent sampling risk reflects a 95 percent confidence level).

3.2 Sampling Risks in Tests of Controls (Attribute Sampling)

3.2.1 Risk of Assessing Control Risk Too Low

The risk of assessing control risk too low is the risk that a properly drawn sample will support the auditor's planned degree of reliance when the true compliance rate does not justify such reliance (risk of overreliance).

3.2.2 Risk of Assessing Control Risk Too High

The risk of assessing control risk too high is the risk that a properly drawn sample will not support the auditor's planned degree of reliance when the true compliance rate does justify such reliance (risk of under-reliance).

Diagram 1: Attribute Sampling Risks

		The true operation of the control is:	
		OK	Not OK
The sample indicates that the operation of the control is:	OK	Correct decision	Incorrect decision **Risk of assessing control risk too low** *Not effective*
	Not OK	Incorrect decision **Risk of assessing control risk too high** *Not efficient*	Correct decision

3.3 Sampling Risks in Substantive Testing (Variables Sampling)

3.3.1 Risk of Incorrect Acceptance

The risk of incorrect acceptance is the risk that a properly drawn sample supports a balance as not being materially misstated when in fact it is materially misstated.

3.3.2 Risk of Incorrect Rejection

The risk of incorrect rejection is the risk that a properly drawn sample supports a balance as materially misstated when in fact it is not materially misstated.

Diagram 2: Variables Sampling Risks

		The recorded value of the population is:	
		OK	Not OK
The sample indicates that the population is:	OK	Correct decision	Incorrect decision **Risk of incorrect acceptance** *Not effective*
	Not OK	Incorrect decision **Risk of incorrect rejection** *Not efficient*	Correct decision

3.4 Effect of Sampling Risk on the Audit

3.4.1 Effectiveness

The risk of assessing control risk too low and the risk of incorrect acceptance are concerned with the effectiveness of the audit. This type of risk is more critical because it can result in the auditor mistakenly relying on an ineffective control or unknowingly accepting a misstatement in the balance being tested and thereby issuing an inappropriate audit opinion.

3.4.2 Efficiency

The risk of assessing control risk too high and the risk of incorrect rejection are concerned with the efficiency of the audit. An audit conclusion in this direction causes the auditor to do more work than is really necessary.

Question 3-1 FR-00006

In assessing sampling risk, the risk of incorrect rejection and the risk of assessing control risk too high relate to the:

1. Efficiency of the audit.
2. Effectiveness of the audit.
3. Selection of the items in the sample.
4. Audit quality controls.

? Related Questions

For related questions, go to the online question bank:

- FR-00056
- FR-00084

4 Steps in the Sampling Process

Attribute Sampling	Variables Sampling
1. Define the objective: This is the purpose of the test.	
Percentage of sales orders missing credit approval (i.e., what is the percentage of control failure).	True dollar value of sales for year 20X5.
2. Define the population: This is the aggregate group or set of items about which the auditor wishes to draw conclusions.	
All new customer sales orders during 20X5.	All sales dollars for year 20X5.
3. Define the sampling unit: This is the actual item or element from which the auditor will collect data.	
Individual sales orders.	Individual sales dollars.
4. Define the attribute of interest: This is the data to be collected.	
Credit approval (e.g., manager's signature). Missing approvals or missing sales orders are deviations.	Sales dollars.
5. Determine the sample size: This is the number of items to be selected for testing. The decision is based on statistical considerations, plus the auditor's judgment.	
Sample size is affected by the risk of assessing control risk too low (inverse relationship), the tolerable deviation rate (inverse), and the expected deviation rate (direct). Population size (>5000 items) generally does not matter.	Sample size is affected by expected misstatement, standard deviation, and the assessed level of risk (direct effects), as well as by tolerable misstatement and the acceptable level of risk (inverse effects).
6. Select the sample: The actual selection of a representative set of items for testing.	
Random selection: Best method (used with prenumbered population). *Systematic selection*: Every nth item (ineffective if population is systematically ordered). *Stratification*: Divide the population into subpopulations based on strata. *Block or cluster*: Not a desirable approach. *PPS*: Every nth dollar, uses a random start, automatically stratifies population but does not test negative or zero balances.	
7. Evaluate the sample results: This tells the auditor if the control can be relied on (attribute sampling) or if the account does not appear to be materially misstated (variables sampling).	
Compare upper deviation rate to tolerable deviation rate. Sample deviation rate + Allowance for sampling risk = **Upper deviation rate** **Tolerable deviation rate:** maximum rate of deviation from prescribed controls that the auditor will tolerate without modifying planned reliance on the control. (Based on professional judgment.) **Sample deviation rate:** error rate in the sample; the auditor's best estimate of the deviation rate in the population from which the sample was selected.	Auditor projects misstatements to population utilizing a projected misstatement (point estimate). An allowance for sampling risk (or precision interval) is added to this estimate. Sample error + recorded balance = point estimate Form conclusions about the account balances/transactions tested: Accept book value if it falls within an acceptable range (point estimate +/− allowance for sampling risk). Likely misstatement = Projected misstatement **Tolerable misstatement:** misstatement in the related account balance or class of transactions that may exist without causing the FS to be materially misstated.
8. Document sampling procedures.	

Question 4-1 FR-00026

A number of factors influence the sample size for a substantive test of details of an account balance. All other factors being equal, which of the following would lead to a larger sample size?

1. Greater reliance on internal control.
2. Greater reliance on analytical procedures.
3. Smaller expected frequency of errors.
4. Smaller measure of tolerable misstatement.

Related Questions

For related questions, go to the online question bank:

➤ FR-00016

5 Example of Evaluating Sample Results for Attribute Sampling

- Sample deviation rate = (Number of errors)/(Sample size)

  10 errors/1000 sample size = 1%

- Sample deviation rate + Allowance for sampling risk = Upper deviation rate

  1.0% + 3.7% = 4.7%

- Compare upper deviation rate (UDR) to tolerable rate (TR).

UDR ≤ TR	Assume TR = 6.0%
	No change in preliminary assessment of control risk is needed
	No change in NET of substantive tests is needed
	4.7% < 6.0% would be a "good" result
UDR > TR	Assume TR = 3.0%
	Increase the assessment of control risk, resulting in a change in NET of substantive tests:
	Nature: Select a more effective substantive test.
	Extent: Increase the substantive test sample size.
	Timing: Apply substantive tests at year-end instead of at interim.
	4.7% > 3.0% would be a "bad" result

Question 5-1 FR-00036

An auditor who uses statistical sampling for attributes in testing internal controls should reduce the planned reliance on a prescribed control when the:

1. Sample rate of deviation plus the allowance for sampling risk equals the tolerable rate.
2. Sample rate of deviation is less than the expected rate of deviation used in planning the sample.
3. Tolerable rate less the allowance for sampling risk exceeds the sample rate of deviation.
4. Sample rate of deviation plus the allowance for sampling risk exceeds the tolerable rate.

Related Questions

For related questions, go to the online question bank:

➤ FR-00075

6 Probability-Proportional-to-Size (PPS) Sampling

Under PPS sampling, the sampling unit is defined as an individual dollar in a population. Once the dollar is selected, the entire account is audited.

6.1 Advantage

Automatically emphasizes larger items, so if no errors are expected, PPS will require a smaller sample than other methods.

6.2 Disadvantage

Zero balances, negative balances, and understated balances generally require special design considerations.

6.3 Steps in PPS Sampling

- Sample size = recorded amount of the population/sampling interval.
- Sampling interval = tolerable misstatement/reliability factor.
- Reliability factors correspond to the risk of incorrect acceptance and are generally obtained from a table.
- **Sample Selection:** A random number between 1 and the sampling interval is selected; it determines the first item selected. The recorded amounts of the logical units throughout the population are then added and individual dollars (and their corresponding units) are selected based on the interval.
- **Evaluation of Sample Results:** If no errors are found, the error projection is zero and the allowance for sampling risk would not exceed the auditor's tolerable error. If errors are found, they need to be projected to the interval. If an account selected has a balance greater than the interval, the actual dollar amount of the error should be used.

Related Questions

For related questions, go to the online question bank:

➤ FR-00102

Probability-Proportional-to-Size							
	A Recorded Amount	*B Audit Amount*	*A–B*	*A*	*(A–B)/A Tainting*	*Sample Interval*	*Projected Error*
	$800	$600	$200	$800	25%	$5,000	$1,250
	4,350	4,350	0	4,350	0%	5,000	0
	4,900	0	4,900	4,900	100%	5,000	5,000
> 5,000	8,500	6,900	1,600	n/a	n/a	n/a	1,600
	1,500	1,200	300	1,500	20%	5,000	1,000
Totals	20,050	13,050	7,000				8,850

Known misstatement (sample errors)	7,000
Projected error	8,850
Allowance for sampling risk (calculation not shown)	2,500
Projected misstatement (likely misstatement)	11,350

If tolerable misstatement is 15,000, the book value is fairly stated (11,350 is less than 15,000)

7 Dual Purpose Samples

Auditors may use the same sample to perform both tests of controls and substantive tests; generally this would only be done when the auditor believes that there is an acceptably low risk that the deviation rate in the population exceeds the tolerable rate.

In evaluating dual-purpose samples, deviations from control procedures and monetary misstatements should be evaluated separately using appropriate risk levels.

Task-Based Simulations

Task-Based Simulation 1: Statistical Sampling

Scroll down to complete all parts of this task.

In discussing his desire to make use of statistical sampling methods, a newly-hired staff accountant made the following statements to the senior on the job. Which of these statements are correct? Check all that apply.

- ☐ 1. Statistical sampling will always result in a smaller sample size than nonstatistical sampling.
- ☐ 2. Statistical sampling allows a greater quantification of risk and reliability than does nonstatistical sampling.
- ☐ 3. Statistical sampling is required by generally accepted auditing standards.
- ☐ 4. Statistical sampling eliminates subjectivity in evaluating sample results.
- ☐ 5. Statistical sampling requires the use of mathematical formulas and/or tables.
- ☐ 6. Statistical sampling should not be used when there is a significant amount of population variability.

Explanation

1. False
Statistical sampling will always result in a smaller sample size than nonstatistical sampling.

While statistical sampling methods can aid the auditor in finding the smallest sample size that achieves the desired level of risk, there is no guarantee that statistical sampling will result in a smaller sample size than nonstatistical sampling.

2. True
Statistical sampling allows a greater quantification of risk and reliability than does nonstatistical sampling.

With statistical sampling, auditors specify the sampling risk they are willing to accept and then calculate the sample size that provides that degree of reliability. Nonstatistical methods use qualitative rather than quantitative judgments of risk and reliability.

3. False
Statistical sampling is required by generally accepted auditing standards.

Either statistical or nonstatistical sampling methods are acceptable under generally accepted auditing standards.

4. False
Statistical sampling eliminates subjectivity in evaluating sample results.

Statistical sampling does not eliminate subjectivity in evaluating sample results. For example, the auditor must still use judgment to evaluate the appropriateness of audit evidence, determine whether a given situation constitutes a deviation, etc.

5. True
Statistical sampling requires the use of mathematical formulas and/or tables.

Statistical sampling involves the use of mathematical formulas and/or tables to determine the sample size that achieves an acceptable level of risk, to evaluate results, etc.

6. False
Statistical sampling should not be used when there is a significant amount of population variability.

Statistical sampling may be used when there is a significant amount of population variability, although the auditor may choose to stratify the population in such cases. Population variability may also affect the determination of sample size.

Task-Based Simulation 2: Attribute Sampling

Scroll down to complete all parts of this task.

An auditor has applied statistical sampling methods in evaluating controls surrounding a client's expenditure cycle. The client's company policy indicates that all purchases over $500 require two signatures, that the accounts payable clerk match the purchase order, receiving report, and vendor invoice before approving the invoice for payment, and that voucher packages be canceled upon payment. The auditor's tolerable deviation rate for all tests of controls is 5%, and his allowance for sampling risk is 2%.

1. The auditor selects a sample consisting of fifty purchases exceeding $500, and notes that two purchases have only one approval signature. Both purchases occurred during the same week. Management states that the second signature was not obtained due to the unexpected illness of the appropriate manager that week, but that the purchases were still appropriate. Which of the following is true?
   - The auditor may rely on this control because the two purchases were appropriate, and therefore they should not be considered deviations.
   - The auditor may rely on this control because the sample deviation rate is less than the tolerable rate.
   - The auditor did not select an appropriate population for this audit test.
   - The auditor should not rely on this control.

2. The auditor selects a sample consisting of forty approved voucher packages, and notes that one is missing the associated purchase order. The auditor may conclude that:
   - The control is functioning adequately.
   - The purchase was unauthorized.
   - The vendor has sent and billed for unsolicited goods.
   - Thirty-nine of the sample purchases were properly recorded.

3. The auditor selects a sample consisting of one hundred paid invoices, and notes that twenty of the associated voucher packages are not properly cancelled after payment. Which of the following is least likely to result?
   - The auditor will perform more substantive testing in this area.
   - The auditor will place less reliance on this control.
   - The auditor will qualify his opinion on the financial statements.
   - The auditor will communicate this weakness to management.

4. Which of the following is true about the auditor's tolerable rate of deviation?
   - It is determined using mathematical formulas and tables.
   - It is the maximum error that can exist in an account balance or class of transactions without causing the financial statements to be materially misstated.
   - It is used in drawing conclusions about the operation of internal controls.
   - It is compared to the sample deviation rate in forming conclusions.

Explanation

1. **Choice 4 is correct—*The auditor should not rely on this control.***
The two purchases that lack appropriate signatures should be considered deviations, despite the fact that the purchases may have been appropriate. In addition, the allowance for sampling risk (2%) must be added to the sample deviation rate (4%) before comparing to the tolerable rate (5%). In this case, 4% + 2% > 5%, so the auditor should not rely on this control. Note that the auditor has selected an appropriate population (purchases exceeding $500) for this audit test.

2. **Choice 1 is correct—*The control is functioning adequately.***
The sum of the sample deviation rate (one divided by forty, or 2.5%) and the allowance for sampling risk (2%) is less than the tolerable deviation rate of 5%, so the control is deemed to be functioning adequately. The lack of a purchase order does not necessarily mean that the purchase was unauthorized, since authorization can occur even if the appropriate documentation is missing. Similarly, although it is possible that the vendor sent unsolicited goods, the auditor would need to investigate further to see if this were actually the case. Finally, although thirty-nine of the voucher packages were complete, this does not necessarily mean that the associated purchases were properly recorded. Remember that a test of controls provides information about the functioning of those controls, not about the proper recording of the associated transactions.

3. **Choice 3 is correct—*The auditor will qualify his opinion on the financial statements.***
The sample deviation rate of 20% clearly represents a control that is not functioning effectively. The auditor would be unlikely to rely on this control, and might choose to perform additional substantive testing in this area. In addition, the auditor would probably let management know that this control was not functioning correctly. However, control deviations do not necessarily result in financial statement misstatements, so this situation alone would be unlikely to result in a qualification of the audit report.

4. **Choice 3 is correct—*It is used in drawing conclusions about the effectiveness of controls.***
The sum of the sample deviation rate and the allowance for sampling risk is compared to the tolerable deviation rate in drawing conclusions about the operation of internal controls. Note that the tolerable deviation rate represents the maximum rate of deviation from prescribed controls that the auditor is willing to tolerate without modifying planned reliance on internal control. This amount is usually determined based on auditor judgment (and not by using mathematical formulas and tables), and it is compared to the upper deviation rate (not the sample deviation rate) in forming conclusions. Note too that the maximum error that can exist in an account balance or class of transactions without causing the financial statements to be materially misstated is tolerable error or tolerable misstatement, not tolerable deviation.

Task-Based Simulation 3: Variables Sampling

Scroll down to complete all parts of this task.

An audit senior has made the following changes to the accounts receivable and accounts payable statistical sampling plans submitted by a staff accountant. How will each of these changes affect the sample size?

	A	B
1	**Revisions to the A/R Plan**	
2	Reduce both the tolerable misstatement and the expected misstatement.	
3	Decrease the assessed risk of material misstatement.	
4	Increase the population variability.	
5	Change from blank confirmation forms to confirmations that state the balance.	
6	**Revisions to the A/P Plan**	
7	Increase the tolerable misstatement.	
8	Decrease both the expected misstatement and the assessed risk of material misstatement.	
9	Increase the population to include another category of payables.	
10	Decrease the population variability.	

Select an option below

- Increase in sample size
- Decrease in sample size
- No effect on sample size
- Indeterminate effect on sample size

RESET CANCEL ACCEPT

Explanation

Revisions to the A/R Plan

Row 2: Indeterminate effect on sample size
A reduction in tolerable misstatement causes an increase in sample size, whereas a reduction in expected misstatement causes a decrease in sample size. The overall effect on sample size is therefore indeterminate.

Row 3: Decrease in sample size
The assessed risk of material misstatement is directly related to sample size, so a decrease in the assessed level of risk results in a smaller sample size.

Row 4: Increase in sample size
Population variability is directly related to sample size, so an increase in population variability causes sample size to increase.

Row 5: No effect on sample size
Changing the form of accounts receivable confirmations has no effect on sample size.

Revisions to the A/P Plan

Row 7: Decrease in sample size
Tolerable misstatement is inversely related to sample size, so an increase in tolerable misstatement results in a decrease in sample size.

Row 8: Decrease in sample size
Since both the expected misstatement and the assessed risk of material misstatement vary directly with sample size, a decrease in these two parameters will result in a decrease in sample size.

Row 9: No effect on sample size
The number of items in the population has virtually no effect on sample size, unless the population is very small. (Note: On the CPA exam, if the question doesn't clearly indicate an unusually small population, assume population size has no effect on sample size.)

Row 10: Decrease in sample size
Population variability is directly related to sample size, so a decrease in population variability causes sample size to decrease.

Task-Based Simulation 4: Research

An auditor has decided to apply statistical sampling techniques to the audit of purchases, and has randomly selected specific purchase order numbers for further testing. However, for some purchase order numbers supporting documentation cannot be located. Where in the AICPA Professional Standards will the auditor find guidance applicable to this situation?

Enter your response in the answer fields below. Guidance on correctly structuring your response appears above and below the answer fields.

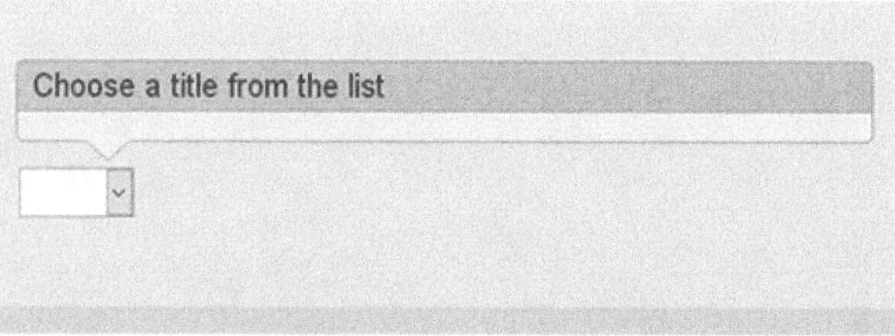

Explanation

Source of answer to this question:

AU-C 530.A19

Keywords: Unexamined items

Tests of Controls

1 Purpose

Tests of controls are used to evaluate the operating effectiveness of internal control in preventing or detecting material misstatements. Tests of controls are necessary when:

- The risk assessment is based on the operating effectiveness of internal control.
- Substantive procedures alone are insufficient because there is extensive use of information technology.

2 Tests of Operating Effectiveness

Testing the operating effectiveness of internal controls includes obtaining evidence regarding:

- Whether the controls were applied at relevant times
- How the controls were applied
- The consistency with which the controls were applied
- By whom or by what means the controls were applied

3 Nature, Extent, and Timing

3.1 Nature

The auditor should use a combination of procedures to obtain sufficient evidence of operating effectiveness. Acceptable procedures include:

- Reperformance
- Inspection
- Observation
- Inquiry

3.2 Extent

The auditor should consider the following factors to determine the extent of a control test:

- Frequency of performance of control
- Length of time over which the auditor intends to rely on the control
- Relevance and reliability of the evidence
- The extent to which other tests provide evidence about the assertion
- The extent to which the auditor intends to rely on the operating effectiveness of the control to reduce substantive procedures
- Expected deviation rate

3.3 Timing

Controls tested at a point in time provide evidence that the control operated effectively at that time, whereas controls tested throughout the period provide evidence of the operating effectiveness during the period.

4 Results

After performing tests of controls, the auditor may conclude that audit evidence indicates that:

- controls are operating effectively and can be relied upon.
- controls are not operating effectively, in which case the auditor can:
  - test alternative controls; or
  - respond to the assessed risk of material misstatement with more reliable and extensive substantive procedures.

Question 4-1 FR-00022

Which of the following is *least* likely to be evidence the auditor examines to determine whether controls are operating effectively?

1. Records documenting usage of computer programs.
2. Canceled supporting documents.
3. Confirmations of accounts receivable.
4. Signatures on authorization forms.

? Related Questions

For related questions, go to the online question bank:

- FR-00013
- FR-00023
- FR-00043
- FR-00944
- FR-00946

Analytical Procedures

1 Use of Analytical Procedures in the Audit

Analytical procedures are evaluations of financial information made by a study of plausible relationships between financial and nonfinancial data.

1.1 Types of Analytical Procedures

Analytical procedures generally involve comparisons of recorded amounts to independent expectations developed by the auditor, including:

- Comparisons of financial data, such as comparison of current and prior year financial statements
- Ratio analysis

1.2 Use During the Audit

Analytical procedures are used during the planning, substantive procedure, and final review stages of the audit.

Phase	Requirement	Purpose
Planning	Required	To assist the auditor in understanding the entity and its environment. Used for risk measurement to alert the auditor to problem areas requiring attention. This serves a vital planning function.
Substantive procedures	Not required	As a substantive test to obtain audit evidence about specific management assertions related to account balances or transactions. The evidence is circumstantial and generally additional corroborating evidence (such as documentation) must be obtained.
Final review	Required	To assist the auditor in the final review of the overall reasonableness of account balances.

D Analytical Procedures

Question 1-1 FR-00952

An auditor notices that interest expense stayed approximately the same as the prior year even though the debt outstanding significantly increased from the prior year. The client only invests in debt that has a fixed interest rate. Which of the following best explains the reason for the above explanation?

1. The company paid off a significant portion of the debt.
2. The company acquired a new loan for construction of a building that began during the year under audit.
3. The Federal Reserve decreased interest rates in the current year.
4. The company acquired a new loan at midyear related to the acquisition of a competitor.

2 Ratio Analysis

2.1 Liquidity Ratios

Measures of a firm's short-term ability to pay maturing obligations.

$$\text{Working capital} = \text{Current assets} - \text{Current liabilities}$$

$$\text{Current ratio (working capital ratio)} = \frac{\text{Current assets}}{\text{Current liabilities}}$$

$$\text{Quick ratio} = \frac{\text{Cash and cash equivalents} + \text{Short-term marketable securities} + \text{Accounts receivable (net)}}{\text{Current liabilities}}$$

- Generally, as the current/quick ratios increase, an entity's ability to meet short-term obligation improves (and vice versa).

2.2 Activity Ratios

Measures of how effectively an enterprise is using its assets.

$$\text{Accounts receivable turnover} = \frac{\text{Sales (net)}}{\text{Average accounts receivables (net)}}$$

- This ratio indicates the receivables' quality and indicates the success of a firm in collecting outstanding receivables. Faster turnover is better.

$$\text{Days sales in accounts receivable} = \frac{\text{Ending accounts receivable (net)}}{\text{(Sales (net) / 365)}}$$

$$\text{Inventory turnover} = \frac{\text{Cost of goods sold}}{\text{Average inventory}}$$

- This ratio measures how quickly inventory is sold. The higher the turnover, the better the performance.

$$\text{Days in inventory} = \frac{\text{Ending inventory}}{\text{(Cost of goods sold / 365)}}$$

$$\text{Operating cycle} = \text{Days sales in accounts receivable} + \text{Days in inventory}$$

- Indicates the number of days between the acquisition of inventory and the realization of cash from selling the inventory—the "cash to cash" cycle.

$$\text{Working capital turnover} = \frac{\text{Sales (net)}}{\text{Average working capital}}$$

- This ratio indicates how effectively working capital is used.

$$\text{Asset turnover} = \frac{\text{Sales (net)}}{\text{Average total assets}}$$

- This ratio is indicative of a firm's effective use of its assets. A high ratio indicates effective asset use to generate sales.

2.3 Profitability Ratios

Measures of the success or failure of an enterprise for a given period of time.

$$\text{Net profit margin} = \frac{\text{Net income}}{\text{Net sales}}$$

$$\text{Net operating margin percentage} = \frac{\text{Net operating income}}{\text{Net sales}}$$

$$\text{Gross (profit) margin} = \frac{\text{Sales (net)} - \text{Cost of goods sold}}{\text{Sales (net)}}$$

$$\text{Return on assets} = \frac{\text{Net income}}{\text{Average total assets}}$$

2.4 Long-Term Debt-Paying Ability Ratios

Measures of security for long-term creditors/investors.

$$\text{Debt to equity} = \frac{\text{Total liabilities}}{\text{Total equity}}$$

$$\text{Total debt ratio} = \frac{\text{Total liabilities}}{\text{Total assets}}$$

These ratios indicate the degree of protection to creditors in case of insolvency. The lower these ratios, the better the company's position.

Question 2-1 FR-00115

Which of the following is *least* likely to be a reasonable explanation for an increase in accounts receivable turnover?

1. Early payment incentives for customers.
2. Tightening of credit policy.
3. Implementation of more aggressive collection policies.
4. Allowance of a new grace period for customer payments.

Related Questions

For related questions, go to the online question bank:

- FR-00065
- FR-00074
- FR-00109

Task-Based Simulations

Task-Based Simulation: Ratios

Scroll down to complete all parts of this task.

As part of the audit of Silva's current year financial statements, Rachel & Shannon, CPAs, calculate various financial statement ratios. For each of the following ratios, identify the interpretation of the ratio by clicking in the associated cell and selecting the appropriate option from the list provided.

	A	B
1	**Ratio**	**Interpretation**
2	Quick ratio	
3	Current ratio	
4	Debt-to-equity ratio	
5	Times interest earned	
6	Accounts receivable turnover	
7	Inventory turnover	
8	Asset turnover	
9	Profit margin	
10	Return on assets	
11	Return on equity	

Select an option below

- The client's ability to cover interest charges
- The client's profit rate
- The client's short-term liquidity
- The client's immediate short-term liquidity
- The client's success in collecting outstanding receivables
- The client's efficiency in using its resources
- How quickly the client's inventory is sold during the year
- How effectively the client makes use of its assets
- The degree of protection afforded to the client's creditors in case of insolvency
- The return earned by the client's shareholders

RESET CANCEL ACCEPT

Explanation

Row 2: The client's immediate short-term liquidity

(Cash equivalents + Marketable securities + Net receivables) / Current liabilities

This ratio provides an indication of Silva's immediate short-term liquidity. Inventory and prepaids are not included.

Row 3: The client's short-term liquidity

Current assets / Current liabilities

This ratio provides an indication of Silva's short-term liquidity.

Row 4: The degree of protection afforded to the client's creditors in case of insolvency

Total liabilities / Total equity

This ratio indicates the degree of protection afforded to creditors in case of insolvency.

Row 5: The client's ability to cover interest charges

(Earnings before interest and taxes) / Interest expense

This ratio reflects Silva's ability to cover interest charges.

Row 6: The client's success in collecting outstanding receivables

Sales (net) / Average accounts receivable (net)

This ratio indicates Silva's success in collecting outstanding receivables.

Row 7: How quickly the client's inventory is sold during the year

Cost of goods sold / Average inventory

This ratio indicates how quickly inventory is sold during the year.

Row 8: How effectively the client makes use of its assets

Sales (net) / Average total assets

This ratio indicates how effectively Silva makes use of its assets.

Row 9: The client's profit rate

Net income / Sales (net)

This ratio indicates Silva's profit rate.

Row 10: The client's efficiency in using its resources

Net income / Average total assets

This ratio indicates Silva's efficiency in using its resources.

Row 11: The return earned by the client's shareholders

Net income / Average total equity

This ratio indicates the return earned by shareholders.

Substantive Procedures

1 Types of Substantive Procedures

Substantive procedures are performed to detect material misstatements at the relevant assertion level. They are required for each material transaction class, account balance, or disclosure.

Substantive procedures include:

- Tests of details of transactions and balances.
- Analytical procedures.

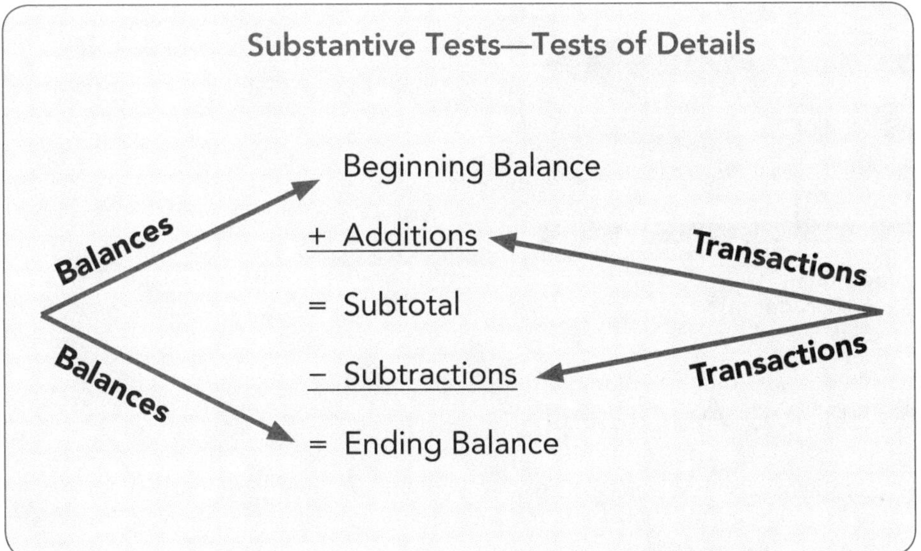

2 Substantive Analytical Procedures

In certain situations, analytical procedures are a more effective and efficient means of gathering evidence than tests of details, and in those cases, analytical procedures may be used as substantive tests.

When using substantive analytical procedures, the auditor considers:

- Designing and performing substantive analytical procedures, including audit data analytics (ADAs) and any associated techniques, tools, graphics, and tables.
- Efficiency and effectiveness of analytical procedures.
- Limitations of analytical procedures.
- Documentation requirements.
- Analytical procedures used as an overall review.

3 Directional Testing

Directional testing refers to testing either forward or backward.

3.1 Tracing Forward

Tracing forward from source documents to journal entries or to the financial statements provides evidence of completeness.

3.2 Vouching Backward

Vouching backward from the financial statements or from journal entries to source documents provides evidence of existence or occurrence.

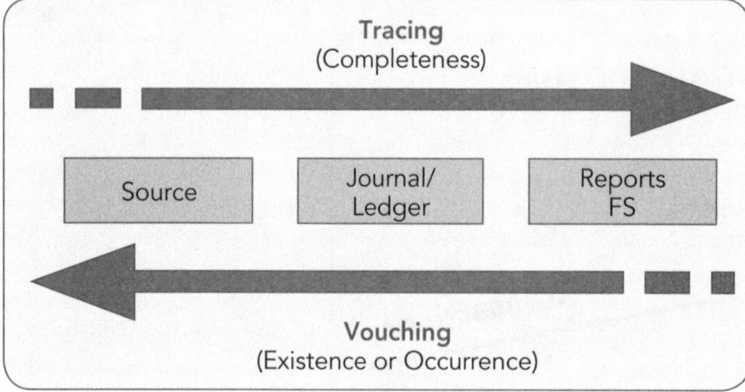

4 Common Substantive Auditing Procedures

- **F**ooting, cross-footing, and recalculation: Adding down and across; testing arithmetical accuracy of statements and schedules (valuation and allocation).
- **I**nquiry: Made of both internal and external sources.
- **V**ouching: Directional testing; looking for support for what has been recorded in the records and statements; going from the financial statement back to supporting documents (existence/occurrence).
- **E**xamination and inspection of documents/records; reading board of directors' (BOD) minutes; reviewing the financial statement (understandability and classification).
- **C**onfirmation: Direct written verification from independent third parties about account balances (existence) and transactions or events (occurrence). Also, perform **c**utoff review of year-end transactions (proper period).
- **A**nalytical procedures: Establish relationships and highlight risk areas. Also, **a**udit related accounts.
- **R**eperformance: Auditor independently performs control procedures.
- **R**econciliation: Substantiates the existence and valuation of accounts. Also, **r**ead necessary information such as meeting minutes from BOD/ shareholder meetings, and obtain management **r**epresentation letter.

- **O**bservation: Provides the auditor with direct knowledge; most persuasive form of evidence in providing assurance as to the existence or occurrence of an item.
- **T**racing: Directional testing; starts with the source documents and traces forward to provide assurance that the event is being given proper recognition in the books and records (completeness; accuracy).
- **C**utoff review: The auditor should perform a cutoff review of year-end transactions, especially inventory, cash, purchases, sales, and accruals.
- **A**uditing related accounts simultaneously: Certain accounts can be audited simultaneously, including long-term liabilities and interest expense, capital additions to PP&E and repairs and maintenance expense, and investments and investment income.
- **R**epresentation letter: At the conclusion of fieldwork, the independent auditor must obtain a management representation letter from the client.
- **S**ubsequent events review: Procedures required for the period after the balance sheet date up to the date of the auditor's report.

Question 4-1 FR-00021

Which financial statement assertion is violated when an expense occurring in one year is *not* recorded until the following year?

1. Accuracy
2. Classification
3. Completeness
4. Occurrence

5 Interim Substantive Procedures

- Performing substantive procedures at an interim date requires additional work to extend audit conclusions to period end.
- Interim substantive procedures should only be performed when the risk of material misstatement is low.

Question 5-1 FR-00935

Which of the following is a substantive procedure?

1. Verifying that the vouchers payable package is appropriately approved.
2. Observing the payroll distribution on an unannounced basis.
3. Observing the preparation of the accounts receivable aging schedule.
4. Examining open vouchers as part of the search for unrecorded liabilities.

E Substantive Procedures

Task-Based Simulations

Task-Based Simulation: Audit Tests

Scroll down to complete all parts of this task.

Vicky is a first year staff accountant who is unsure of the difference between tests of controls and substantive testing.

For each of the following tests in column A, indicate whether it is more likely to be used as a "test of controls" or as a "substantive test" by selecting the appropriate option from the list provided in column B.

	A	B
1	Compare current year actual sales to the current year forecasted sales.	
2	Verify that voucher packages indicate agreement of purchase order, receiving report, and invoice.	
3	Confirm accounts receivable.	
4	Trace the auditor's test counts of inventory into the client's inventory schedule.	
5	Perform sales cutoff test.	
6	Examine subsequent cash collections.	
7	Inspect checks for restrictive endorsement prior to deposit.	
8	Observe the use of time clocks and time cards.	
9	Inquire regarding access controls to the client's computer systems.	
10	Recalculate interest expense for reasonableness.	
11	Calculate interest income as a percentage of average investment in bonds.	

Select an option below

- Test of controls
- Substantive test

RESET CANCEL ACCEPT

Explanation

Tests of controls are procedures performed to evaluate the effectiveness of either the design or the operation of a control.

Substantive tests are of tests of the details of transactions and balances, and analytical review procedures.

Row 1: Substantive test
Comparing actual sales to forecasted sales is an analytical review procedure.

Row 2: Test of controls
Verifying that voucher packages indicate agreement of purchase order, receiving report, and invoice allows the auditor to determine whether the control is operating effectively.

Row 3: Substantive test
Confirmation of accounts receivable is a test of the details of the receivables balance.

Row 4: Substantive test
Tracing the auditor's test counts of inventory into the client's inventory schedule is a test of the details of the inventory balance.

Row 5: Substantive test
Performing a sales cutoff test is a test of the details of sales transactions.

Row 6: Substantive test
Examining subsequent cash collections is a means of testing the details of the receivables balance.

Row 7: Test of controls
Inspecting checks for restrictive endorsement prior to deposit is a means of determining whether the control is operating effectively.

Row 8: Test of controls
Observation of the use of time clocks and time cards is a means of determining whether the control is operating effectively.

Row 9: Test of controls
Inquiring regarding access controls to the client's computer system is a means of determining whether the control is operating effectively.

Row 10: Substantive test
Recalculating interest expense for reasonableness is a test of the details of interest transactions.

Row 11: Substantive test
Calculating interest income as a percentage of average investment in bonds is an analytical review procedure.

Confirmations

1 Auditing Accounts Receivable

1.1 Accounts Receivable Confirmations

Confirmation of accounts receivable is required unless:

- receivables are immaterial; or
- confirmation would be ineffective; or
- inherent and control risks are very low and evidence provided by other procedures sufficiently reduces audit risk.

The auditor must document the basis for omission of confirmation procedures.

1.2 Positive Confirmations

Positive confirmations should be used for large receivables. The customers are requested to return a statement to the auditor indicating that they agree with the amount. Positive confirmations should be sent for:

- Large individual accounts
- Expected errors
- Items in dispute
- Weak internal control
- Old balances

1.3 Negative Confirmations

Negative confirmations are less effective than positive confirmations. When negative confirmations are used, an answer is requested only if the amount stated is incorrect. Negative confirmations may be used when:

- inherent and control risks are low; and
- a large number of small balances are being confirmed; and
- there is no reason to expect that the recipients will ignore the confirmations.

1.4 Confirmation Nonresponses

When the auditor has not received replies to positive confirmation requests, the auditor should apply alternative procedures to the nonresponsive accounts to reduce audit risk to an acceptably low level. The nature of alternative procedures varies with the account and the assertion.

The omission of alternative procedures may be warranted when:

- the auditor has not identified unusual qualitative factors or systematic characteristics related to the nonresponses; and
- treating the aggregate nonresponses as 100 percent misstatements would not affect the auditor's conclusion about whether the financial statements are materially misstated.

1.5 Accounts Receivable Confirmation Exceptions

Confirmation exceptions occur when there is a disparity between the amount of the receivable recorded in the client's accounting records and the amount of the receivable confirmed by the client's customer. For confirmation exceptions, the auditor should determine whether the exception is due to a timing difference or a misstatement.

1.6 Evaluating Results

- The auditor should evaluate the evidence provided by confirmations and alternative procedures to determine whether sufficient evidence has been obtained about all the applicable financial statement assertions.
- If the evidence gathered is not sufficient, the auditor should request additional confirmations or extend other tests.

Question 1-1 FR-00929

After multiple attempts, an auditor is unable to obtain a response for several positive requests for year-end accounts receivable confirmations. An appropriate alternative procedure to verify the existence of accounts receivable is:

1. Visit the customer selected for confirmation and review documents in their possession.
2. Obtain the aging of accounts receivable and trace it to the general ledger control account.
3. Examine the applicable sales order, shipping document, and subsequent cash receipts.
4. Examine subsequent cash disbursements and related receiving reports.

Related Questions

For related questions, go to the online question bank:

- FR-00014
- FR-00054
- FR-00073
- FR-00928
- FR-00934

2 Auditing Cash

2.1 Bank Confirmations

Bank confirmations should be sent to all banks with whom the entity has done business. Bank transfer schedules, bank reconciliations, and cutoff bank statements should also be used.

2.2 Fraudulent Cash Schemes

The auditor should look for fraudulent cash schemes during the audit.

2.2.1 Kiting

- Kiting occurs when a check drawn on one bank is deposited in another bank and no record is made of the first disbursement.
- To detect kiting, cash deposits at the end of a period and paid checks returned with the bank statements of the next period should be examined (bank transfer schedule). Check dates will indicate whether the receiving bank recorded the receipt before the recorded disbursement date.

2.2.2 Lapping

- Lapping occurs when current receipts of cash/checks are withheld (i.e., stolen) and not recorded. Subsequent receipts are applied to the prior accounts.
- Safeguard—Use a lockbox system.
- To detect lapping, use the deposit slip test—trace deposit items from the deposit slip to posting in the customer account.

F Confirmations

Question 2-1 FR-00931

At KRM Corporation, an employee performed the following scheme:

Customer	*Employee*
Andrew Vent came in with $100 cash to pay off his outstanding receivable.	The employee stole the $100 cash.
Bob Butterfield paid off $100 of his outstanding receivable.	The employee credited Andrew Kent's account for $100.
Chris Copper paid off $200 of his outstanding receivable.	The employee credited Bob Butterfield's account for $100 and stole the remainder $100.

What best describes this scheme?

1. Kiting
2. Lapping
3. Identity theft
4. Fraudulent financial reporting

Related Questions

For related questions, go to the online question bank:

➤ FR-00114

1 Auditing Revenue

1.1 Flowchart—Cash Receipts and Accounts Receivable

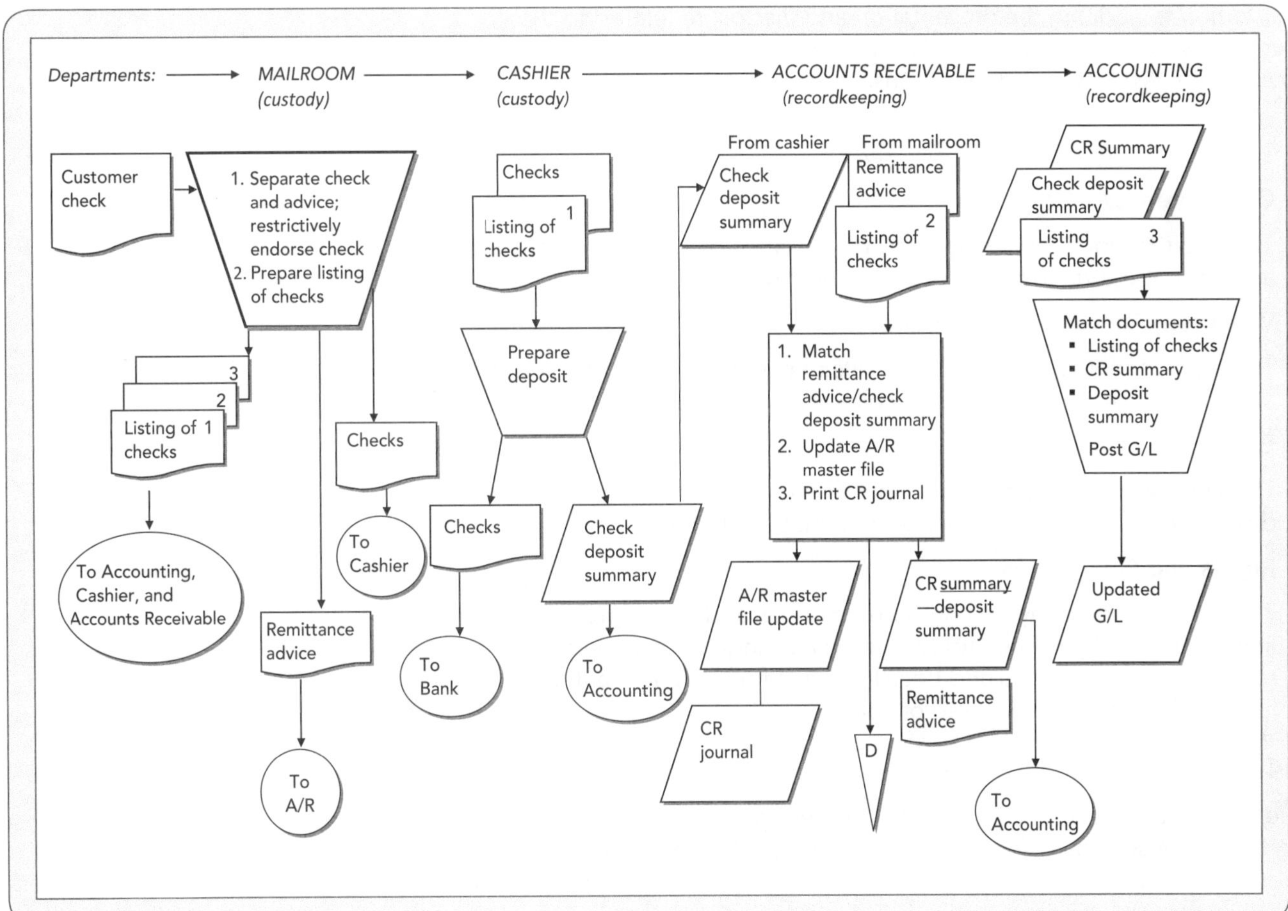

1.2 Segregation of Duties

- **Authorization:** Sales order and credit
- **Record Keeping:** Billing/accounts receivable/accounting
- **Custody:** Warehouse and shipping

1.3 Risk of Overstatement

Management may be pressured to overstate revenues to meet EPS targets and improve balance sheet ratios. For these reasons, management may:

- Record fictitious sales (existence assertion).
- Hold open the sales journal into next year (cutoff).
- Ship goods not ordered, which will be returned next year (improper revenue recognition).

1.4 Substantive Procedures

In addition to auditing the presentation and disclosure related to the revenue cycle, the auditor should perform the following procedures related to accounts receivable and sales transactions.

1.4.1 Auditing Accounts Receivable

- **Completeness**

  The auditor should obtain an aged trial balance of accounts receivable and trace the total to the general ledger control account.

- **Valuation, Allocation, and Accuracy**

  The auditor should examine the results of confirmations and test the adequacy of the allowance for uncollectible accounts.

- **Existence and Occurrence**

  The auditor should confirm a sample of accounts receivable (see the discussion of accounts receivable confirmations below).

- **Rights and Obligations**

  The auditor should review bank confirmations and debt agreements for liens on receivables. The auditor should also inquire of management and review debt agreements and board minutes for evidence that accounts receivable have been factored or sold.

1.4.2 Auditing Sales Transactions

The following tests of details may also be performed as tests of controls or dual-purpose tests. The cutoff procedure is performed most often as a substantive procedure.

- **Completeness**

  The auditor should trace a sample of shipping documents to the corresponding sales invoices and to the sales journal and accounts receivable subsidiary ledger.

- **Cutoff**

  The auditor should compare a sample of sales invoices from shortly before and after year-end with the shipment dates and with the dates the sales were recorded in the sales journal. The auditor should also analyze the record of sales returns after year-end.

- **Valuation, Allocation, and Accuracy**

  The auditor should compare prices and terms on a sample of sales invoices with authorized price lists and terms of trade to determine whether sales are recorded at the appropriate amount.

- **Existence and Occurrence**

  The auditor should vouch a sample of sales transactions from the sales journal to the sales invoice back to the customer order and shipping documents.

- **Understandability and Classification**

  The auditor should examine a sample of sales invoices for proper classification into the appropriate revenue accounts.

Question 1-1 FR-00003

Which of the following controls most likely would assure that all billed sales are correctly posted to the accounts receivable ledger?

1. Daily sales summaries are compared to daily postings to the accounts receivable ledger.
2. Each sales invoice is supported by a prenumbered shipping document.
3. The accounts receivable ledger is reconciled daily to the control account in the general ledger.
4. Each shipment on credit is supported by a prenumbered sales invoice.

Question 1-2 FR-00943

Tracing shipping documents to sales invoices provides evidence that:

1. Sales billed to customers were actually shipped.
2. Shipments to customers were properly invoiced.
3. Shipments to customers were recorded as sales.
4. All goods ordered by customers were shipped.

2 Auditing Expenditures

2.1 Segregation of Duties

- **Purchasing Department:** Approve and prepare purchase order.
- **Receiving Department:** Receive goods, match with purchase order (blind copy), and prepare receiving reports.
- **Vouchers Payable Department:** Match documents, purchase order, receiving reports, invoice; prepare and approve voucher, verify accuracy.
- **Treasury Department:** Review documents, prepare check & remittance advice, sign checks, cancel voucher package.

2.2 Substantive Procedures

In addition to auditing the presentation and disclosure related to the expenditure cycle, the auditor should perform the following procedures related to accounts payable and purchase transactions.

2.2.1 Auditing Accounts Payable

- **Completeness**

  The auditor should perform a search for unrecorded liabilities.

- **Valuation, Allocation, and Accuracy**

  The auditor should obtain the accounts payable listing, foot the listing, and agree the listing to the general ledger, obtain a sample of vendor statements and agree the amounts to the vendor accounts, and review the results of any accounts payable confirmations.

- **Existence and Occurrence**

  The auditor should vouch selected amounts from the accounts payable listing to the voucher packages. The auditor may also confirm accounts payable. Accounts payable confirmations are not required because good external evidence to support accounts payable is generally available. However, confirmations of accounts payable may be sent when internal control is weak, when there are disputed amounts, or when monthly vendor statements are not available. Typically, vendors with small or zero balances would be selected for confirmation.

- **Rights and Obligations**

  The auditor should review a sample of voucher packages for the presence of the purchase requisition, purchase order, receiving report and vendor invoice to verify that the accounts payable are owed by the entity.

2.2.2 Auditing Purchase Transactions

The following substantive tests may also be performed as tests of controls or dual-purpose tests.

- **Completeness**

  The auditor should trace a sample of vouchers to the purchase journal.

- **Cutoff**

  The auditor should compare dates on a sample of vouchers with the dates the transactions were recorded in the purchase journal. The auditor should also examine purchases before and after year-end to determine if they were recorded in the proper period.

- **Valuation, Allocation, and Accuracy**

  The auditor should recompute the mathematical accuracy of a sample of vendor invoices.

- **Existence and Occurrence**

  The auditor should test a sample of vouchers for authorization and the presence of the receiving report.

- **Understandability and Classification**

  The auditor should verify the account classification of a sample of purchases.

Question 2-1 FR-00945

An auditor searching for unrecorded payables most likely would:

1. Obtain a sample of vendor invoices and recalculate the invoice amount.
2. Obtain the accounts payable listing and agree to subsequent cash payments.
3. Compare cash disbursements made prior to year-end with vendor invoices.
4. Compare subsequent bank statements with the accounts payable listing.

3 Auditing PP&E

The property, plant, and equipment cycle includes all tangible long-term asset functions (e.g., purchasing, maintenance and repair, depreciation, retirement).

- **Purchases and Retirements:** Verify that proper authorization was obtained, and that proper procedures were followed. The auditor should vouch additions to fixed assets by examining documentation and inspecting the actual asset (existence). The auditor should also select older fixed assets from the subsidiary ledger and try to locate the assets as a means of testing for unrecorded retirements (existence). The auditor should review related repair and maintenance accounts for any improper classification of additions and repairs as expenses (completeness and classification).
- **Authorization:** Verify Board approval of substantial purchases.
- **Physical Security:** Serially numbered plates should be on assets; the control account should include all appropriate information.
- **Depreciation:** Verify that written policies and records are maintained; recalculate expense and ensure conformity with GAAP (valuation and accuracy).
- **Impairments:** Check for adjustments for impairments (valuation and accuracy).

Question 3-1 FR-00053

An auditor analyzes repair and maintenance accounts primarily to obtain evidence in support of the audit assertion that all:

1. Noncapitalizable expenditures for repairs and maintenance have been recorded in the proper period.
2. Expenditures for property and equipment have been recorded in the proper period.
3. Noncapitalizable expenditures for repairs and maintenance have been properly charged to expense.
4. Expenditures for property and equipment have not been charged to expense.

4 Auditing Payroll

4.1 Segregation of Duties

Controls including proper segregation of duties are essential to prevent common problems in the payroll and personnel cycle—fictitious employees and falsification of hours.

4.1.1 Authorization

- **Authorization to Employ and Pay:** The human resource department's function is to hire new employees and maintain personnel records (hire date, salary, and position).
- **Supervision:** All pay base data (hours, absences, and time off) should be approved by an employee's immediate supervisor.

4.1.2 Record Keeping

- **Timekeeping and Cost Accounting:** Data on which pay is based should be accumulated independent of any other function. Hourly employees should use time clocks. Supervisors should compare job time tickets to signed employee clock cards.
- **Payroll Check Preparation:** The payroll department computes salary based on information received. This department is responsible for issuing the unsigned payroll checks.

4.1.3 Custody of Assets

The treasurer is responsible for signing the payroll checks.

4.1.4 Auditing Payroll and Personnel

- The auditor reviews the payroll account to determine that only authorized people are being paid, and that they are receiving the right amounts. The auditor should verify time records, and perform recalculations of payroll amounts and any year-end accruals (valuation assertion).
- A person who has no other payroll function should distribute the payroll checks. This person is often referred to as the paymaster. Employees should be required to show ID before receiving paychecks.

4.2 Substantive Procedures

When internal control over payroll is effective, the auditor generally focuses substantive procedures on the valuation and accuracy assertion. The following audit procedures should be performed to verify the accuracy of payroll amounts:

- Vouch time on payroll summaries by selecting a payroll register entry and comparing to time cards and approved time reports.
- Compare total recorded payroll with total payroll checks issued.

- Test extensions and footings of payroll.
- Verify pay rates and payroll deductions with employee records from personnel.
- Recalculate gross and net pay on a test basis.
- Recalculate any year-end accruals.
- Compare payroll costs with standards or budgets.

Substantive tests should be extended if unusual fluctuations or significant errors are noted.

Question 4-1 FR-00033

In auditing the payroll function of a client, an auditor would least likely:

1. Request specific management representations related to payroll.
2. Verify proper segregation of duties.
3. Recalculate year-end payroll accruals.
4. Apply analytical procedures.

5 Auditing Liabilities

When auditing debt, the auditor reviews board minutes for evidence of new debt, obtains new debt agreements, and traces new debt to the financial statements (completeness), recomputes gains and losses, interest expense and interest payable (valuation and accuracy), and verifies proper presentation and disclosure.

6 Auditing Owners' Equity and Treasury Stock

The audit of owners' equity and treasury stock includes examining transactions related to the sale and repurchase of stock, related payments, dividends, and retained earnings.

6.1 Substantive Procedures

- **Treasury Stock:** Examine and reconcile the number of shares in the treasury stock account, and trace all transactions to the accounting records and the board minutes (existence and completeness).
- **Stock Transactions:** Vouch all transactions to supporting documentation (existence).
- **Minutes of Board Meetings:** Verify that all stock issuances, dividends declared, and treasury stock transactions have been authorized by the board.
- **Articles of Incorporation:** Read the articles and prepare excerpts for the permanent file.
- **Stock Transfer Agents:** Use third-party confirmations to provide evidence of shares authorized, issued, and outstanding (completeness and existence).
- **Stock Certificate Book:** If there is no transfer agent, review the stock certificate book to provide evidence of proper stock transaction accounting (completeness and existence).
- **Retained Earnings:** Analyze retained earnings account since inception (or since the last audit) and review the propriety of any direct entries to retained earnings (valuation), and determine whether any appropriations are necessary (understandability and classification).

Question 6-1 FR-00063

An audit program for the examination of the retained earnings account should include a step that requires verification of the:

1. Market value used to charge retained earnings to account for a two-for-one stock split.
2. Approval of the adjustment to the beginning balance as a result of a write-down of an account receivable.
3. Authorization for both cash and stock dividends.
4. Gain or loss resulting from disposition of treasury shares.

Specific Matters That Require Special Consideration: Inventory and Investments

Topic **H**

1 Auditing Inventory

- **Controls:** Good controls should exist between purchasing, receiving, storage, and shipping.
- **Observation:** Observation of the physical inventory count is required, although failure to observe can be mitigated by alternative procedures. Observation and test counts provide evidence related to existence and completeness.
- **Calculation:** The auditor should test the physical inventory report by tracing test counts and verifying mathematical accuracy.
- **Consigned Goods:** The auditor should ascertain that consigned inventory on hand is excluded from the physical count, while goods out on consignment are included in inventory.
- **Related Accounts:** Simultaneous procedures should be undertaken for accounts related to inventory (purchases, sales, returns, and allowances).
- **Quantity:** Cutoff procedures should be performed for purchases and sales.
- **Presentation:** GAAP (lower of cost or market) should be followed.
- **Analytical Review:** Overall reasonableness of amounts and disclosures should be evaluated; ratio analysis may be used.
- **Obsolete or Damaged Goods:** The inventory listing should be reviewed for slow-moving items; inquiries should be made regarding obsolete or damaged goods.

Question 1-1 FR-00926

In auditing a manufacturing entity, which of the following procedures would an auditor most likely perform to determine whether slow-moving, defective, and obsolete items included in inventory are properly identified?

1. Test the mathematical accuracy of the inventory report.
2. Inquire of management about whether inventory has been pledged or assigned.
3. Tour the manufacturing plant or production facility.
4. Test the computation of standard overhead rates.

Related Questions

For related questions, go to the online question bank:

➤ FR-00082

2 Auditing Investments

The auditor must ensure that GAAP is consistently applied, gains and losses are accurately computed and disclosed, investment income is properly reported, valuation is fairly stated and disclosed, and the investments in fact exist and are owned by the entity under audit.

- **Segregation of Duties:** Authorization (usually the board of directors), the custodial function, and record keeping should be segregated.
- **Confirmation From Third Parties:** This should be obtained if investments are held by an independent, third-party custodian.
- **Physical Inspection:** For securities on hand, a physical inspection should be performed.
- **Cutoff Procedures:** These procedures should be applied to purchases, sales, and investment income.
- **Conformance With GAAP:** Derivative, cost/equity method, trading, available-for-sale, and held-to-maturity classifications should be used.
- **Computations:** Gains, losses, discount or premium amortization, and interest or dividend income should be independently calculated.
- **Management Representations:** The auditor should inquire of management and obtain written representation concerning management's intent and ability to hold or to exercise significant influence over investments.
- **Reasonableness and Appropriateness:** These factors should be evaluated as they relate to assumptions, market variables, valuation models, and any decline in fair value.
- **Special Skill or Knowledge:** The auditor may need special skill or knowledge to plan and perform auditing procedures for certain assertions about derivatives and securities.

Question 2-1 FR-00064

Which of the following provides the best evidence supporting the existence of marketable securities included in the client's financial statements?

1. A custodial statement received and held by the client.
2. The client's securities ledger.
3. Broker's advice regarding purchases and sales of marketable securities.
4. A year-end listing of market prices for the securities obtained by reference to the Wall Street Journal.

Related Questions

For related questions, go to the online question bank:

➤ FR-00024

Task-Based Simulations

Task-Based Simulation: Evaluating Results

Scroll down to complete all parts of this task.

Davis & Smith, CPAs, have performed a variety of audit tests as part of their audit of Silva Inc. and must now evaluate their results. For each of the following situations, identify whether the selected balance (shown in parentheses) is "overstated," "understated," or "fairly stated" by clicking in the associated cell and selecting the appropriate option from the list provided.

	A	B
1	One of Silva's suppliers shipped goods to Silva on December 26, Year 1, FOB destination, with a scheduled arrival date of December 30, Year 1. The goods did not arrive at Silva's receiving dock until January 2, Year 2. The goods were included in Silva's ending inventory based on the scheduled arrival date of December 30. (inventory)	
2	On December 31, a major customer of Silva's requested a rush order of goods. Silva shipped the goods just before the close of business on the 31st, FOB shipping point. Silva did not include the goods in its year-end inventory balance. (inventory)	
3	One of Silva's customers is holding goods on consignment for Silva. The goods were delivered to the customer on December 31, Year 1. Silva has included the retail value of these goods in its sales for Year 1. (sales)	
4	December 31, Year 1 falls on a Wednesday, but Silva pays its employees on Fridays. The payroll expense for the year includes all checks written through December 31. (expense)	
5	On December 31, Silva sold goods to a related party. The goods were sold above Silva's cost but below the normal retail value. (sales)	

Select an option below

- Overstated
- Understated
- Fairly stated

RESET CANCEL ACCEPT

Explanation

Row 1: Overstated
Title does not transfer until the goods have arrived at Silva's receiving dock, regardless of the scheduled arrival date. Therefore, these goods should not be included in Year 1 inventory.

Row 2: Fairly stated
Silva properly excluded the goods from inventory as title transferred to the buyer as soon as the goods were shipped.

Row 3: Overstated
Silva's sales will be overstated. Goods held on consignment (which have not yet been sold) still properly belong to Silva. No sale has taken place.

Row 4: Understated
Payroll expense should properly be accrued for the last three days of the year, even though no money will be paid until January Year 2.

Row 5: Fairly stated
Related party transactions are by definition not considered to be consummated at arm's-length, and such transactions must be disclosed in the financial statements. However, this does not imply that there is an error in sales.

Specific Matters That Require Special Consideration: Attorney Letter

Topic I

1 Overview

When audit procedures indicate that there are actual or potential litigation, claims, or assessments, the auditor should seek direct communication with the entity's external legal counsel through a letter of inquiry regarding litigation, claims and assessments.

- The auditor should inquire about specific litigation (if identified), including the timing and the degree of probability of an unfavorable outcome.
- The lawyer's response is sent directly to the auditor.
- No response or a refusal to cooperate is considered a scope limitation.

Question 1-1 FR-00947

Which limitation on response from an attorney in response to auditor's inquiry may result in a qualified opinion?

1. The client's refusal to permit inquiry of the attorney.
2. The attorney's refusal to respond when the attorney has given substantial attention to the matter.
3. An inherent uncertainty making it difficult for a lawyer to form conclusions regarding pending litigation.
4. The attorney limits replies to matters to which he or she has given substantial attention.

Question 1-2 FR-00091

Which of the following best describes the purpose of an auditor's external inquiry sent to the client's attorney?

1. To develop an appropriate understanding of controls in place with respect to the recognition of litigation, claims, and assessments.
2. To evaluate the operating effectiveness of controls in place with respect to the recognition of litigation, claims, and assessments.
3. To corroborate information provided by management with respect to litigation, claims, and assessments.
4. To obtain reasonable assurance from the client's attorney regarding fair presentation of litigation, claims, and assessments in the financial statements.

? Related Questions

For related questions, go to the online question bank:

➤ FR-00044

2 Sample Attorney Letter

Letter of Audit Inquiry

[*Company Letterhead*]

[*Appropriate Addressee*]:

In connection with an audit of our financial statements at (balance sheet date) and for the (period) then ended, management of the Company has prepared, and furnished to our auditors (name and address of auditors), a description and evaluation of certain contingencies, including those set forth below involving matters with respect to which you have been engaged and to which you have devoted substantive attention on behalf of the Company in the form of legal consultation or representation. These contingencies are regarded by management of the Company as material for this purpose (management may indicate a materiality limit if an understanding has been reached with the auditor). Your response should include matters that existed at (balance sheet date) and during the period from that date to the date of your response.

Pending or Threatened Litigation

[*Ordinarily management's information would include (i) the nature of the litigation, (ii) the progress of the case to date, (iii) how management is responding or intends to respond to the litigation, and (iv) an evaluation of the likelihood of an unfavorable outcome and an estimate, if one can be made, of the amount or range of potential loss.*]

This letter will serve as our consent for you to furnish to our auditor all the information requested therein. Accordingly, please furnish to our auditors such explanation, if any, that you consider necessary to supplement the foregoing information, including an explanation of those matters as to which your views may differ from those stated and an identification of the omission of any pending or threatened litigation, claims, and assessments or a statement that the list of such matters is complete.

Unasserted Claims and Assessments

[*Ordinarily management's information would include (i) the nature of the matter, (ii) how management intends to respond if the claim is asserted, and (iii) an evaluation of the likelihood of an unfavorable outcome and an estimate, if one can be made, of the amount or range of potential loss.*]

Please furnish to our auditors such explanation, if any, that you consider necessary to supplement the foregoing information, including an explanation of those matters as to which your views may differ from those stated.

We understand that whenever, in the course of performing legal services for us with respect to a matter recognized to involve an unasserted possible claim or assessment that may call for financial statement disclosure, if you have formed a professional conclusion that we should disclose or consider disclosure concerning such possible claim or assessment, as a matter of professional responsibility to us, you will so advise us and will consult with us concerning the question of such disclosure and the applicable requirements of Financial Accounting Standards Board (FASB) Accounting Standards Codification (ASC) 450, Contingencies. Please specifically confirm to our auditors that our understanding is correct.

Please specifically identify the nature of and reasons for any limitations on your response.

Very truly yours,

[*Name*]

Specific Matters That Require Special Consideration: Going Concern

Topic **J**

1 Auditor Responsibility

The auditor is responsible for evaluating audit evidence to determine whether there is *"substantial doubt"* that the client will be able to continue as a going concern for a reasonable period of time, as defined by the financial reporting framework used (FASB—one year after financial statements are issued or available to be issued; GASB—one year beyond the date of the financial statements).

2 Emphasis-of-Matter or Explanatory Paragraph

If substantial doubt exists, an *emphasis-of-matter paragraph* (nonissuer) or explanatory paragraph (issuer) stating the auditor's concerns should be added to the auditor's opinion. The words *"substantial doubt"* and *"going concern"* must be included.

Emphasis of Matter

The accompanying financial statements have been prepared assuming that the Company will continue as a going concern. As discussed in Note X to the financial statements, the Company has suffered recurring losses from operations and has a net capital deficiency, and has stated that substantial doubt exists about the Company's ability to continue as a going concern. Management's evaluation of the events and conditions and management's plans regarding these matters are also described in Note X. The financial statements do not include any adjustments that might result from the outcome of this uncertainty. Our opinion is not modified with respect to this matter.

Question 2-1 FR-00057

Calibro, CPA, believes that there is substantial doubt about the ability of Canto Company, a nonissuer, to continue as a going concern. This matter is appropriately disclosed in Canto's financial statements. Calibro should:

1. Issue an unmodified opinion with an other-matter paragraph describing the situation.
2. Issue a qualified opinion due to the fact that there is substantial doubt about the ability of Canto Company to continue as a going concern.
3. Issue an unmodified opinion with an emphasis-of-matter paragraph describing the situation.
4. Withdraw from the engagement, to minimize the association with financial statements that may be misleading.

3 Audit Approach

3.1 Audit Procedures

The following audit procedures (ADMITS) may indicate that there is a problem with the entity's ability to continue as a going concern:

- **A**nalytical procedures
- Review of compliance with terms of **d**ebt/loan agreements
- Review of the **m**inutes of stockholder/board meetings
- **I**nquiry of client's legal counsel
- Confirmation of the details of financial support arrangements with **t**hird parties
- Review of **s**ubsequent events

3.2 Conditions

Conditions (FINE) that may indicate a problem include:

- **F**inancial difficulties
- **I**nternal matters (e.g., work stoppages, labor difficulties)
- **N**egative financial trends
- **E**xternal matters (e.g., legal proceedings, new legislation)

3.3 Mitigating Factors

The auditor should consider *mitigating factors*. Both intent and ability are required.

3.4 Subsequent Periods

If doubt is removed in a subsequent period, the going concern paragraph need not be repeated.

Question 3-1 FR-00037

Davis, CPA, believes there is substantial doubt about the ability of Hill Co. to continue as a going concern for a reasonable period of time. In evaluating Hill's plans for dealing with the adverse effects of future conditions and events, Davis most likely would consider, as a mitigating factor, Hill's plans to:

1. Accelerate research and development projects related to future products.
2. Accumulate treasury stock at prices favorable to Hill's historic price range.
3. Purchase equipment and production facilities currently being leased.
4. Negotiate reductions in required dividends being paid on preferred stock.

Internal Control Deficiencies

Topic **K**

1 Control Deficiency

A control deficiency exists when the design or operation of a control does not allow management or employees, in the normal course of their assigned functions, **to prevent, or detect and correct** [*prevent and detect*], misstatements on a timely basis.

Note

Wording for nonissuers is shown in **bold**; wording for issuers is shown in [*brackets*].

2 Significant Deficiency

A significant deficiency is a deficiency (or a combination of deficiencies) in internal control [*over financial reporting*] that is less severe than a material weakness, yet important enough to merit attention by **those charged with governance** [*responsible for oversight of the company's financial reporting*].

3 Material Weakness

A material weakness is a deficiency (or a combination of deficiencies) in internal control [*over financial reporting*] such that there is a reasonable possibility that a material misstatement of the **entity's** [*company's annual or interim*] financial statements will not be **prevented, or detected and corrected,** [*prevented or detected*] on a timely basis.

3.1 Reasonable Possibility

"Reasonable possibility" implies that the likelihood of an event is either reasonably possible or probable.

3.2 Indicators of Material Weakness

The following situations are indicators of material weakness in internal control:

- Identification of any level of fraud (even immaterial fraud) perpetrated by senior management.
- Restatement of previously issued financial statements to correct a material misstatement.
- Identification by the auditor of a material misstatement that would not have been detected by the entity's internal control.
- Ineffective oversight by those charged with governance.

Question 3-1 FR-00803

Significant deficiencies are control deficiencies that come to an auditor's attention that are:

1. Disclosures of information that significantly contradict the auditor's going concern assumption.
2. Material fraud or illegal acts perpetrated by high-level management.
3. Important enough to merit attention by those charged with governance.
4. Manipulation or falsification of accounting records or documents from which financial statements are prepared.

Related Questions

For related questions, go to the online question bank:

- FR-00119

Written Representations

Topic
L

1 Overview

At the conclusion of fieldwork, the auditor must obtain a letter (signed by the CEO and CFO), dated as of the date of the auditor's report.

1.1 Purpose

The purposes of the representation letter are:

- to ensure that management accepts its responsibility for the assertions in the entity's financial statements; and
- to document the client's representations and responses to inquiries concerning various aspects of the audit.

1.2 Timing

The representation letter is the final piece of audit evidence. When reporting on comparative financial statements, it should address all periods covered by the report. This letter is mandatory; omission of this letter constitutes a scope limitation.

Question 1-1 FR-00930

According to U.S. GAAS, the date of the management representation letter should be:

1. As near as possible to, but not after, the date of the auditor's report.
2. The same as the date of the auditor's report.
3. As near as possible to, but not after, the date of the financial statements.
4. The same as the date of the financial statements.

? Related Questions

For related questions, go to the online question bank:

- FR-00034
- FR-00936

2 Sample Representation Letter

Management Representation Letter

[*Entity Letterhead*]

To [*Auditor*] [*Date*]

This letter is provided in connection with your audit of the financial statements of ABC Company, which comprise the balance sheet as of December 31, 20XX, and the related statements of income, changes in stockholders' equity, and cash flows for the year then ended, and the related notes to the financial statements, for the purpose of expressing an opinion on whether the financial statements are presented fairly, in all material respects, in accordance with accounting principles generally accepted in the United States (U.S. GAAP).

Certain representations in this letter are described as being limited to matters that are material. Items are considered material, regardless of size, if they involve an omission or misstatement of accounting information that, in the light of surrounding circumstances, makes it probable that the judgment of a reasonable person relying on the information would be changed or influenced by the omission or misstatement.

Except where otherwise stated below, immaterial matters less than $[*insert amount*] collectively are not considered to be exceptions that require disclosure for the purpose of the following representations. This amount is not necessarily indicative of amounts that would require adjustment to or disclosure in the financial statements.

We confirm that, [*to the best of our knowledge and belief, having made such inquiries as we considered necessary for the purpose of appropriately informing ourselves*] [*as of (date of auditor's report)*]:

Financial Statements

1. We have fulfilled our responsibilities, as set out in the terms of the audit engagement dated [*insert date*], for the preparation and fair presentation of the financial statements in accordance with U.S. GAAP.

2. We acknowledge our responsibility for the design, implementation, and maintenance of internal control relevant to the preparation and fair presentation of financial statements that are free from material misstatement, whether due to fraud or error.

3. We acknowledge our responsibility for the design, implementation, and maintenance of internal control to prevent and detect fraud.

4. Significant assumptions used by us in making accounting estimates, including those measured at fair value, are reasonable.

5. Related party relationships and transactions have been appropriately accounted for and disclosed in accordance with the requirements of U.S. GAAP.

6. All events subsequent to the date of the financial statements and for which U.S. GAAP requires adjustment or disclosure have been adjusted or disclosed.

7. The effects of uncorrected misstatements are immaterial, both individually and in the aggregate, to the financial statements as a whole. A list of the uncorrected misstatements is attached to the representation letter.

8. The effects of all known or possible litigation and claims have been accounted for and disclosed in accordance with U.S. GAAP.

[*Any other matters that the auditor may consider appropriate.*]

(continued)

(continued)

Information Provided

9. We have provided you with:

   a. Access to all information, of which we are aware that is relevant to the preparation and fair presentation of the financial statements such as records, documentation and other matters;

   b. Additional information that you have requested from us for the purpose of the audit; and

   c. Unrestricted access to persons within the entity from whom you determined it necessary to obtain audit evidence.

10. All transactions have been recorded in the accounting records and are reflected in the financial statements.

11. We have disclosed to you the results of our assessment of the risk that the financial statements may be materially misstated as a result of fraud.

12. We have [*no knowledge of any*] [*disclosed to you all information that we are aware of regarding*] fraud or suspected fraud affecting the entity and involves:

    a. Management,

    b. Employees who have significant roles in internal control, or

    c. Others where the fraud could have a material effect on the financial statements.

13. We have [*no knowledge of any*] [*disclosed to you all information that we are aware of regarding*] allegations of fraud, or suspected fraud, affecting the entity's financial statements communicated by employees, former employees, analysts, regulators, or others.

14. We disclosed to you all known instances of noncompliance or suspected noncompliance with laws and regulations whose effects should be considered when preparing financial statements.

15. We [*have disclosed to you all known actual or possible*][*are not aware of any pending or threatened*] litigation and claims whose effects should be considered when preparing financial statements [*and we have not consulted legal counsel concerning litigation or claims*].

16. We have disclosed to you the identity of the entity's related parties and all the related party relationships and transactions of which we are aware.

[*Any other matters that the auditor may consider necessary.*]

____

[*Name of Chief Executive Officer and Title*]

____

[*Name of Chief Financial Officer and Title*]

Subsequent Events

1 Types of Subsequent Events

A subsequent event occurs between the balance sheet date and the date the financial statements are issued. Subsequent events may require either adjustment to the financial statements or additional disclosure. Subsequent events are divided into two categories.

1.1 Recognized Events

Recognized events are conditions existing on or before the balance sheet date. Recognized events usually require adjustment to the financial statements.

1.2 Nonrecognized Events

Nonrecognized events are conditions existing after the balance sheet date. Nonrecognized events usually require disclosure, but no financial statement adjustment.

Question 1-1 FR-00027

A client acquired 25% of its outstanding capital stock after year-end but prior to the date of the auditor's report. The auditor should:

1. Advise management to adjust the balance sheet to reflect the acquisition.
2. Issue pro forma financial statements giving effect to the acquisition as if it had occurred at year-end.
3. Advise management to disclose the acquisition in the notes to the financial statements.
4. Disclose the acquisition in the opinion paragraph of the auditor's report.

2 Auditor's Responsibility

The auditor has an active responsibility to investigate subsequent events during the period from the balance sheet date to the date of the auditor's report. Responsibilities include:

- Reviewing **p**ost balance sheet transactions.
- Obtaining a **r**epresentation letter from management.
- **I**nquiry
- Reading the **m**inutes of stockholder, director, and other committee meetings.
- **E**xamining the latest available interim statements.

3 Responsibility After the Auditor's Report Date

The auditor has no active responsibility after the date of the auditor's report, but cannot ignore information coming to his/her attention. If subsequent events result in adjustments or disclosures that are made after the original date of the auditor's report, the auditor may dual date the report to extend responsibility only for the particular subsequent event.

Question 3-1 FR-00094

An auditor issues a report dated 2/12/Year 2 on financial statements for the year ended 12/31/Year 1. Which best describes the auditor's responsibility for an event occurring on 2/1/Year 2 and an event occurring on 3/1/Year 2?

1. The auditor has an active responsibility to investigate both events.
2. The auditor has an active responsibility to investigate the 2/1/Year 2 event, but no responsibility concerning the 3/1/Year 2 event.
3. The auditor has an active responsibility to investigate the 2/1/Year 2 event, and must also consider the effect of the 3/1/Year 2 event if it comes to his/her attention.
4. The auditor has no responsibility for either event, since both occur after the date of the financial statements.

Task-Based Simulations

Task-Based Simulation: Subsequent Events

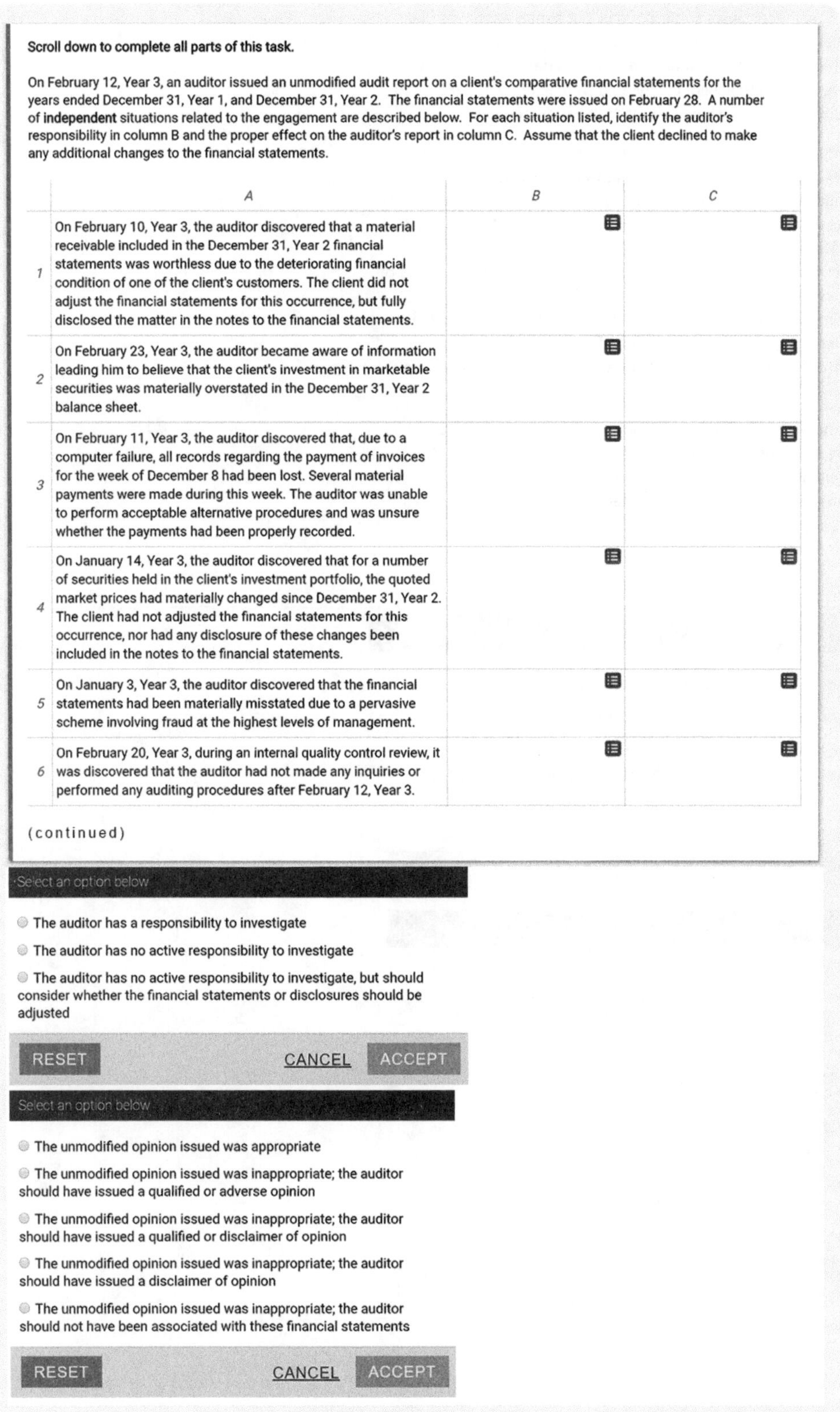

Scroll down to complete all parts of this task.

On February 12, Year 3, an auditor issued an unmodified audit report on a client's comparative financial statements for the years ended December 31, Year 1, and December 31, Year 2. The financial statements were issued on February 28. A number of **independent** situations related to the engagement are described below. For each situation listed, identify the auditor's responsibility in column B and the proper effect on the auditor's report in column C. Assume that the client declined to make any additional changes to the financial statements.

	A	B	C
1	On February 10, Year 3, the auditor discovered that a material receivable included in the December 31, Year 2 financial statements was worthless due to the deteriorating financial condition of one of the client's customers. The client did not adjust the financial statements for this occurrence, but fully disclosed the matter in the notes to the financial statements.		
2	On February 23, Year 3, the auditor became aware of information leading him to believe that the client's investment in marketable securities was materially overstated in the December 31, Year 2 balance sheet.		
3	On February 11, Year 3, the auditor discovered that, due to a computer failure, all records regarding the payment of invoices for the week of December 8 had been lost. Several material payments were made during this week. The auditor was unable to perform acceptable alternative procedures and was unsure whether the payments had been properly recorded.		
4	On January 14, Year 3, the auditor discovered that for a number of securities held in the client's investment portfolio, the quoted market prices had materially changed since December 31, Year 2. The client had not adjusted the financial statements for this occurrence, nor had any disclosure of these changes been included in the notes to the financial statements.		
5	On January 3, Year 3, the auditor discovered that the financial statements had been materially misstated due to a pervasive scheme involving fraud at the highest levels of management.		
6	On February 20, Year 3, during an internal quality control review, it was discovered that the auditor had not made any inquiries or performed any auditing procedures after February 12, Year 3.		

(continued)

Select an option below

- The auditor has a responsibility to investigate
- The auditor has no active responsibility to investigate
- The auditor has no active responsibility to investigate, but should consider whether the financial statements or disclosures should be adjusted

RESET CANCEL ACCEPT

Select an option below

- The unmodified opinion issued was appropriate
- The unmodified opinion issued was inappropriate; the auditor should have issued a qualified or adverse opinion
- The unmodified opinion issued was inappropriate; the auditor should have issued a qualified or disclaimer of opinion
- The unmodified opinion issued was inappropriate; the auditor should have issued a disclaimer of opinion
- The unmodified opinion issued was inappropriate; the auditor should not have been associated with these financial statements

RESET CANCEL ACCEPT

(continued)

7	On February 27, Year 3, during an internal quality control review, it was discovered that the staff accountant on the job never actually mailed any receivables confirmations, but simply assumed that receivables were fairly stated. However, all outstanding receivables at year-end were paid within 30 days, and material cash receipts subsequent to year-end were audited and traced to the receivables worksheet as part of the audit of cash.		
8	On February 4, Year 3, the auditor discovered that the client was the defendant in a product liability lawsuit. The client's management asserted its innocence, and its attorney agreed with this assessment. However, the attorney also noted that it would be significantly less costly to settle out of court than to proceed to trial, and the client's management was likely to follow the advice of counsel. Settlement costs could not be reasonably estimated at that time, but they were likely to be material. The client had not accrued this cost or made mention of this matter in its financial statements, as it did not wish to give an appearance of guilt in any way.		
9	On January 19, Year 3, the auditor became aware that the client was recalling one of its products due to a design defect that posed a potential safety hazard. The potential cost of the recall program was material and could be estimated with a reasonable degree of precision. The client had accrued this cost in its financial statements.		

Select an option below

- The auditor has a responsibility to investigate
- The auditor has no active responsibility to investigate
- The auditor has no active responsibility to investigate, but should consider whether the financial statements or disclosures should be adjusted

RESET CANCEL ACCEPT

Select an option below

- The unmodified opinion issued was appropriate
- The unmodified opinion issued was inappropriate; the auditor should have issued a qualified or adverse opinion
- The unmodified opinion issued was inappropriate; the auditor should have issued a qualified or disclaimer of opinion
- The unmodified opinion issued was inappropriate; the auditor should have issued a disclaimer of opinion
- The unmodified opinion issued was inappropriate; the auditor should not have been associated with these financial statements

RESET CANCEL ACCEPT

Explanation

The auditor has an active responsibility to investigate subsequent events between the date of the financial statements and the date of the auditor's report (12/31/Y2 through 2/12/Y3, in this case). The auditor would also be responsible for investigating the effects of any omitted audit procedures discovered after the submission of the audit report.

The auditor has no active responsibility to make inquiries or perform any further auditing procedures after the date of the auditor's report (2/12/Y3), but should consider the implications of any information coming to his or her attention.

Row 1: The auditor has a responsibility to investigate | The unmodified opinion issued was inappropriate; the auditor should have issued a qualified or adverse opinion
Because this discovery took place prior to the date of the auditor's report, the auditor was responsible to investigate. Additionally, this condition likely existed at the date of the financial statements and because the loss was probable and estimable, a financial statement adjustment is required. Because no adjustment was made, a qualified or adverse opinion would have been appropriate

Row 2: The auditor has no active responsibility to investigate, but should consider whether the financial statements or disclosures should be adjusted | The unmodified opinion issued was inappropriate; the auditor should have issued a qualified or adverse opinion
The auditor had no responsibility to make inquiries or perform any further auditing procedures after February 12, but could not ignore information that came to his attention. Given the new information, a qualified or adverse opinion would have been appropriate. (At this point, however, the client would more likely be advised to revise the financial statements, since they have not yet been issued.)

Row 3: The auditor has a responsibility to investigate | The unmodified opinion issued was inappropriate; the auditor should have issued a qualified or disclaimer of opinion.
Because this discovery took place prior to the date of the auditor's report, the auditor was responsible to investigate. Because the auditor was unable to perform acceptable alternative procedures and was unsure whether the payments had been properly recorded, a qualified or disclaimer of opinion would have been appropriate.

Row 4: The auditor has no active responsibility to investigate | The unmodified opinion issued was appropriate
The auditor is only required to investigate certain subsequent events between year-end and the date of the auditor's report. Changes in the market prices of securities are not among these items. Such changes are to be expected and would not require adjustment to or disclosure in the financial statements. The unmodified opinion issued was therefore appropriate.

Row 5: The auditor has a responsibility to investigate | The unmodified opinion issued was inappropriate; the auditor should not have been associated with these financial statements
Because this discovery took place prior to the date of the auditor's report, the auditor was responsible to investigate. Additionally, since this situation posed serious concerns about both the financial statements and management's integrity, the auditor should have withdrawn from the engagement and should not have been associated with these financial statements.

(continued)

Explanation

(continued)

Row 6: The auditor has no active responsibility to investigate | The unmodified opinion issued was appropriate
The auditor had no responsibility to make inquiries or perform any further auditing procedures after February 12. Because no problems had come to his attention, the unmodified opinion remained the appropriate option.

Row 7: The auditor has a responsibility to investigate | The unmodified opinion issued was appropriate
The auditor is responsible for investigating the effects of any omitted audit procedures discovered after the submission of the audit report. In this case, it appears that other audit procedures tended to compensate for the omitted audit procedure, so the unmodified opinion remains the appropriate option.

Row 8: The auditor has a responsibility to investigate | The unmodified opinion issued was inappropriate; the auditor should have issued a qualified or adverse opinion
Because this discovery took place prior to the date of the auditor's report, the auditor was responsible to investigate. The incurrence of this cost was probable but not estimable, so GAAP requires footnote disclosure. Because the company neglected to disclose the situation, a qualified or adverse opinion should have been expressed.

Row 9: The auditor has a responsibility to investigate | The unmodified opinion issued was appropriate
Because this discovery took place prior to the date of the auditor's report, the auditor was responsible to investigate. The cost was both probable and estimable, so the company properly accrued this amount. Because GAAP was followed, an unmodified opinion remains the appropriate option.

Subsequent Discovery of Facts

Topic **N**

1 Auditor Action

If the auditor becomes aware of material information after the report's issuance and knows persons are currently relying or likely to rely on the financial statements, the auditor should advise the client to immediately disclose the information and its impact on the financial statements. If the financial impact cannot be timely ascertained, notification should be made that the financial statements cannot be relied upon.

2 Client Refuses to Follow Procedures

The auditor must be satisfied with the client's action; if not, the auditor should notify the board of directors and the client that the audit report cannot be associated with the financial statements. The auditor should also notify any regulatory agencies and any persons known to be relying on the statements and report.

Question 2-1 FR-00871

Which of the following events occurring after the issuance of the auditor's report most likely would cause the auditor to make further inquiries about the previously issued financial statements?

1. The company issues a bond for a material amount.
2. Loss of a plant as the result of a fire.
3. Purchase of a business that has revenues equivalent to the entity.
4. The discovery of information regarding a material unrecorded expense that occurred during the year under audit.

Related Questions

For related questions, go to the online question bank:

➤ FR-00872

IV Forming Conclusions and Reporting

Reports on Auditing Engagements

1 Opinion Types

1.1 Unmodified (Unqualified) Opinion

An unmodified opinion states that the financial statements present fairly, in all material respects, the financial position, results of operations, and cash flows of the entity, in conformity with the applicable financial reporting framework.

1.1.1 Emphasis-of-Matter, Other-Matter, Explanatory, and Critical Audit Matters Paragraphs

These are additional communications added to the auditor's report without modifying the auditor's opinion.

1.2 Modified Opinions

The auditor's report is modified when the auditor concludes that the financial statements as a whole are materially misstated (GAAP issue) or when the auditor is unable to obtain sufficient appropriate audit evidence to conclude that the financial statements as a whole are free from material misstatement (GAAS issue).

1.2.1 Qualified Opinion

A qualified opinion states that *except for* the effects of the matter(s) to which the qualification relates, "the financial statements present fairly..." It is used for GAAS or GAAP issues.

1.2.2 Adverse Opinion

An adverse opinion states that the financial statements do not present fairly. It is used for GAAP issues.

1.2.3 Disclaimer of Opinion

A disclaimer of opinion states that auditor does not express an opinion on the financial statements. It is used for GAAS issues.

2 Unmodified Opinion (Nonissuer)

Financial statements are presented fairly in all material respects. The following is an unmodified option for a nonissuer reporting on a single year.

Independent Auditor's Report

[*Appropriate Addressee*]

Report on the Financial Statements[1]

We have audited the accompanying financial statements of ABC Company, which comprise the balance sheet as of December 31, 20X1, and the related statements of income, changes in stockholders' equity, and cash flows for the year then ended, and the related notes to the financial statements.

Management's Responsibility for the Financial Statement

Management is responsible for the preparation and fair presentation of these financial statements in accordance with accounting principles generally accepted in the United States of America; this includes the design, implementation, and maintenance of internal control relevant to the preparation and fair presentation of financial statements that are free from material misstatement whether due to fraud or error.

Auditor's Responsibility

Our responsibility is to express an opinion on these financial statements based on our audit. We conducted our audit in accordance with auditing standards generally accepted in the United States of America. Those standards require that we plan and perform the audit to obtain reasonable assurance about whether the financial statements are free from material misstatement.

An audit involves performing procedures to obtain audit evidence about the amounts and disclosures in the financial statements. The procedures selected depend on the auditor's judgment, including the assessment of the risks of material misstatement of the financial statements, whether due to fraud or error. In making those risk assessments, the auditor considers internal control relevant to the entity's preparation and fair presentation of the financial statements in order to design audit procedures that are appropriate in the circumstances, but not for the purpose of expressing an opinion on the effectiveness of the entity's internal control. Accordingly, we express no such opinion. An audit also includes evaluating the appropriateness of accounting policies used and the reasonableness of significant accounting estimates made by management, as well as evaluating the overall presentation of the financial statements.

We believe that the audit evidence we have obtained is sufficient and appropriate to provide a basis for our audit opinion.

Opinion

In our opinion, the financial statements referred to above present fairly, in all material respects, the financial position of ABC Company as of December 31, 20X1, and the results of its operations and its cash flows for the year then ended in accordance with accounting principles generally accepted in the United States of America.

Report on Other Legal and Regulatory Requirements

[*Form and content of this section of the auditor's report will vary depending on the nature of the auditor's other reporting responsibilities.*]

[*Auditor's signature*]

[*Auditor's city and state*]

[*Date of the auditor's report*]

[1] "Report on the Financial Statements" is unnecessary in circumstances when the second subtitle, "Report on Legal and Regulatory Requirements," is not used.

3 Audits of Group Financial Statements

When an auditor acts as the auditor of group financial statements, the auditor must determine whether to make reference to any component auditors in the auditor's report on the group financial statements.

3.1 Making Reference to the Component Auditor

When making reference to the component auditor, the auditor's report on the group financial statements should clearly indicate that the component was audited by the component auditor and should include the magnitude of the portion of the financial statements audited by the component auditor.

3.1.1 U.S. GAAS

Under U.S. GAAS, the name of the component auditor may be included in the auditor's report only if permission is granted by the component auditor and the component auditor's report is presented with the auditor's report on the group financial statements.

3.1.2 Auditor's Report Referencing the Audit of a Component Auditor (Nonissuer)

Independent Auditor's Report

[Appropriate Addressee]

We have audited the accompanying consolidated financial statements of ABC Company and its subsidiaries, which comprise the consolidated balance sheets as of December 31, 20X1 and 20X0, and the related consolidated statements of income, changes in stockholders' equity, and cash flows for the year then ended, and the related notes to the financial statements.

Management's Responsibility for the Financial Statements

Management is responsible for the preparation and fair presentation of these consolidated financial statements in accordance with accounting principles generally accepted in the United States of America; this includes the design, implementation, and maintenance of internal control relevant to the preparation and fair presentation of consolidated financial statements that are free from material misstatement whether due to fraud or error.

Auditor's Responsibility

Our responsibility is to express an opinion on these consolidated financial statements based on our audits. We did not audit the financial statements of B Company, a wholly-owned subsidiary, which statements reflect total assets constituting 20 percent and 22 percent, respectively, of consolidated total assets at December 31, 20X1 and 20X0, and total revenues constituting 18 percent and 20 percent, respectively, of consolidated total revenues for the years then ended. Those statements were audited by other auditors, whose report has been furnished to us, and our opinion, insofar as it relates to the amounts included for B Company, is based solely on the report of the other auditors. We conducted our audit in accordance with auditing standards generally accepted in the United States of America. Those standards require that we plan and perform the audit to obtain reasonable assurance about whether the financial statements are free from material misstatement.

An audit involves performing procedures to obtain audit evidence about the amounts and disclosures in the consolidated financial statements. The procedures selected depend on the auditor's judgment, including the assessment of the risks of material misstatement of the consolidated financial statements, whether due to fraud or error. In making those risk assessments, the auditor considers internal control relevant to the entity's preparation and fair presentation of the consolidated financial statements in order to design audit procedures that are appropriate in the circumstances, but not for the purpose of expressing an opinion on the effectiveness of the entity's internal control. Accordingly, we express no such opinion. An audit also includes evaluating the appropriateness of accounting policies used and the reasonableness of significant accounting estimates made by management, as well as evaluating the overall presentation of the consolidated financial statements. We believe that the audit evidence we have obtained is sufficient and appropriate to provide a basis for our audit opinion.

Opinion

In our opinion, based on our audit and the report of the other auditors, the consolidated financial statements referred to above present fairly, in all material respects, the financial position of ABC Company and its subsidiaries as of December 31, 20X1 and 20X0, and the results of their operations and their cash flows for the year then ended in accordance with accounting principles generally accepted in the United States of America.

[Auditor's signature]
[Auditor's city and state]
[Date of the auditor's report]

3.2 Assumption of Responsibility

When the group auditor decides to assume responsibility for the work of a component auditor, no reference to the component auditor is made in the auditor's report.

Question 3-1 FR-00865

According to GAAS, which of the following procedures is *not* required when the group auditor decides to make reference to the component auditor in the auditor's report on the group financial statements?

1. The group auditor should be satisfied with the independence of the component auditor.
2. The component auditor's report is not restricted.
3. The group auditor should be satisfied with the competence of the component auditor.
4. The group auditor should determine the type of work to be performed on the financial information of the components.

Related Questions

For related questions, go to the online question bank:

- FR-00868
- FR-00869

4 Emphasis-of-Matter, Other-Matter, Explanatory, and Critical Audit Matters Paragraphs

4.1 Emphasis-of-Matter Paragraphs

An emphasis-of-matter paragraph is included in the auditor's report when required by GAAS or at the auditor's discretion. An emphasis-of-matter paragraph is used when referring to a matter that is appropriately presented or disclosed in the financial statements and is of such importance that it is fundamental to the users' understanding of the financial statements.

4.1.1 Report Requirements

When an emphasis-of-matter paragraph is included in the auditor's report, the auditor should:

- place the emphasis-of-matter paragraph immediately after the opinion paragraph;
- use the heading "Emphasis of Matter" or other appropriate heading;
- describe the matter and the location of relevant disclosures; and
- state that the auditor's report is not modified with respect to the matter emphasized.

4.1.2 Lack of Consistency—Justified (Acceptable/Justified Change in Accounting Principle)

Consistency is implied in the auditor's report. *If a material change in GAAP has occurred* between periods and such change is justified, the auditor should *add an emphasis-of-matter paragraph* to the auditor's opinion describing the change and referring the reader to the note describing the change in detail.

4.2 Other-Matter Paragraphs

An other-matter paragraph is included in the auditor's report when required by GAAS or at the auditor's discretion. Other-matter paragraphs refer to matters other than those presented or disclosed in the financial statements that are relevant to the users' understanding of the audit, the auditor's responsibilities, or the auditor's report.

4.2.1 Report Requirements

When an other-matter paragraph is included in the auditor's report, the auditor should:

- place the other-matter paragraph immediately after the opinion paragraph and after any emphasis-of-matter paragraph;
- use the heading "Other Matter" or other appropriate heading; and
- describe the matter and the location of relevant disclosures.

4.2.2 Alert That Restricts the Use of the Auditor's Written Communication

The auditor may be required by GAAS or may decide that it is necessary to include language in the auditor's report (or other written communication) that restricts the use of the auditor's written communication. In the auditor's report, such language is included in an *other-matter paragraph.*

4.3 Explanatory Paragraphs

An explanatory paragraph is included in the auditor's report when required by PCAOB auditing standards or at the auditor's discretion. The inclusion of an explanatory paragraph in the auditor's report does not affect the auditor's opinion.

4.3.1 Report Requirements

When an explanatory paragraph is included in the auditor's report, the auditor generally should place the explanatory paragraph immediately after the opinion paragraph and describe the matter.

4.4 Critical Audit Matters (Issuers Only)

The auditor's report for audits of issuers must include any critical audit matters (CAMs) arising from the current period's audit of the financial statements, or state that the auditor determined that there were no CAMs.

A critical audit matter is a matter that was communicated or required to be communicated to the audit committee and that:

1. relates to accounts or disclosures that are material to the financial statements; and
2. involved especially challenging, subjective, or complex auditor judgment.

4.4.1 Reporting Requirements

For each CAM identified, the audit report should include:

- **identification** of the CAM;
- description of the **principal** considerations that led the auditor to determine that the matter was a CAM;
- description of how the CAM was **addressed** in the audit; and
- reference to the relevant financial statement accounts or **disclosures**.

Question 4-1 FR-00864

Which of the following circumstances requires the use of an emphasis-of-matter paragraph?

1. An alert in the audit report restricts the use of the audit report.
2. Prior to the audit report date, the auditor identifies a material inconsistency in other information that is included in the document containing audited financial statements that management refuses to revise.
3. The financial statements are prepared in accordance with a special purpose framework.
4. The auditor chooses to report on supplementary information presented with the financial statements in the auditor's report, rather than in a separate report.

? Related Questions

For related questions, go to the online question bank:

➤ FR-00863

5 GAAP Issues: Qualified or Adverse Opinion

The auditor uses professional judgment to determine whether to issue a qualified opinion or an adverse opinion when audit evidence indicates that there is material misstatement of the financial statements.

Materiality of Problem		Financial Statements Are Materially Misstated (GAAP Issues)	Inability to Obtain Sufficient Appropriate Audit Evidence (GAAS Issues)
None or immaterial	=	Unmodified	Unmodified
Material but not pervasive	=	Qualified opinion	Qualified opinion
Material and pervasive	=	Adverse opinion	Disclaimer of opinion

5.1 Qualified Opinion

A qualified opinion should be expressed when the auditor concludes that misstatements, individually or in the aggregate, are material but not pervasive to the financial statements.

5.2 Adverse Opinion

An adverse opinion should be expressed when the auditor concludes that misstatements, individually or in the aggregate, are both material and pervasive to the financial statements.

5.3 Form and Content of Auditor's Report

Nonissuers: When the auditor expresses a qualified or adverse opinion due to a material misstatement of the financial statements, the "Auditor's Responsibility" paragraph is modified and the auditor's report includes a "Basis for Modification" paragraph and a "Qualified Opinion" or "Adverse Opinion" paragraph, as appropriate.

Issuers: When the auditor expresses a qualified or adverse opinion due to material misstatement of the financial statements, the auditor's report will include an additional paragraph immediately following the opinion paragraph and the opinion paragraph will be modified. The auditor is not required to report critical audit matters in the auditor's report when the auditor expresses an adverse opinion.

5.3.1 Qualified Opinion—GAAP Problem (Nonissuer)

Independent Auditor's Report

[Appropriate Addressee]

We have audited the accompanying financial statements of ABC Company, which comprise the balance sheets as of December 31, 20X1 and 20X0, and the related statements of income, changes in stockholders' equity, and cash flows for the years then ended, and the related notes to the financial statements.

Management's Responsibility for the Financial Statements

Management is responsible for the preparation and fair presentation of these financial statements in accordance with accounting principles generally accepted in the United States of America; this includes the design, implementation, and maintenance of internal control relevant to the preparation and fair presentation of financial statements that are free from material misstatement whether due to fraud or error.

Auditor's Responsibility

Our responsibility is to express an opinion on these financial statements based on our audits. We conducted our audits in accordance with auditing standards generally accepted in the United States of America. Those standards require that we plan and perform the audit to obtain reasonable assurance about whether the financial statements are free from material misstatement.

An audit involves performing procedures to obtain audit evidence about the amounts and disclosures in the financial statements. The procedures selected depend on the auditor's judgment, including the assessment of the risks of material misstatement of the financial statements, whether due to fraud or error. In making those risk assessments, the auditor considers internal control relevant to the entity's preparation and fair presentation of the financial statements in order to design audit procedures that are appropriate in the circumstances, but not for the purpose of expressing an opinion on the effectiveness of the entity's internal control. Accordingly, we express no such opinion. An audit also includes evaluating the appropriateness of accounting policies used and the reasonableness of significant accounting estimates made by management, as well as evaluating the overall presentation of the financial statements.

We believe that the audit evidence we have obtained is sufficient and appropriate to provide a basis for our qualified audit opinion.

Basis for Qualified Opinion

The Company has stated inventories at cost in the accompanying balance sheets. Accounting principles generally accepted in the United States of America require inventories to be stated at the lower of cost or market. If the Company stated inventories at the lower of cost or market, a write down of $XXX and $XXX would have been required as of December 31, 20X1 and 20X0, respectively. Accordingly, costs of sales would have increased by $XXX and $XXX, and net income, income taxes, and stockholders' equity would have been reduced by $XXX, $XXX, and $XXX, and $XXX, $XXX, and $XXX, as of and for the years ended December 31, 20X1 and 20X0, respectively.

Qualified Opinion

In our opinion, except for the effects of the matter described in the Basis for Qualified Opinion paragraph, the financial statements referred to above present fairly, in all material respects, the financial position of ABC Company as of December 31, 20X1 and 20X0, and the results of its operations and its cash flows for the years then ended in accordance with accounting principles generally accepted in the United States of America.

[Auditor's signature]
[Auditor's city and state]
[Date of the auditor's report]

5.3.2 Adverse Opinion (Nonissuer)

Independent Auditor's Report

[*Appropriate Addressee*]

We have audited the accompanying consolidated financial statements of ABC Company and its subsidiaries, which comprise the balance sheet as of December 31, 20X1, and the related consolidated statements of income, changes in stockholders' equity, and cash flows for the year then ended, and the related notes to the financial statements.

Management's Responsibility for the Financial Statements

Management is responsible for the preparation and fair presentation of these consolidated financial statements in accordance with accounting principles generally accepted in the United States of America; this includes the design, implementation, and maintenance of internal control relevant to the preparation and fair presentation of consolidated financial statements that are free from material misstatement whether due to fraud or error.

Auditor's Responsibility

Our responsibility is to express an opinion on these consolidated financial statements based on our audits. We conducted our audits in accordance with auditing standards generally accepted in the United States of America. Those standards require that we plan and perform the audit to obtain reasonable assurance about whether the financial statements are free from material misstatement.

An audit involves performing procedures to obtain audit evidence about the amounts and disclosures in the consolidated financial statements. The procedures selected depend on the auditor's judgment, including the assessment of the risks of material misstatement of the consolidated financial statements, whether due to fraud or error. In making those risk assessments, the auditor considers internal control relevant to the entity's preparation and fair presentation of the consolidated financial statements in order to design audit procedures that are appropriate in the circumstances, but not for the purpose of expressing an opinion on the effectiveness of the entity's internal control. Accordingly, we express no such opinion. An audit also includes evaluating the appropriateness of accounting policies used and the reasonableness of significant accounting estimates made by management, as well as evaluating the overall presentation of the consolidated financial statements.

We believe that the audit evidence we have obtained is sufficient and appropriate to provide a basis for our adverse audit opinion.

Basis for Adverse Opinion

As described in Note X, the Company has not consolidated the financial statements of subsidiary XYZ Company that it acquired during 20X1 because it has not yet been able to ascertain the fair value of certain of the subsidiary's material assets and liabilities at the acquisition date. This investment is therefore accounted for on a cost basis by the Company. Under accounting principles generally accepted in the United States of America, the subsidiary should have been consolidated because it is controlled by the Company. Had XYZ Company been consolidated, many elements in the accompanying consolidated financial statements would have been materially affected. The effects on the consolidated financial statements of the failure to consolidate have not been determined.

Adverse Opinion

In our opinion, because of the significance of the matter discussed in the Basis for Adverse Opinion paragraph, the consolidated financial statements referred to above do not present fairly the financial position of ABC Company and its subsidiaries as of December 31, 20X1, or the results of their operations or their cash flows for the year then ended.

[*Auditor's signature*]

[*Auditor's city and state*]

[*Date of the auditor's report*]

6 GAAS Issues—Qualified Opinion or Disclaimer

The auditor uses professional judgment to determine whether to issue a qualified opinion or a disclaimer of opinion due to a limitation on the scope of the audit. A scope limitation occurs when the auditor is unable to obtain sufficient appropriate audit evidence to conclude that the financial statements are free of material misstatement.

Materiality of Problem		Financial Statements Are Materially Misstated (GAAP Issues)	Inability to Obtain Sufficient Appropriate Audit Evidence (GAAS Issues)
None or immaterial	=	Unmodified	Unmodified
Material but not pervasive	=	Qualified opinion	Qualified opinion
Material and pervasive	=	Adverse opinion	Disclaimer of opinion

6.1 Qualified Opinion

A qualified opinion due to a GAAS issue should be expressed when the auditor is unable to obtain sufficient appropriate audit evidence on which to base an opinion and the auditor concludes that the possible effects of any undetected misstatements could be material but not pervasive.

6.2 Disclaimer of Opinion

A disclaimer of opinion should be expressed when the auditor is unable to obtain sufficient appropriate audit evidence on which to base an opinion and the auditor concludes that the possible effects of any undetected misstatements could be both material and pervasive.

6.3 Form and Content of the Auditor's Report

Nonissuer: When the auditor expresses a qualified opinion or disclaimer of opinion due to scope limitation, the Auditor's Responsibility paragraph is modified and the auditor's report will include a Basis for Modification paragraph and a Qualified Opinion or Disclaimer of Opinion paragraph, as appropriate. A disclaimer of opinion will also include a modification to the introductory paragraph of the auditor's report.

Issuer: When the auditor expresses a qualified opinion or disclaimer of opinion, a paragraph immediately following the opinion paragraph is added and the opinion paragraph is modified. A qualified opinion and disclaimer of opinion will include modified language in the basis for opinion section. The auditor is not required to report critical audit matters in the auditor's report when the auditor expresses a disclaimer of opinion.

6.3.1 Qualified Opinion—GAAS Problem (Nonissuer)

Independent Auditor's Report

[Appropriate Addressee]

We have audited the accompanying financial statements of ABC Company, which comprise the balance sheets as of December 31, 20X1, and the related statements of income, changes in stockholders' equity, and cash flows for the year then ended, and the related notes to the financial statements.

Management's Responsibility for the Financial Statements

Management is responsible for the preparation and fair presentation of these financial statements in accordance with accounting principles generally accepted in the United States of America; this includes the design, implementation, and maintenance of internal control relevant to the preparation and fair presentation of financial statements that are free from material misstatement whether due to fraud or error.

Auditor's Responsibility

Our responsibility is to express an opinion on these financial statements based on our audits. We conducted our audits in accordance with auditing standards generally accepted in the United States of America. Those standards require that we plan and perform the audit to obtain reasonable assurance about whether the financial statements are free from material misstatement.

An audit involves performing procedures to obtain audit evidence about the amounts and disclosures in the financial statements. The procedures selected depend on the auditor's judgment, including the assessment of the risks of material misstatement of the financial statements, whether due to fraud or error. In making those risk assessments, the auditor considers internal control relevant to the entity's preparation and fair presentation of the financial statements in order to design audit procedures that are appropriate in the circumstances, but not for the purpose of expressing an opinion on the effectiveness of the entity's internal control. Accordingly, we express no such opinion. An audit also includes evaluating the appropriateness of accounting policies used and the reasonableness of significant accounting estimates made by management, as well as evaluating the overall presentation of the financial statements.

We believe that the audit evidence we have obtained is sufficient and appropriate to provide a basis for our qualified audit opinion.

Basis for Qualified Opinion

ABC Company's investment in XYZ Company, a foreign affiliate acquired during the year and accounted for under the equity method is carried at $XXX on the balance sheet at December 31, 20X1, and ABC Company's share of XYZ Company's net income of $XXX is included in ABC Company's net income for the year then ended. We were unable to obtain sufficient appropriate audit evidence about the carrying amount of ABC Company's investment in XYZ Company as of December 31, 20X1 and ABC Company's share of XYZ Company's net income for the year then ended because we were denied access to the financial information, management, and the auditors of XYZ Company. Consequently, we were unable to determine whether any adjustments to these amounts were necessary.

Qualified Opinion

In our opinion, except for the possible effects of the matter described in the Basis for Qualified Opinion paragraph, the financial statements referred to above present fairly, in all material respects, the financial position of ABC Company as of December 31, 20X1, and the results of its operations and its cash flows for the year then ended in accordance with accounting principles generally accepted in the United States of America.

[Auditor's signature]

[Auditor's city and state]

[Date of the auditor's report]

6.3.2 Disclaimer of Opinion (Nonissuer)

Independent Auditor's Report

[*Appropriate Addressee*]

We were engaged to audit the accompanying financial statements of ABC Company, which comprise the balance sheets as of December 31, 20X1, and the related statements of income, changes in stockholders' equity, and cash flows for the year then ended, and the related notes to the financial statements.

Management's Responsibility for the Financial Statements

Management is responsible for the preparation and fair presentation of these financial statements in accordance with accounting principles generally accepted in the United States of America; this includes the design, implementation, and maintenance of internal control relevant to the preparation and fair presentation of financial statements that are free from material misstatement whether due to fraud or error.

Auditor's Responsibility

Our responsibility is to express an opinion on these financial statements based on conducting the audit in accordance with auditing standards generally accepted in the United States of America. Because of the matters described in the Basis for Disclaimer of Opinion paragraph, however, we were not able to obtain sufficient appropriate audit evidence to provide a basis for an audit opinion.

Basis for Disclaimer of Opinion

We were not engaged as auditors of the Company until after December 31, 20X1, and, therefore, did not observe the counting of physical inventories at the beginning or end of the year. We were unable to satisfy ourselves by other auditing procedures concerning the inventory held at December 31, 20X1, which is stated in the balance sheet at $XXX. In addition, the introduction of a new computerized accounts receivable system in September 20X1 resulted in numerous misstatements in accounts receivable. As of the date of our audit report, management was still in the process of rectifying the system deficiencies and correcting the misstatements. We were unable to confirm or verify by alternative means accounts receivable included in the balance sheet at a total amount of $XXX at December 31, 20X1. As a result of these matters, we were unable to determine whether any adjustments might have been found necessary in respect of recorded or unrecorded inventories and accounts receivable, and the elements making up the statements of income, changes in stockholder's equity, and cash flows.

Disclaimer of Opinion

Because of the significance of the matters described in the Basis for Disclaimer of Opinion paragraph, we have not been able to obtain sufficient appropriate audit evidence to provide a basis for an audit opinion. Accordingly, we do not express an opinion on these financial statements.

[*Auditor's signature*]
[*Auditor's city and state*]
[*Date of the auditor's report*]

Question 6-1 FR-00860

Under which of the following situations would the expression of a disclaimer of opinion be inappropriate?

1. The entity's going concern disclosures are adequate.
2. Management refuses to allow the auditor to send a letter of inquiry to their attorneys.
3. The auditor is not independent.
4. Management fails to disclose a significant subsequent event.

Related Questions

For related questions, go to the online question bank:

- FR-00007
- FR-00047
- FR-00067
- FR-00861
- FR-00862

7 Comparative Financial Statements

7.1 Change in Opinion

A prior opinion may be changed. The auditor should update (i.e., either reaffirm or change) the opinion on any previously issued financial statements shown in comparative statements.

If the updated opinion differs from the previous opinion, the auditor should disclose the reason(s) in an *emphasis-of-matter or other-matter paragraph* (nonissuer) or *explanatory paragraph* (issuer) that discloses the following:

- **D**ate of the previous auditor's report.
- **O**pinion type previously issued.
- **R**eason for the prior opinion.
- **C**hanges that have occurred.
- **S**tatement that "opinion … is different."

7.1.1 Sample Other-Matter Paragraph—Updating Prior Opinion

Other Matter

In our report dated March 1, 20X1, we expressed an opinion that the 20X0 financial statements did not fairly present the financial position, results of operations, and cash flows of ABC Company in accordance with accounting principles generally accepted in the United States of America because of two departures from such principles: (1) ABC Company carried its property, plant, and equipment at appraisal values, and provided for depreciation on the basis of such values; and (2) ABC Company did not provide for deferred income taxes with respect to differences between income for financial reporting purposes and taxable income. As described in Note X, the Company has changed its method of accounting for these items and restated its 20X0 financial statements to conform with accounting principles generally accepted in the United States of America. Accordingly, our present opinion on the restated 20X0 financial statements, as presented herein, is different from that expressed in our previous report.

7.2 Different Opinions

Some comparative reports will have different opinions for each year presented. Depending upon the situation, the appropriate paragraphs will be modified.

7.2.1 Report on Comparative Financial Statements—Different Opinions (Nonissuer)

Independent Auditor's Report

[*Appropriate Addressee*]

We have audited the accompanying financial statements of ABC Company, which comprise the balance sheets as of December 31, 20X1 and 20X0, and the related statements of income, changes in stockholders' equity, and cash flows for the years then ended, and the related notes to the financial statements.

Management's Responsibility for the Financial Statements

Management is responsible for the preparation and fair presentation of these financial statements in accordance with accounting principles generally accepted in the United States of America; this includes the design, implementation, and maintenance of internal control relevant to the preparation and fair presentation of financial statements that are free from material misstatement whether due to fraud or error.

Auditor's Responsibility

Our responsibility is to express an opinion on these financial statements based on our audits. We conducted our audit in accordance with auditing standards generally accepted in the United States of America. Those standards require that we plan and perform the audit to obtain reasonable assurance about whether the financial statements are free from material misstatement.

An audit involves performing procedures to obtain audit evidence about the amounts and disclosures in the financial statements. The procedures selected depend on the auditor's judgment, including the assessment of the risks of material misstatement of the financial statements, whether due to fraud or error. In making those risk assessments, the auditor considers internal control relevant to the entity's preparation and fair presentation of the financial statements in order to design audit procedures that are appropriate in the circumstances, but not for the purpose of expressing an opinion on the effectiveness of the entity's internal control. Accordingly, we express no such opinion. An audit also includes evaluating the appropriateness of accounting policies used and the reasonableness of significant accounting estimates made by management, as well as evaluating the overall presentation of the financial statements.

We believe that the audit evidence we have obtained is sufficient and appropriate to provide a basis for our qualified audit opinion.

Basis for Qualified Opinion

The company has excluded, from property and debt in the accompanying 20X1 balance sheet, certain capital lease obligations that were entered into in 20X1 which, in our opinion, should be capitalized in accordance with accounting principles generally accepted in the United States of America. If these lease obligations were capitalized, property would be increased by $XXX, long-term debt by $XXX, and retained earnings by $XXX as of December 31, 20X1, and net income and earnings per share would be increased (decreased) by $XXX and $XXX, respectively, for the year then ended.

Qualified Opinion

In our opinion, except for the effects on the 20X1 financial statements of not capitalizing certain lease obligations as described in the Basis for Qualified Opinion paragraph, the financial statements referred to above present fairly, in all material respects, the financial position of ABC Company as of December 31, 20X1 and 20X0, and the results of its operations and its cash flows for the years then ended in accordance with accounting principles generally accepted in the United States of America.

[*Auditor's signature*]

[*Auditor's city and state*]

[*Date of the auditor's report*]

Question 7-1 FR-00085

In Year 1, Randall, CPA, issued a qualified opinion on the financial statements of Celadon Industries, a nonissuer, due to the improper recording of lease obligations. During Year 2, Celadon restated the Year 1 financial statements to correct the error, and now plans to issue comparative financial statements for Year 1 and Year 2. Which of the following is true about Randall's report on the comparative financial statements?

1. Randall may not change the prior opinion, but may add an other-matter paragraph to the report indicating that the previous error has been corrected.
2. Randall may revise the prior opinion, but must include an emphasis-of-matter or other-matter paragraph describing the situation.
3. Randall may not change the prior opinion, and should not issue a report on the comparative financial statements.
4. Randall may revise the prior opinion and need not make mention of the change, as long as the comparative financial statements include the revised statements (and not the original statements) for Year 1.

8 Required Auditor Reporting of Certain Audit Participants

8.1 Filing of Form AP

An issuer must file Form AP with the PCAOB for each audit report issued. This form includes information about the audit, such as:

- Name of the firm.
- Name of the issuer whose financial statements are audited.
- Date of the audit report.
- The end date of the most recent period's financial statements identified in the audit report.
- The name of the engagement partner on the most recent period's audit and his/her current and prior ID number(s).
- The city and state (or city and country) of the office of the firm issuing the audit report.
- Whether the audit report is dual-dated.
- Whether other accounting firms participated in the audit.
- Whether the firm divided responsibility for the audit.
- Signature of partner or authorized officer.

Form AP must be filed by the 35th day after the audit report is first filed in a document with the SEC or within 10 days if the audit report is included in a registration statement.

8.2 Optional Inclusions

Although not required, the auditor of an issuer may elect to include in the auditor's report information regarding the engagement partner and/or other accounting firms participating in the audit.

Task-Based Simulations

Task-Based Simulation 1: Audit Opinion

Scroll down to complete all parts of this task.

A manager is explaining to a staff auditor how various situations might affect the audit opinion. For each of the following scenarios, identify the appropriate reporting option by clicking in the associated cell and selecting the appropriate option from the list provided. Assume that any financial statement effect is material and that U.S. auditing standards are followed.

	A	B
1	The scope of the auditor's examination is affected by conditions that preclude the application of a necessary auditing procedure.	
2	The auditor decides to make reference to the report of a component auditor as a basis, in part, for expressing an opinion on group financial statements.	
3	The company changed its method of accounting for long-term construction contracts, but management was justified in making the change. The new method is acceptable under GAAP, and the change was accounted for prospectively.	
4	Doubt about the company's ability to continue as a going concern is fully disclosed in the notes to the financial statements.	
5	The financial statements are subject to an uncertainty that will likely result in a material loss. Management has been unable to estimate the amount of potential loss, but has properly disclosed the details of the situation.	
6	The company changed its method of valuing inventory, but management did not have appropriate justification for the change. The change had a material but not pervasive effect on the financial statements and is properly disclosed.	
7	A predecessor auditor's unmodified opinion for a prior year's report on comparative financial statements is not presented.	
8	Required supplementary information is omitted from the financial statements.	

Select an option below

- Unmodified opinion
- Unmodified opinion with emphasis-of-matter paragraph
- Unmodified opinion with other-matter paragraph
- Qualified opinion
- Qualified opinion or adverse opinion
- Qualified opinion or disclaimer of opinion
- Adverse opinion
- Disclaimer of opinion
- Adverse opinion or disclaimer of opinion

RESET CANCEL ACCEPT

A Reports on Auditing Engagements

Explanation

	A	B
1	The scope of the auditor's examination is affected by conditions that preclude the application of a necessary auditing procedure.	Qualified opinion or disclaimer of opinion
2	The auditor decides to make reference to the report of a component auditor as a basis, in part, for expressing an opinion on group financial statements.	Unmodified opinion
3	The company changed its method of accounting for long-term construction contracts, but management was justified in making the change. The new method is acceptable under GAAP, and the change was accounted for prospectively.	Qualified opinion or adverse opinion
4	Doubt about the company's ability to continue as a going concern is fully disclosed in the notes to the financial statements.	Unmodified opinion with emphasis-of-matter paragraph
5	The financial statements are subject to an uncertainty that will likely result in a material loss. Management has been unable to estimate the amount of potential loss, but has properly disclosed the details of the situation.	Unmodified opinion
6	The company changed its method of valuing inventory, but management did not have appropriate justification for the change. The change had a material but not pervasive effect on the financial statements and is properly disclosed.	Qualified opinion
7	A predecessor auditor's unmodified opinion for a prior year's report on comparative financial statements is not presented.	Unmodified opinion with other-matter paragraph
8	Required supplementary information is omitted from the financial statements.	Unmodified opinion with other-matter paragraph

Row 1: Qualified opinion or disclaimer of opinion
When the scope of the auditor's examination is affected by conditions that preclude the application of a necessary auditing procedure, a qualified opinion or disclaimer of opinion would be appropriate.

Row 2: Unmodified opinion
When an auditor decides to make reference to a component auditor in the auditor's report on group financial statements, the auditor will issue an unmodified opinion with references to the component auditor in the Auditor's Responsibility paragraph and the Opinion paragraph.

Row 3: Qualified opinion or adverse opinion
Although management was justified in making the change to an acceptable accounting principle, the method of accounting for the change was not correct. The cumulative effect of a change in accounting principle should be recognized as an adjustment in the retained earnings statement (retrospective adjustment), not accounted for prospectively. Because the entity has not complied with requirements for accounting for changes in accounting principle, the auditor's report must contain a qualified or adverse opinion.

Row 4: Unmodified opinion with emphasis-of-matter paragraph
Doubt about the company's ability to continue as a going concern results in an unmodified opinion with an emphasis-of-matter paragraph, as long as the situation is fully disclosed in the notes to the financial statements.

Row 5: Unmodified opinion
Since the potential loss is probable but not estimable, the proper treatment is disclosure only. Management has properly disclosed this situation, so an unmodified opinion is appropriate.

Row 6: Qualified opinion
Since management lacked appropriate justification for the change, GAAP has been violated despite the financial statement disclosure. A qualified opinion will be issued because the change had a material but not pervasive effect on the financial statements.

Row 7: Unmodified opinion with other-matter paragraph
When a predecessor auditor's unmodified opinion for a prior year's report on comparative financial statements is not presented, the successor auditor would express an unmodified opinion on the current period financial statements with an other-matter paragraph describing the report of the predecessor auditor.

Row 8: Unmodified opinion with other-matter paragraph
When required supplementary information is omitted from the financial statements, the audit report on the financial statements should include an other-matter paragraph explaining the situation.

Task-Based Simulation 2: Review Notes

Scroll down to complete all parts of this task.

Charles, CPA, is the group auditor for the consolidated financial statements of Raleigh Industries, a nonissuer, and all but two of its subsidiaries for the years ended December 31, Year 1, and December 31, Year 2. Tyler is the staff accountant assigned to the Raleigh engagement.

Charles expressed a qualified opinion on the Year 1 financial statements because Raleigh capitalized certain research and development expenditures that should have been expensed, but Raleigh has corrected this error in Year 2. The Year 1 financial statements have been appropriately restated, and an unmodified opinion is currently being expressed on both sets of financial statements.

Karl & Karla, CPAs, is the component auditor that audited the financial statements of Newton, Inc., and of Capricorn Consulting, both of which are consolidated subsidiaries of Raleigh. Charles has decided not to assume responsibility for the work of Karl & Karla with respect to the Newton engagement, but will assume responsibility for the work of Karl & Karla with respect to the Capricorn job.

Raleigh is currently being investigated for possible securities law violations. This is adequately disclosed in the notes to the consolidated financial statements, but the ultimate outcome of these matters cannot presently be determined. Therefore, no provision for any liability that may result has been recorded.

Raleigh experienced a net loss in Year 2 and is currently in default under substantially all of its debt agreements. Management's plans in regard to these matters are adequately disclosed, although no financial statement adjustments have been made. These matters raise substantial doubt about Raleigh's ability to continue as a going concern.

Charles reviewed Tyler's draft of the auditor's report and indicated in his review notes that there were several deficiencies in the report. Based only on the review notes, select those items which Charles has *correctly* identified as deficiencies in the report by clicking the box beside the appropriate options. Select all that apply.

☐ 1. The reference to the subsidiary, Newton, and the magnitude of its financial statements should be in the Introductory paragraph rather than in the Auditor's Responsibility paragraph.
☐ 2. The component auditors, Karl & Karla, should be named in the auditor's report.
☐ 3. The reference in the Management's Responsibility paragraph to "financial statements that are free from material misstatement" should be followed by the phrase, "whether due to fraud or error."
☐ 4. There should be a reference in the Auditor's Responsibility paragraph to evaluating "significant accounting estimates made by management."
☐ 5. The reference in the Auditor's Responsibility paragraph to "assessing fraud risk" is inappropriate and should be omitted from the report
☐ 6. The Auditor's Responsibility paragraph should include a reference to "evaluating the overall presentation" of the "financial statements."
☐ 7. An emphasis-of-matter paragraph describing the investigation into possible violations of securities laws is required to be placed between the Auditor's Responsibility and Opinion paragraphs.

(continued)

(continued)

☐ 8. The reference in the other-matter paragraph (between the Auditor's Responsibility and Opinion paragraphs) to the qualified opinion on the Year 1 financial statements is not properly placed. Other-matter paragraphs should be placed after the opinion paragraph and after any emphasis-of-matter paragraphs.

☐ 9. The reference to the component auditor in the opinion paragraph is incomplete. It should specifically include the words "unqualified opinion" to describe the type of opinion expressed by Karl & Karla.

☐ 10. The emphasis-of-matter paragraph following the opinion paragraph does not include the terms "substantial doubt" and "going concern." These terms are required to be used in this paragraph under these circumstances.

Explanation

1. Incorrect
Reference to the subsidiary that was not audited by the group auditor and the magnitude of its financial statements is included in the Auditor's Responsibility paragraph.

2. Incorrect
The component auditors can only be named with their express permission and if their report is being presented together with that of Charles, CPA.

3. Correct
The Management's Responsibility paragraph includes the phrase "financial statements that are free from material misstatement whether due to fraud or error."

4. Correct
There should be a reference in the Accountant's Responsibility paragraph to "significant accounting estimates made by management."

5. Correct
Reference to the assessment of fraud risk is not part of the auditor's report and should be removed.

6. Correct
The auditor's report should include a reference in the Auditor's Responsibility paragraph to "evaluating the overall presentation of the financial statements."

7. Incorrect
Since Raleigh has provided adequate disclosure in the notes to its financial statements, the auditor is not required to make mention of the uncertainty. If the auditor chose to use an emphasis-of-matter paragraph to describe the uncertainty, the paragraph would be placed after the opinion paragraph.

8. Correct
The substantive reasons for the different opinion should be disclosed in an other-matter paragraph **following** the opinion paragraph and following any emphasis-of-matter paragraph.

9. Incorrect
The type of opinion expressed by the other auditor need not be specifically identified in the opinion paragraph. Rather, the group auditor provides his opinion on the consolidated financial statements taken as a whole, and simply mentions that a portion of the work was performed by "other auditors."

10. Correct
The terms "substantial doubt" and "going concern" are **required** to be used in situations where substantial doubt exists about an entity's ability to continue as a going concern.

Task-Based Simulation 3: Research

What guidance is provided by AICPA Professional Standards with respect to matters that should be disclosed in the auditor's report when the auditor's opinion in the current period on prior period financial statements differs from the opinion previously expressed by the auditor?

Enter your response in the answer fields below. Guidance on correctly structuring your response appears above and below the answer fields.

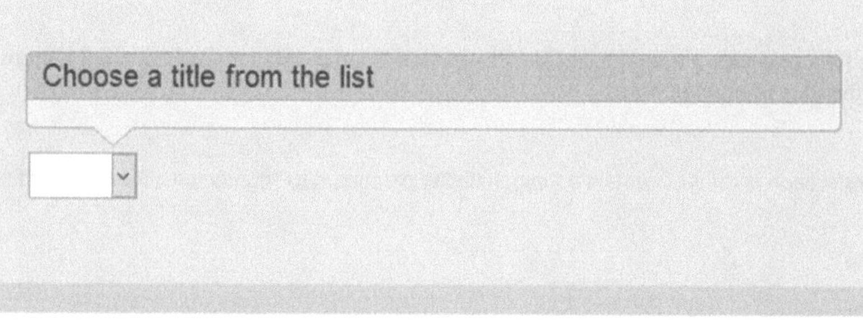
Choose a title from the list

Explanation

Source of answer for this question:

AU-C 700.53

Keywords: Prior period financial statements

Integrated Audit Reports

1 Integrated Audits of Issuers

PCAOB standards, which apply to issuers, require that auditors perform an "integrated audit," auditing internal control in conjunction with the audit of the financial statements. The Dodd-Frank Act amended this rule, providing that integrated audits are required only for large accelerated filers and accelerated filers.

2 Integrated Audits of Nonissuers

SASs allow an auditor to audit and report on a nonissuer's internal control over financial reporting that is integrated with a financial statement audit. The rules governing integrated audits of nonissuers are very similar to the rules for issuers.

3 Impact on Tests of Controls

In both issuer and nonissuer integrated audits, tests of controls should be designed to provide sufficient appropriate evidence to support both the opinion on internal control and the control risk assessment in the financial statement audit.

3.1 Top-Down Approach

A top-down approach is used to select the controls to test. The auditor should:

- Evaluate overall risk at the financial statement level.
- Consider controls at the entity level.
- Focus tests of controls on accounts, disclosures, and assertions for which there is a reasonable possibility of material misstatement.

B Integrated Audit Reports

Question 3-1 FR-00960

In an integrated audit of an issuer, which of the following most likely would be considered an entity-level control?

1. The auditor's adherence to a system of quality control.
2. Management's procedures used to initiate, authorize, and record journal entries into the general ledger.
3. An aging schedule that is prepared by the accounts receivable department.
4. Upon receiving checks from customers by mail, an employee prepares a duplicate listing of checks received.

Related Questions

For related questions, go to the online question bank:

- FR-00959

Reports on Internal Controls

1 Communications With Management and Those Charged With Governance

The auditor is not required to search for control deficiencies or significant deficiencies in a financial statement audit only, but those that are identified should be communicated.

- Control deficiencies, significant deficiencies, and material weaknesses should be communicated to management in writing.
- Significant deficiencies and material weaknesses must also be communicated to the audit committee in writing.
- For issuers, material weaknesses should be communicated to management and the audit committee before the issuance of the auditor's report on internal control.
- For nonissuers, communication of significant deficiencies and material weaknesses should be made by the report release date and communication of control deficiencies should be made within 60 days of the report release date.

Question 1-1 FR-00110

With respect to the expression of an opinion regarding whether a client maintained effective internal control over financial reporting:

1. The auditor of a nonissuer may express an opinion as a result of an audit engagement.
2. The auditor of a nonissuer may express an opinion as a result of a financial statement audit.
3. The auditor of a nonissuer must express an opinion in every financial statement audit.
4. The auditor of a nonissuer must express an opinion whenever significant deficiencies or material weaknesses are noted.

2 Opinion on Internal Control

The auditor must express an opinion on the company's internal control over financial reporting in an integrated audit.

2.1 Separate or Combined Reports

This report may be combined with the report on the financial statements, or it may be presented separately. If separate reports are issued, each report should contain an explanatory paragraph making reference to the other report.

2.1.1 Sample Combined Report (Issuer)

Report of Independent Registered Public Accounting Firm

To the shareholders and the board of directors of W Company:

Opinions on the Financial Statements and Internal Control Over Financial Reporting

We have audited the accompanying balance sheets of W Company (the "Company") as of December 31, 20X8 and 20X7, and the related statements of income, comprehensive income, stockholders' equity, and cash flows for each of the years in the two-year period ended December 31, 20X8, and the related notes [*and schedules*] (collectively referred to as the "financial statements"). We also have audited the Company's internal control over financial reporting as of December 31, 20X8, based on [*identify control criteria, for example, "criteria established in Internal Control-Integrated Framework: (20XX) issued by the Committee of Sponsoring Organizations of the Treadway Commission (COSO)"*].

In our opinion, the financial statements referred to above present fairly, in all material respects, the financial position of the Company as of December 31, 20X8 and 20X7, and the results of its operations and its cash flows for each of the years in the two-year period ended December 31, 20X8, in conformity with accounting principles generally accepted in the United States of America. Also in our opinion, the Company maintained, in all material respects, effective internal control over financial reporting as of December 31, 20X8, based on [*identify control criteria, for example, "criteria established in Internal Control-Integrated Framework: (20XX) issued by COSO"*].

Basis for Opinion

The Company's management is responsible for these financial statements, for maintaining effective internal control over financial reporting, and for its assessment of the effectiveness of internal control over financial reporting, included in the accompanying [title of management's report]. Our responsibility is to express an opinion on the Company's financial statements and an opinion on the Company's internal control over financial reporting based on our audits. We are a public accounting firm registered with the Public Company Accounting Oversight Board (United States) (PCAOB) and are required to be independent with respect to the Company in accordance with the U.S. federal securities laws and the applicable rules and regulations of the Securities and Exchange Commission and the PCAOB.

We conducted our audits in accordance with the standards of the PCAOB. Those standards require that we plan and perform the audits to obtain reasonable assurance about whether the financial statements are free of material misstatement, whether due to error or fraud, and whether effective internal control over financial reporting was maintained in all material respects.

(continued on next page)

(continued)

Our audits of the financial statements included performing procedures to assess the risks of material misstatement of the financial statements, whether due to error or fraud, and performing procedures that respond to those risks. Such procedures included examining, on a test basis, evidence regarding the amounts and disclosures in the financial statements. Our audits also included evaluating the accounting principles used and significant estimates made by management, as well as evaluating the overall presentation of the financial statements. Our audit of internal control over financial reporting included obtaining an understanding of internal control over financial reporting, assessing the risk that a material weakness exists, and testing and evaluating the design and operating effectiveness of internal control based on the assessed risk. Our audits also included performing such other procedures as we considered necessary in the circumstances. We believe that our audits provide a reasonable basis for our opinions.

Definition and Limitations of Internal Control Over Financial Reporting

A company's internal control over financial reporting is a process designed to provide reasonable assurance regarding the reliability of financial reporting and the preparation of financial statements for external purposes in accordance with generally accepted accounting principles. A company's internal control over financial reporting includes those policies and procedures that (1) pertain to the maintenance of records that, in reasonable detail, accurately and fairly reflect the transactions and dispositions of the assets of the company; (2) provide reasonable assurance that transactions are recorded as necessary to permit preparation of financial statements in accordance with generally accepted accounting principles, and that receipts and expenditures of the company are being made only in accordance with authorizations of management and directors of the company; and (3) provide reasonable assurance regarding prevention or timely detection of unauthorized acquisition, use, or disposition of the company's assets that could have a material effect on the financial statements.

Because of its inherent limitations, internal control over financial reporting may not prevent or detect misstatements. Also, projections of any evaluation of effectiveness to future periods are subject to the risk that controls may become inadequate because of changes in conditions, or that the degree of compliance with the policies or procedures may deteriorate.

Critical Audit Matters

[*Include critical audit matters*]

[*Signature*]
We have served as the Company's auditor since [year].
[*City and State or Country*]
[*Date*]

2.1.2 Sample Combined Report (Nonissuer)

Independent Auditor's Report

[*Appropriate addressee*]

We have audited the financial statements of W Company, which comprise the balance sheet as of December 31, 20XX, and the related statements of income, changes in stockholder's equity, and cash flows for the year then ended, and the related notes to the financial statements. We also have audited W Company's internal control over financial reporting as of December 31, 20XX, based on [*identify criteria*].

Management's Responsibility for the Financial Statements and Internal Control Over Financial Reporting

Management is responsible for the preparation and fair presentation of these financial statements in accordance with accounting principles generally accepted in the United States of America, for maintaining internal control over financial reporting including the design, implementation, and maintenance of controls; this includes the design, implementation, and maintenance of effective internal control over financial reporting relevant to the preparation and fair presentation of these financial statements that are free from material misstatement, whether due to error of fraud. Management is also responsible for its assertion about the effectiveness of internal control over financial reporting, included in the accompanying [*title of management's report*].

Auditor's Responsibility

Our responsibility is to express an opinion on these financial statements and an opinion on W Company's internal control over financial reporting based on our audits. We conducted our audit of the financial statements in accordance with auditing standards generally accepted in the United States of America and our audit of internal control over financial reporting in accordance with attestation standards established by the American Institute of Certified Public Accountants. Those standards require that we plan and perform the audits to obtain reasonable assurance about whether the financial statements are free of material misstatement and whether effective internal control over financial reporting was maintained in all material respects.

An audit of financial statements involves performing procedures to obtain audit evidence about the amounts and disclosures in the financial statements. The procedures selected depend on the auditor's judgment, including assessment of the risks of material misstatement of the financial statements, whether due to fraud or error. In making those risk assessments, the auditor considers internal control relevant to the entity's preparation and fair presentation of the financial statements in order to design audit procedures that are appropriate in the circumstances. An audit of internal control over financial reporting involves obtaining an understanding of internal control over financial reporting, assessing the risk that a material weakness exists, and testing and evaluating the design and operating effectiveness of internal control over financial reporting based on the assessed risk, and performing such other procedures as we considered necessary in the circumstances.

We believe that the audit evidence we obtained is sufficient and appropriate to provide a basis for our audit opinions.

Definitions and Inherent Limitations of Internal Control Over Financial Reporting

An entity's internal control over financial reporting is a process effected by those charged with governance, management, and other personnel, designed to provide reasonable assurance regarding the preparation of reliable financial statements in accordance with [*applicable financial reporting framework, such as accounting principles generally accepted in the United States of America*]. An entity's internal control over financial reporting includes those policies and procedures that (1) pertain to the maintenance of records that, in reasonable detail, accurately and fairly reflect the transactions and dispositions of the assets of the entity; (2) provide reasonable assurance that transactions are recorded as necessary to permit preparation of financial statements in accordance with [*applicable financial reporting framework, such as accounting principles generally accepted in the United States of America*], and that receipts and expenditures of the entity are being made only in accordance with authorizations of management and those charged with governance; and (3) provide reasonable assurance regarding prevention, or timely detection and correction of unauthorized acquisition, use, or disposition of the entity's assets that could have a material effect on the financial statements.

Because of its inherent limitations, internal control over financial reporting may not prevent, or detect and correct misstatements. Also, projections of any evaluation of effectiveness to future periods are subject to the risk that controls may become inadequate because of changes in conditions, or that the degree of compliance with the policies or procedures may deteriorate.

(continued on next page)

(continued)

Opinions

In our opinion, the financial statements referred to above present fairly, in all material respects, the financial position of W Company as of December 31, 20XX, and the results of its operations and its cash flows for the year then ended in accordance with accounting principles generally accepted in the United States of America. Also in our opinion, W Company maintained, in all material respects, effective internal control over financial reporting as of December 31, 20XX, based on [*identify criteria*].

[*Auditor's signature*]
[*Auditor's city and state*]
[*Date of the auditor's report*]

2.2 Modified Audit Opinions

2.2.1 Scope Limitation

A scope limitation requires the auditor to disclaim an opinion or to withdraw from the engagement.

2.2.2 Material Weakness

A material weakness requires the auditor to issue an adverse opinion. The adverse opinion should include:

- the definition of material weakness.
- a statement that a material weakness has been identified.
- an identification of the material weakness described in management's own assessment of internal control.

If the material weakness is not included in management's assessment, the report should state this and should include a description of the material weakness.

2.2.3 Absence of Control Deficiencies or Significant Deficiencies

The auditor should not report the absence of control deficiencies or significant deficiencies.

Question 2-1 FR-00957

During an integrated audit, an auditor uncovers one control deficiency in internal control such that there is a reasonable possibility that a material misstatement of the entity's financial statements will not be prevented, or detected and corrected on a timely basis. In this situation, the auditor should issue an opinion on internal control that is:

1. Unmodified
2. Qualified
3. Adverse
4. A disclaimer

Related Questions

For related questions, go to the online question bank:

- FR-00087
- FR-00104

Reports on Attestation Engagements

1 Statements on Standards for Attestation Engagements

Statements on Standards for Attestation Engagements (SSAE) apply to engagements in which a practitioner is engaged to issue, or does issue, an examination, review, or agreed-upon procedures report on subject matter (or an assertion thereon) that is another party's responsibility. Independence is required.

1.1 Levels of Reports

There are three levels of reports that may be issued on the assertion or the associated subject matter:

1. Examination (reasonable assurance, with positive opinion)
2. Review (limited assurance, with conclusion)
3. Agreed-upon procedures (no assurance, with list of findings)

Report Type			
Attestation Service	*Examination*	*Review*	*Agreed-Upon Procedures*
Agreed-upon procedures			✓
Prospective financial statements	✓		✓
Pro forma financial statements	✓	✓	
Compliance	✓		✓
MD&A	✓	✓	
Service organizations	✓		

Note that preparations and compilations are also allowed for prospective financial statements. However, with the issuance of SSAE 18, preparations and compilations of prospective financial statements are no longer addressed in the attestation standards and are instead governed by the SSARS standards.

? Related Questions

For related questions, go to the online question bank:

- FR-00889
- FR-00890

2 "Agreed-Upon" Procedures Engagements

The practitioner is engaged to report findings using specific, agreed-upon procedures. Required conditions:

- **I**ndependence of the practitioner.
- **A**greement of parties—the practitioner and specified parties agree regarding procedures to be performed, the criteria to be used in the determination of findings, and any materiality limits used for reporting.
- **M**easurability and consistency—subject matter should be capable of reasonably consistent measurement, procedures should be expected to result in reasonably consistent findings, and evidential matter to support the report should be expected to exist.
- **S**ufficiency of procedures—specified parties take responsibility for the sufficiency of procedures for their purposes.
- **U**se of the report is restricted to specified parties.
- **R**esponsibility for subject matter. Either:
  - the client is responsible for (or has a reasonable basis for providing an assertion about) the subject matter; or
  - the client is able to provide evidence of a third party's responsibility for the subject matter.
- **E**ngagements to perform agreed-upon procedures on prospective financial statements.
  - Prospective financial statements must include a summary of significant assumptions.

Question 2-1 FR-00888

Which of the following should a practitioner perform as part of an engagement for agreed-upon procedures in accordance with *Statements on Standards for Attestation Engagements*?

1. Ensure the engagement procedures are comparable to those performed in a compilation.
2. Express a disclaimer of opinion on the subject matter.
3. Express positive assurance on findings of work performed.
4. Disclose responsibility for the sufficiency of procedures.

? Related Questions

For related questions, go to the online question bank:

➤ FR-00887

3 Financial Forecasts and Projections

Financial forecasts and projections are prospective financial statements. Allowable engagements for prospective financial statements are preparation, compilation, examination, and agreed-upon procedures. No review engagement is allowed.

Note: SSARS provides guidance for preparations and compilations of financial forecasts and projections. SSAE provides guidance for examinations and agreed-upon procedure engagements of financial forecasts and projections.

3.1 Financial Forecast

Financial forecasts are based on expected conditions and expected courses of action. Financial forecasts are available for general use or may be limited use.

3.1.1 Report on Compilation of a Financial Forecast*

[The responsible party] is responsible for the accompanying financial forecast of XYZ Company, which comprises the forecasted balance sheet as of December 31, 20X2, and the related forecasted statements of income, changes in stockholders' equity, and cash flows for the year then ending, and the related summaries of significant assumptions and accounting policies in accordance with guidelines for the presentation of a financial forecast established by the American Institute of Certified Public Accountants (AICPA). We have performed a compilation engagement in accordance with Statements on Standards for Accounting and Review Services promulgated by the Accounting and Review Services Committee of the AICPA. We did not examine or review the financial forecast nor were we required to perform any procedures to verify the accuracy or completeness of the information provided by management. Accordingly, we do not express an opinion, a conclusion, nor provide any form of assurance on the accompanying financial statements or assumptions.

The forecasted results may not be achieved as there will usually be differences between the forecasted and actual results, because events and circumstances frequently do no occur as expected, and these differences may be material. We have no responsibility to update this report for events and circumstances occurring after the date of this report.

[*Signature of practitioner's firm or accountant, as appropriate*]

[*Practitioner's city and state*]

[*Date of the practitioner's report*]

*With the issuance of SSAE 18, compilations of prospective financial statements are no longer addressed in the attestation standards and are instead governed by AR-C section 80 of the SSARS standards.

3.1.2 Report on Examination of a Financial Forecast

Independent Accountant's Report

[*Appropriate Addressee*]

We have examined the accompanying forecast of XYZ Company, which comprises, the forecasted balance sheet as of December 31, 20XX, and the related forecasted statements of income, stockholders' equity, and cash flows for the year then ending, based on the guidelines for the presentation of a forecast established by the American Institute of Certified Public Accountants. XYZ Company's management is responsible for preparing and presenting the forecast in accordance with the guidelines for the presentation of a forecast established by the American Institute of Certified Public Accountants. Our responsibility is to express an opinion on the forecast based on our examination.

Our examination was conducted in accordance with attestation standards established by the American Institute of Certified Public Accountants. Those standards require that we plan and perform the examination to obtain reasonable assurance about whether the forecast is presented in accordance with the guidelines for the presentation of a forecast established by the American Institute of Certified Public Accountants, in all material respects. An examination involves performing procedures to obtain evidence about the forecast. The nature, timing, and extent of the procedures selected depend on our judgment, including an assessment of the risks of material misstatement of the forecast, whether due to fraud or error. We believe that the evidence we obtained is sufficient and appropriate to provide a reasonable basis for our opinion.

In our opinion, the accompanying forecast is presented, in all material respects, in accordance with the guidelines for the presentation of a forecast established by the American Institute of Certified Public Accountants, and the underlying assumptions are suitably supported and provide a reasonable basis for management's forecast.

There will usually be differences between the forecasted and actual results because events and circumstances frequently do not occur as expected, and those differences may be material. We have no responsibility to update this report for events and circumstances occurring after the date of this report.

[*Practitioner's signature*]

[*Practitioner's city and state*]

[*Date of practitioner's report*]

3.2 Financial Projection

Financial projections are based on hypothetical ("what if") assumptions. Reports on financial projections are restricted use only and cannot be made available for general use.

3.2.1 Report on Compilation of a Financial Projection

The report on the compilation of a financial projection would be similar to the report on the compilation of a financial forecast, except that it would refer to a "financial projection" rather than "financial forecast."

3.2.2 Report on Examination of a Financial Projection

The report on an examination of a financial projection would be similar to the report on the examination of a financial forecast, except it would include a description of the purpose of the projection in the first paragraph, a reference to the hypothetical assumption in the third and fourth paragraphs, and a paragraph restricting the use of the report.

3.3 Prospective Financial Statement (PFS) Summary

General Procedures	Compilation Report*	Examination Report	Agreed-Upon Procedures
Prospective financial statements	Assemble	Evaluate	Apply specific procedures
Responsible party's assumptions	Assemble	Evaluate	Should be included in PFS
Are financial statements and significant assumptions in conformance with AICPA guidelines?	Look for obvious errors	Opinion	Disclaimer
Obtain agreed-upon scope from specified users	—	—	Yes

Reports Include a Statement Regarding:	Compilation Report*	Examination Report	Agreed-Upon Procedures
Identification of PFS	Yes	Yes	Yes
Compliance with AICPA standards	Yes	Yes	Yes
Limitation of scope	Yes	—	Yes
An enumeration of procedures performed	—	—	Yes
A caveat that prospective results may not be achieved	Yes	Yes	Yes
CPA has no responsibility for updating report	Yes	Yes	Yes
Opinion on PFS accordance with AICPA presentation guidelines	—	Yes	—
Limited use of report	Only required for projection	Only required for projection	Yes (always)

*With the issuance of SSAE 18, compilations of prospective financial statements are no longer addressed in the attestation standards and are instead governed by AR-C section 80 of the SSARS standards.

Question 3-1 FR-00038

Which of the following is a prospective financial statement for general use upon which an accountant may appropriately report?

1. Financial projection
2. Partial presentation
3. Pro forma financial statement
4. Financial forecast

For related questions, go to the online question bank:

➤ FR-00086

1 Statements on Standards for Accounting and Review Services

SSARS (Statements on Standards for Accounting and Review Services) are issued by the AICPA Accounting and Review Services Committee. SSARS provide guidance with respect to preparations, compilations, and reviews of financial statements of nonissuers.

1.1 Engagement Letter

- All SSARS engagements require a written understanding with management and, when appropriate, those charged with governance, regarding the services to be performed.
- This engagement letter (or other suitable form of written agreement) should be signed by the accountant or the accountant's firm as well as management or those charged with governance.

1.2 Review Engagements

- Independence is required.
- Each page of the financial statements should be marked, "See accountant's review report."
- Review procedures, consisting principally of inquiry and analytical procedures, should be tailored to the specific engagement.

1.2.1 Inquiry

In a review engagement, inquiries should be made about:

- Accounting principles and practices used.
- Procedures for recording, classifying, and summarizing transactions.
- How footnote information is accumulated.
- Changes in business or accounting.
- Subsequent events.
- Whether the financial statements have been prepared and fairly presented in accordance with the applicable financial reporting framework.
- Actions authorized by stockholders or board of directors.
- Unusual or complex situations that may affect the financial statements.
- Significant transactions near the end of the period.
- The status of uncorrected misstatements from previous engagements.
- Material fraud or suspected fraud.
- Significant journal entries and adjustments.
- Communications from regulatory agencies.
- Litigation, claims, and assessments.

- Entity's ability to continue as a going concern (and, if applicable, management's plans to mitigate the going concern issue).
- Whether management has disclosed all known instances of noncompliance with laws and regulations.
- Whether management believes that significant assumptions used for accounting estimates are reasonable.

1.2.2 Analytical Procedures

The accountant should compare current statements with prior statements, compare actual with budgets, and study specific predictable items. The accountant should also compare:

- Financial and relevant nonfinancial information.
- Ratios and indicators with those of other entities in the industry.
- Relationships among elements in the financial statements within the period and with corresponding prior period relationships.

1.2.3 Other Procedures

The accountant should also:

- Obtain an understanding of the client's business.
- Become familiar with the accounting principles used in the client's industry.
- Read the client's financial statements.
- Obtain reports of other accountants who have been engaged to audit or review significant components of the reporting entity.
- Obtain evidence that the financial statements agree or reconcile with accounting records.
- Obtain a representation letter. Management representations should include:
  - Acknowledgment of responsibility to prevent/detect fraud.
  - Knowledge of any material fraud or suspected fraud.
- Issue a review report.

1.3 Compilation Engagements

- No independence is required and no assurance is expressed. Lack of independence must be disclosed in the compilation report. The accountant is permitted, but not required, to disclose the reason(s) for the lack of independence.
- The CPA presents in the form of financial statements, information that is management's representation.

1.3.1 Procedures

- Obtain knowledge of the client industry's accounting principles practices.
- Obtain an understanding of the client's business.
- Read the financial statements to ensure they are free of obvious clerical errors and obvious mistakes related to GAAP.
- Disclose lack of independence, if applicable.
- Issue a compilation report.

1.4 Preparation Engagements

- A preparation does not provide assurance.
- A preparation is considered a non-attest service, therefore, it does not require a determination of whether the accountant is independent of the entity.
- In a preparation, the CPA prepares financial statements in accordance with a specified financial reporting framework.
- The accountant may prepare financial statements that omit disclosures as long as the financial statements clearly indicate the omission.

1.4.1 Procedures

- Obtain knowledge of the client industry's accounting principles/practices.
- Obtain an understanding of the client's business.
- Prepare the financial statements.
- Ensure a statement on each page at a minimum stating "no assurance is provided" or issue a disclaimer that makes clear no assurance is provided on the financial statements. The accountant or accountant's firm name is not required to be included in prepared financial statements.

1.5 Change in Engagement

- If the client wishes to change an audit to a compilation or a review, the accountant should:
  - Inquire about the reasons for the change (e.g., a change in client requirements, a misunderstanding as to the service to be rendered, a scope restriction).
  - Consider the estimated additional cost/effort required to complete the engagement.
- If the accountant decides that the change in engagement is justified, he/she must comply with standards for a compilation or review and issue an appropriate report.

E Accounting and Review Service Engagements

Question 1-1 FR-00008

Which of the following accounting services may an accountant perform without being required to issue a compilation or review report under Statements on Standards for Accounting and Review Services?

I. Preparing a working trial balance.

II. Preparing standard monthly journal entries.

1. I only.
2. II only.
3. Both I and II.
4. Neither I nor II.

Question 1-2 FR-00095

Which of the following procedures would most likely be performed during an engagement to compile the financial statements of a nonissuer?

1. Read the financial statements and consider whether they are appropriate in form and free from obvious material errors.
2. Perform inquiry and analytical review procedures.
3. Obtain a representation letter from management.
4. Send accounts receivable confirmations.

Question 1-3 FR-00885

A client requests to change an engagement from an audit to a review of financial statements. Which of the following is most likely to be considered by the auditor as an acceptable reason for the change?

1. Management is unwilling to sign the representation letter because management was not present for the entire period covered by the engagement.
2. Management does not want the auditor to correspond with legal counsel.
3. The bank the client is obtaining a loan from has changed the assurance required on the financial statements from positive to negative assurance.
4. Audit procedures might discover that land is materially overstated.

Question 1-4 FR-00884

Before reissuing a compilation report on the financial statements of a nonissuer for the prior year, the predecessor accountant is required to perform all the following procedures, *except* for:

1. Read the financial statements and the report of the current period.
2. Obtain a letter of representation from management.
3. Compare the prior period financial statements with those issued previously and currently.
4. Obtain a letter from the successor accountants.

? Related Questions

For related questions, go to the online question bank:

- FR-00882
- FR-00883

2 Review of Interim Financial Statements

A review of interim financial statements provides a basis for reporting whether the auditor is aware of any needed material modifications to interim financial information for GAAP conformity. Procedures include inquiries, analytical procedures, and other procedures.

2.1 Procedures

- The required procedures are:
  - **U**nderstanding with the client must be established.
  - **L**earn and/or obtain an understanding of the entity and its environment, including its internal control.
  - **I**nquiries should be addressed to appropriate individuals, including the predecessor auditor.
  - **A**nalytical procedures should be performed.
  - **R**eview—other procedures should be performed.
  - **C**lient representation letter should be obtained from management.
  - **P**rofessional judgment should be used to evaluate results.
  - **A**ccountant (CPA) should communicate results.
- In addition to the standard review analysis of aggregated amounts, analytical procedures should be applied to disaggregated revenue data (by month, by product line, etc.).
- The auditor is required to obtain evidence that interim data reconciles to accounting records.
- In addition to the usual representations, the auditor should also obtain management's written representations related to internal controls and fraud.

3 Letters for Underwriters

"Comfort letters" are provided to an underwriter or other party (i.e., broker-dealer) just before the registration of the client's securities.

- The CPA is required to perform a review of interim financial information.
- The letter must include a restriction on its use (requesting party only).
- Negative assurance is provided for most financial information.
- Positive assurance is provided on the CPA's independence and compliance of financial statements with Securities Acts, assuming financial statements were audited; otherwise, negative assurance is provided.

Question 3-1 FR-00886

When issuing letters for underwriters, an accountant may provide positive assurance related to:

1. Unaudited financial statements that have been reviewed.
2. Compliance of management's discussion and analysis (MD&A) with SEC rules and regulations.
3. Compliance of the form of the audited financial statements with the requirements of the SEC Act.
4. Qualitative disclosures and market-sensitive instruments.

? Related Questions

For related questions, go to the online question bank:

➤ FR-00103

4 Comparison of SSARS and SAS Engagements

	Preparation Engagement	Compilation Engagement	Review Engagement			Audit Engagement
	SSARS	*SSARS*	*SSARS*	*SAS*	*PCAOB*	*SAS/PCAOB*
Level of Assurance	None	None	Limited			Reasonable.
Entities	Nonissuers only	Nonissuers only	Nonissuers	Nonissuers: Interim	Issuers: Interim	Nonissuers/Issuers
Knowledge Required	Knowledge of accounting principles and practices of industry; general understanding of client's business	Knowledge of accounting principles and practices of industry; general understanding of client's business	Same as compilation plus increased knowledge of client's business			Extensive knowledge of economy, industry, and client's business
Inquiry and Analytical Procedures Required	None unless information is questionable	None unless information is questionable	Inquiries of internal personnel Analytical procedures			Inquiries of external parties and internal personnel Analytical procedures Audit procedures
GAAP Disclosure Omitted	May omit, but need to disclose in the financial statement	May omit most without restricting use; warn with ending paragraph	All are required or modify review report			All required or "qualified/adverse" opinion
GAAP Departures	May depart from GAAP, but need to disclose in the financial statement	Modify report to discuss GAAP departure	Modify report to discuss GAAP departure			Modify report "qualified/adverse" opinion
Independence	Not required (non-attest engagement)	Not required but disclosure is required	Required			Required
Engagement Letter	Presumptively mandatory	Presumptively mandatory	Presumptively mandatory			Presumptively mandatory
Representation Letter	Not required	Not required	Required			Required
Understanding of Internal Control	Not required (no test work)	Not required (no test work)	Not required (no test work)	Required		Required
Errors and Irregularities Detection	Only obvious errors found when preparing financial statements	Only obvious errors found when reading financial statements	Only errors discovered through inquiry and analytical procedures			Must be designed to provide reasonable assurance of detection of material misstatements
Noncompliance with Laws and Regulations Detection	None, but known acts must be evaluated	None, but known acts must be evaluated	Only direct and material effect, that could be disclosed by inquiry and analytical procedures			Must be designed to reasonably assure detection of direct and material noncompliance with laws and regulations
FS Reported on (BS/IS/RE/CF)	One or more financial statements allowed to be prepared	One or more financial statements allowed to be reported on	One or more financial statements allowed if scope of inquiry and analytical procedures has not been restricted			One or more financial statements allowed if scope of audit is not limited and all necessary procedures are applied
Communication with Predecessor	Not required	Not required	Not required	Required		Required
Subsequent Event Inquiries	Not required	Not required	Required			Required

Accounting and Review Service Engagement Reports

Topic **F**

1 SSARS Review Report

- The review report provides limited assurance (less assurance than is provided by an audit) that no material modifications to the financial statements are required for conformity with GAAP (or other appropriate financial reporting framework).
- GAAP departures should be disclosed in a separate final paragraph in the review report titled "Known Departures from the [identify the applicable financial reporting framework]," or the accountant may withdraw from the engagement.

SSARS Review Report

Independent Accountant's Review Report

[*Appropriate addressee*]

We have reviewed the accompanying balance sheet of XYZ Company as of December 31, 20XX, and the related statements of income, retained earnings, and cash flows for the year then ended. A review includes primarily applying analytical procedures to management's financial data and making inquiries of company management. A review is substantially less in scope than an audit, the objective of which is the expression of an opinion regarding the financial statements as a whole. Accordingly, we do not express such an opinion.

Management's Responsibility for the Financial Statements

Management is responsible for the preparation and fair presentation of the financial statements in accordance with [*the applicable financial reporting framework (for example, accounting principles generally accepted in the United States of America)*]; and this includes the design, implementation, and maintenance of internal control relevant to the preparation and fair presentation of the financial statements that are free from material misstatement, whether due to fraud or error.

Accountant's Responsibility

Our responsibility is to conduct the review in accordance with Statements on Standards for Accounting and Review Services promulgated by the Accounting and Review Services Committee of the AICPA. Those standards require us to perform procedures to obtain limited assurance as a basis for reporting whether we are aware of material modifications that should be made to the financial statements for them to be in accordance with accounting principles generally accepted in the United States of America. We believe that the results of our procedures provide a reasonable basis for our report.

Accountant's Conclusion

Based on our review, **we are not aware of any material modifications** that should be made to the accompanying financial statements in order for them to be in accordance with [*the applicable financial reporting framework*].

[*Signature of accounting firm or accountant*]

[*Accountant's city and state*]

[*Date*]

F Accounting and Review Service Engagement Reports

Question 1-1 FR-00048

Financial statements of a nonissuer that have been reviewed by an accountant should be accompanied by a report stating that a review:

1. Provides only limited assurance that the financial statements are fairly presented.
2. Includes examining, on a test basis, information that is the representation of management.
3. Includes primarily applying analytical procedures to management's financial data and making inquiries of company management.
4. Does not contemplate obtaining corroborating audit evidence or applying certain other procedures ordinarily performed during an audit.

Related Questions

For related questions, go to the online question bank:

- FR-00068

2 SSARS Compilation Report

SSARS Compilation Report

Management is responsible for the accompanying financial statements of XYZ Company, which comprise the balance sheets as of December 31, 20X2 and 20X1 and the related statements of income, changes in stockholders' equity, and cash flows for the years then ended, and the related notes to the financial statements in accordance with accounting principles generally accepted in the United States of America. We have performed compilation engagements in accordance with Statements on Standards for Accounting and Review Services promulgated by the Accounting and Review Services Committee of the AICPA. We did not audit or review the financial statements nor were we required to perform any procedures to verify the accuracy or completeness of the information provided by management. Accordingly, we do not express an opinion, a conclusion, nor provide any form of assurance on these financial statements.

[*Signature of accounting firm or accountant*]

[*Accountant's city and state*]

[*Date*]

- GAAP departures should be disclosed in a separate paragraph of the report, or the accountant may withdraw from the engagement.
- If substantially all required disclosures are omitted, the accountants report should clearly indicate this omission.

3 Comparative Reporting

Different services may be provided in different years.

- Increase in level of service—If a service upgrade (from compiled to reviewed) occurs:
  - The prior year report should be updated and issued as the last paragraph of the current period report.
- Decrease in level of service—If a service downgrade (from reviewed to compiled) occurs, three options exist:
  - Issue a compilation report and add a paragraph to the report describing the responsibility for the prior period statements. Include the date of original report, and a statement that no review procedures were performed after that date.
  - Issue two separate reports.
  - Issue a combined report presenting both full reports with an added statement to the review report indicating that no review procedures have since been performed.
- Decrease in level of service—If a service downgrade to a preparation engagement (from reviewed or compiled to preparation) occurs, there is no requirement to reference the prior period service performed.

4 Interim Review Report

- The auditor expresses limited assurance on interim financial information covering the period from the last audit to the date of the interim statements.
- GAAP departures must be disclosed.
- If the auditor determines that the disclosure related to substantial doubt about the entities' ability to continue as a going concern is inadequate, resulting in a departure from the applicable financial reporting framework, the auditor should modify the report.
- For issuers: As long as going concern disclosure is adequate, the auditor is not required to include an explanatory paragraph.
- For nonissuers: Add an emphasis-of-matter paragraph if management has included a statement that substantial doubt exists in its financial statements or (1) a going concern emphasis-of-matter paragraph was included in the prior year audit report, (2) the conditions of going concern still exist at interim, and (3) management's plans do not alleviate the substantial doubt.
- A lack of consistency paragraph is optional if there is adequate disclosure.

SAS Review of Interim Financial Statements

Independent Auditor's Review Report

[Appropriate Addressee]

Report on the Financial Statements

We have reviewed the accompanying [*describe the interim financial information or statements reviewed*] of ABC Company and subsidiaries as of September 30, 20X1, and for the three-month and nine-month periods then ended.

Management's Responsibility

The Company's management is responsible for the preparation and fair presentation of the interim financial information in accordance with [*identify the applicable financial reporting framework; for example, accounting principles generally accepted in the United States of America*]; this responsibility includes the design, implementation, and maintenance of internal control sufficient to provide a reasonable basis for the preparation and fair presentation of interim financial information in accordance with [*identify the applicable financial reporting framework; for example, accounting principles generally accepted in the United States of America*].

Auditor's Responsibility

Our responsibility is to conduct our review in accordance with auditing standards generally accepted in the United States of America applicable to reviews of interim financial information. A review of interim financial information consists principally of applying analytical procedures and making inquiries of persons responsible for financial and accounting matters. It is substantially less in scope than an audit conducted in accordance with auditing standards generally accepted in the United States, the objective of which is the expression of an opinion regarding the financial information. Accordingly, we do not express such an opinion.

Conclusion

Based on our review, we are not aware of any material modifications that should be made to the accompanying interim financial information for it to be in accordance with [*identify the applicable financial reporting framework; for example, accounting principles generally accepted in the United States of America*].

[Auditor's Signature]

[Auditor's city and state]

[Date of the auditor's report]

Other Information

1 Other Information in Documents Containing Audited Financial Statements

The auditor must read the information and should try to resolve any material inconsistencies or material misstatements of fact directly with the client. The auditor may issue a disclaimer of opinion, or may be engaged to express an opinion on such information.

Question 1-1 FR-00870

In its annual report to shareholders, Walsh Co. included a letter to shareholders that contained financial summaries of the past two years. Walsh's auditor is expressing an unmodified opinion on Walsh's financial statements but has not been engaged to examine and report on this additional information. What is the auditor's responsibility concerning the financial summaries?

1. The auditor should express a qualified or adverse opinion because all financial statement information should be audited.
2. The auditor should include an emphasis-of-matter paragraph that includes a disclaimer of opinion on this information.
3. The auditor should inquire of management regarding the purpose of the supplementary information and the criteria used to prepare the information.
4. The auditor should read the letter to the shareholders and verify the information is materially consistent with the information presented in the audited financial statements.

? Related Questions

For related questions, go to the online question bank:

➤ FR-00060

2 Reporting on Supplementary Information in Relation to the Financial Statements as a Whole

An auditor may be engaged to report on supplementary information in relation to the financial statements as a whole.

2.1 Engagement Objectives

The auditor has two objectives in such engagements:

- to evaluate the presentation of the supplementary information in relation to the financial statements as a whole; and
- to report whether the supplementary information is fairly stated, in all material respects, in relation to the financial statements as a whole.

2.2 Auditor's Report

The auditor's report on the supplementary information may either be presented:

- in a separate report; or
- in the auditor's report on the financial statements as an other-matter paragraph (nonissuer) or as an additional paragraph (issuer).

3 Required Supplementary Information

Limited procedures should be performed. The auditor's report on the financial statements should include an other-matter paragraph related to the required supplementary information. An opinion is permitted but not required.

Question 3-1 FR-00088

Jorge, CPA, has been asked to audit the financial statements of Capri Industries, which include supplementary information required by generally accepted accounting principles. Which best describes an appropriate response to this situation?

1. Jorge should not accept this engagement, since auditing information outside the basic financial statements goes beyond the scope of an audit.
2. Jorge may accept this engagement, but need not apply procedures specifically to the supplementary information, since it is outside the basic financial statements.
3. Jorge should not accept this engagement unless he is also hired to perform a separate attest engagement on the supplementary information.
4. Jorge may accept this engagement, but would need to perform certain procedures specifically with respect to the supplementary information.

4 Reports on Application of the Requirements of an Applicable Financial Reporting Framework

A reporting accountant may report on the application of the requirements of an applicable financial reporting framework to a specific transaction or the type of report that may be rendered on a specific entity's financial statements. The report should be restricted in use.

5 Reporting on Financial Statements Prepared in Accordance With a Financial Reporting Framework Generally Accepted in Another Country

A auditor practicing in the United States may be engaged to report on financial statements that have been prepared in accordance with a financial reporting framework generally accepted in another country that has not been adopted by a body designed by the AICPA to establish generally accepted accounting principles, when such audited financial statements are intended to be used outside the United States.

5.1 Distribution Outside the U.S. Only

Use either the other country's report, the report set out in the ISAs, or a U.S. form report that reflects that the financial statements being reported on have been prepared in accordance with a financial reporting framework generally accepted in another country.

5.2 Distribution Within the U.S.

Use the U.S. form report with an emphasis-of-matter paragraph that identifies the financial reporting framework, refers to the note in the financial statements that describes the framework, and indicates that the framework differs from accounting principles generally accepted in the United States of America.

Question 5-1 FR-00097

Which would most likely determine the appropriate form of audit report when financial statements are prepared in accordance with a financial reporting framework generally accepted in another country?

1. The other country's auditing standards.
2. The geographic location of the company.
3. The expected distribution of the financial statements.
4. The reciprocity agreement between that country and the United States.

Reports Required by Government Auditing Standards

Topic **H**

1 Government Auditing—Standards and Supplementary Requirements

In performing an audit of government entities, the auditor may be responsible for meeting the requirements of as many as three sources of guidance:

- GAAS
- GAGAS (Generally Accepted Government Auditing Standards, also referred to as the Yellow Book)
- The Single Audit Act (2 CFR 200), which presents supplementary requirements only applicable if the entity spends federal financial assistance in excess of a specific amount.

2 GAAS Requirements for Compliance Audits

2.1 Objectives of Compliance Audits

- Obtain sufficient evidence to form an opinion on whether the entity complied, in all material respects, with the compliance requirements applicable to their programs.
- Report at the level specified in the governmental audit requirement.
- Identify audit and reporting requirements supplementary to GAAS and GAGAS and address those requirements (e.g., Single Audit Act requirements).

2.2 Overall Standards for Compliance Audits

- Perform a risk assessment (audit risk of noncompliance model)
- Design responses to the risk assessment
- Determine if supplementary audit requirements exist
- Obtain written representations from management
- Prepare reports
- Document risk and materiality

2.3 The Audit Risk of Noncompliance Model

The audit risk of noncompliance model adapts the terminology and relationships of the audit risk model. The risk of material noncompliance consists of inherent risk of noncompliance and control risk of noncompliance:

Risk of Material Noncompliance	Acceptable Level of Detection Risk	Determine "NET" of Testing
High ↑ (Bad)	Low ↓	High ↑
Low ↓ (Good)	High ↑	Low ↓

2.3.1 Inherent Risk of Noncompliance

The susceptibility of a compliance requirement to noncompliance that could be material assuming that there are no related controls.

- Inherent risk exists independent of the audit.
- The auditor cannot change this risk, but can change his/her assessment of the risk based on evidence gathered during the audit.

2.3.2 Control Risk of Noncompliance

The risk that noncompliance with a compliance requirement that could be material will not be prevented or detected on a timely basis by an entity's internal control over compliance.

- Control risk exists independent of the audit.
- The auditor cannot change this risk, but can change his/her assessment of the risk based on evidence gathered during the audit.
- The stronger the system of controls over compliance, the greater the reliance that may be placed on those controls, and the fewer the tests of details (or the lower the quality) required.

2.3.3 Detection Risk of Noncompliance

The risk that the auditor will not detect noncompliance that exists and that undetected noncompliance could be material.

- Detection risk relates to the auditor's procedures.
- The auditor can change this risk by varying the nature, extent, or timing of audit procedures.
- As the acceptable level of detection risk decreases, the assurance provided from tests of details (including tests of implementation of corrective actions from previous audits) should increase.

2.4 Design Responses to Risk Assessment

- The auditor should design audit procedures, including tests of details of the entity's compliance with program requirements.
- The risk assessment, tests of controls, and analytical procedures are not sufficient to address the risk of material noncompliance. Tests of details must be performed.
- Tests of controls may be required if any one of the following conditions exist:
  - The risk assessment includes an expectation of the operating effectiveness of controls over compliance.
  - Substantive procedures do not provide enough evidence to support a conclusion.
  - Tests of controls are required by the applicable governmental audit requirements.

2.5 Determine if Supplementary Audit Requirements Exist

- The entity may have audit requirements that go beyond GAAS and GAGAS. The auditor must make that determination.
- A common example of supplementary audit requirements is the Single Audit requirements related to federal financial assistance described below.

2.6 Obtain a Written Management Representation Letter

Auditors must obtain a written management representation letter that includes statements that management:

- takes responsibility for compliance.
- takes responsibility for maintaining controls over compliance.
- asserts that they have disclosed all programs to the auditor.
- asserts that they have disclosed any known noncompliance or states that no such noncompliance exists.

2.7 Prepare Reports

The auditor may report in several ways, depending on the audit requirement. Possible reports include a(n):

- Opinion on compliance
- Report on internal control over compliance
- Combined report on compliance and internal control over compliance

2.8 Document Risk and Materiality

The auditor is responsible for documenting the following:

- The assessed risk of material noncompliance
- Responses to the risk assessment
- Materiality levels

3 Government Auditing Standards (GAGAS)

3.1 GAGAS: Source and Content Organization

- GAGAS are contained in the Government Auditing Standards, a publication of the Government Accountability Office (GAO) The publication is sometimes called the Yellow Book.
- Generally Accepted Government Auditing Standards (GAGAS) include ethical principles, general standards, standards for financial audits and attest engagements, and field work and reporting standards for performance audits.

3.2 Ethical Principles

The ethical principles that guide the work of auditors who conduct audits in accordance with GAGAS are:

- serving the public interest;
- integrity;
- objectivity;
- proper use of government information, resources, and positions; and
- professional behavior.

3.3 General Standards

The general standards provide guidance for performing financial audits, attestation engagements, and performance audits under GAGAS. The general standards include:

- independence (of mind and appearance);
- professional judgment;
- competence; and
- quality control and assurance (including maintenance of a quality control system and securing an external peer review at least once every three years).

3.4 Standards for Financial Audits: Additional GAGAS Requirements for Performing Financial Audits

- GAGAS describes a number of standards for financial audits in addition to the GAAS requirements.
- Additional standards include consideration of previous audits and attestation engagements, additional attention to fraud and noncompliance and abuse, development of findings to be reported to the entity and others, and audit documentation that provides evidence of supervision, supports findings, and describes the impact of departures from GAGAS.

3.5 Standards for Financial Audits: Additional GAGAS Requirements for Reporting on Financial Audits

- Auditors should include a statement in the auditor's report that they complied with GAGAS.
- Reporting should include a report on internal control over financial reporting and a report on compliance with provisions of laws, regulations, contracts or grant agreements that have a material effect on the financial statements.
- Auditors must report fraud and noncompliance with laws or regulations that have a material effect on the financial statements, noncompliance with provisions of contracts or grant agreements that have a material effect on the financial statements, and report abuse that is material either quantitatively or qualitatively.
- Auditors should report directly to outside parties when entity management fails to satisfy legal or regulatory requirements to report or when an entity's management fails to take time and appropriate steps to respond to known or likely fraud, noncompliance, or abuse.
- Auditors must report their findings and also solicit and report the views of responsible officials along with any planned corrective actions.
- GAGAS auditors should consider reducing materiality thresholds in response to public accountability issues, various legal and regulatory requirements, and the visibility and sensitivity of government programs.
- GAGAS auditors should consider reporting deficiencies early when the urgency or significance of findings requires faster corrective actions or follow-up or when ongoing noncompliance undetected by management should be stopped.

3.6 Reporting Standards and Requirements

3.6.1 Reporting on Compliance

When reporting on compliance under GAGAS, the report should include the following components:

- A statement that the audit complied with GAAS as well as GAGAS for financial audits.
- A report that states the auditor performed tests of compliance with provisions of laws, regulations, contracts, and grant agreements.
- Identification of noncompliance issues discovered during the audit.

3.6.2 Reporting on Internal Control

When reporting on internal control under GAGAS, the report should include the following components:

- A statement that the audit complied with GAAS as well as GAGAS for financial audits.
- The auditor asserts that internal control over financial reporting was considered as part of planning and performing the audit of the financial statements, but not for the purpose of expressing an opinion on internal control. The internal control reporting requirement under GAGAS differs from the objective of an audit of internal control (as part of an integrated audit).

  (*Note*: An integrated audit is not required for nonissuers under SAS. A nonissuer may engage an auditor to perform a financial statement audit only. In a financial statement audit only under SAS, an auditor will report on internal control only if deficiencies are discovered during the financial statement audit.)

  - An audit of internal control (as part of an integrated audit) requires the auditor to provide a high level of assurance about internal control over financial reporting in the form of an opinion.
  - GAGAS does not require the auditor to render an opinion on the effectiveness of internal control over financial reporting. However, the auditor is not precluded from rendering an opinion on internal control if sufficient procedures have been performed.
- A statement that no opinion is expressed on internal control.
- The definition of deficiency in internal control and material weakness in internal control.
- A description of identified material weakness and significant deficiencies in internal control.
- A statement that no material weaknesses were found if none were found.

3.6.3 Reporting Noncompliance

Material instances of noncompliance should be reported in a separate communication to the entity and should be noted in the auditor's report.

- Material instances are defined as:
  - failure to follow requirements; or
  - violations of rules contained in statutes, regulations, contracts, or grants.
- Reporting illegal acts is required.

Question 3-1 FR-00059

Reporting standards associated with government audits include requirements in addition to those associated with generally accepted auditing standards. A requirement that distinguishes audits performed in accordance with government auditing standards from audits that are not subject to these standards is:

1. An opinion on the financial statements taken as a whole.
2. A written communication of the auditor's work on internal control.
3. An opinion on internal control over financial reporting.
4. No opinion on the financial statements is required.

Related Questions

For related questions, go to the online question bank:

➤ FR-00078

4 Single Audit Act (2 CFR 200) Requirements

4.1 Criteria

- The Single Audit Act applies to entities that receive and spend total financial awards equal to or in excess of $750,000 in a fiscal year.
- The Single Audit Act allows for either a single audit that covers the entire entity, or program specific audits associated with an individual award. Program-specific audits are only available to grant recipients who only have one federal program and who are not required to have a financial statement audit.

4.2 Materiality Determinations

- Materiality of a transaction or other compliance finding is considered separately in relation to each major program, not just in relation to the financial statement as a whole.
- Programs classified as major are generally those that expend $750,000 or more in federal financial assistance. Smaller programs may be classified as major if they are deemed to be high risk.

Question 4-1 FR-00069

The requirements to perform a Single Audit under the provisions of 2 CFR 200 apply to entities that:

1. Receive $500,000 in federal financial assistance in a fiscal year.
2. Receive $750,000 in federal financial assistance in a fiscal year.
3. Receive and expend $500,000 in federal financial assistance in a fiscal year.
4. Receive and expend $750,000 in federal financial assistance in fiscal year.

Related Questions

For related questions, go to the online question bank:

➤ FR-00029

5 GAAS, GAGAS, and SAA: Comparison of Reports

Single Audit Act (2 CFR 200)—

Required reports based on federal programs

1. Compliance (opinion)
2. Internal control over compliance applicable to each major program (report—no opinion)
3. Schedule of findings and questioned costs

GAGAS—

Required reports based on the financial statements

1. Compliance (report—no opinion)
2. Internal control over financial reporting (report—no opinion)

GAAS—

1. Opinion on all financial statements

Question 5-1

FR-00009

A government audit may extend beyond an examination leading to the expression of an opinion on the fairness of financial presentation to include:

	Program Results	*Compliance*	*Economy & Efficiency*
1.	Yes	Yes	No
2.	Yes	Yes	Yes
3.	No	Yes	Yes
4.	Yes	No	Yes

Related Questions

For related questions, go to the online question bank:

- FR-00019
- FR-00049

H Reports Required by Government Auditing Standards

Task-Based Simulations

Task-Based Simulation 1: Audit Standards

Scroll down to complete all parts of this task.

Changes to the financial support of Kanine Kennel Dog Shelter, Inc. may create additional requirements for Smith, Smythe, & Smathers as they complete their audit. For each of the additional circumstances or responsibilities described below, identify the most likely combination of audit types by clicking in the associated cells and selecting the appropriate options from the lists provided. Assume each item is independent of the other items and all items are material.

	A	B
1	The auditors discover that Kanine Kennel Dog Shelter has received over $750,000 in federal financial assistance.	
2	The auditors discover that Kanine Kennel Dog Shelter has expended over $300,000 in federal financial assistance.	
3	The auditors are obligated to evaluate materiality based upon major programs.	
4	The auditors are obligated to report on internal control over compliance applicable to each major program.	
5	The auditors must report on the fair presentation on the financial statements of Kanine Kennel Dog Shelter, Inc. taken as a whole.	
6	The auditors must expand their report to include whether federal financial assistance has been administered in accordance with laws and regulations.	
7	Firm standards should include a mandatory peer review every three years.	

Select an option below

- GAAS Audit
- GAAS and GAGAS Audit
- GAAS, GAGAS, and Single Audit

RESET CANCEL ACCEPT

Explanation

Row 1: GAAS and GAGAS Audit
An entity that receives in excess of $750,000 of federal financial assistance would likely be required to have an audit in accordance with GAGAS. If the entity spent $750,000 in federal financial assistance, it would qualify for a single audit.

Row 2: GAAS and GAGAS Audit
An entity that spends in excess of $300,000 of federal financial assistance would likely be required to have an audit in accordance with GAGAS. If the entity spent $750,000 in federal financial assistance, it would qualify for a single audit.

Row 3: GAAS, GAGAS, and Single Audit
Evaluation of materiality for each major program is a characteristic of single audits.

Row 4: GAAS, GAGAS, and Single Audit
Reports on compliance associated with major programs is a characteristic of single audits.

Row 5: GAAS Audit
Reporting on fair presentation of an entity's financial statements taken as a whole is a characteristic of a GAAS audit.

Row 6: GAAS and GAGAS Audit
Expansion of reports to include representations regarding whether federal financial assistance has been administered in accordance with laws and regulations is a characteristic of a GAGAS audit.

Row 7: GAAS and GAGAS Audit
Additional peer review standards are a characteristic of a GAGAS audit. GAGAS sets peer review, CPE, and independence standards that are in excess of GAAS audits.

H Reports Required by Government Auditing Standards

Task-Based Simulation 2: Responsibilities

Scroll down to complete all parts of this task.

Which of the following correctly identify the expanded responsibilities that a CPA firm will face when auditing government financial assistance programs requiring the application of generally accepted government audit standards? Check all that apply.

☐ 1. Identify applicable laws and regulations with compliance requirements.
☐ 2. Obtain absolute assurance that the financial statements are completely free of any misstatement resulting from violations of laws and regulations.
☐ 3. Obtain an understanding of the possible effects on the financial statements of laws and regulations that are generally recognized to have a direct and material effect on the determination of the financial statements.
☐ 4. Prepare supplementary financial reports, including a "Schedule of Expenditures and Federal Awards."
☐ 5. Communicate to decision makers of the entity that an audit in conformity with GAAS may not be sufficient to meet the entity's audit requirements if the engagement does not address governmental audit requirements.
☐ 6. Obtain sufficient evidence to form an opinion on whether the entity complied in all material respects with the compliance requests applicable to their programs.
☐ 7. Obtain sufficient evidence to form an opinion on the effectiveness of internal controls over compliance.
☐ 8. Perform appropriate risk assessment relative to compliance to ensure that detection risks are increased to meet the increases in risk of material noncompliance to decrease audit risk of noncompliance.
☐ 9. Obtain a written management representation letter.
☐ 10. Prepare separate reports on compliance and internal control over compliance and take appropriate measures to ensure they are never combined.

Explanation

1. False
Responsibility for identification of laws and regulations with compliance requirements rests with management. Management is then charged with designing appropriate controls to ensure compliance. While the auditor is responsible for obtaining an understanding of laws and regulations generally recognized to have a direct and material effect on financial statements, the auditor is primarily charged with assessing if management has properly identified applicable laws and regulations with compliance requirements.

2. False
The auditor is charged with obtaining reasonable (not absolute) assurance that the financial statements are free of misstatements that have a direct and material effect on the financial statements (not completely free of any misstatements). This selection overstates the auditor's responsibilities.

3. True
The auditor's responsibilities include obtaining an understanding of the possible effects on the financial statements of laws and regulations that are generally recognized to have a direct and material effect on the determination of financial statement amounts.

4. False
Preparation of supplementary financial reports, like the financial statements, is the responsibility of management, not the auditor.

5. True
Upon discovery that an entity requires the expanded auditing procedures and reporting that result from the entity's receipt of government financial assistance, the auditor must communicate to management and the audit committee that an audit in accordance with GAAS may not be sufficient.

6. True
The auditor must obtain sufficient evidence to form an opinion on compliance when performing an audit in conformity with GAGAS.

7. False
The auditor will not express an opinion regarding the effectiveness of internal control over compliance.

8. False
As risk of material risk of noncompliance increases, the auditor should take measures to reduce, not increase, detection risk.

9. True
The auditor should obtain a written management representation letter.

10. False
The report on compliance and report on internal control over compliance may be either separate or combined.

Notes

1 Special Purpose Frameworks

1.1 Types of Special Purpose Frameworks

Special purpose frameworks include:

- Cash basis.
- Income tax basis.
- Basis required by regulatory agency.
- Basis required by contract.
- Any other basis of accounting that uses a definite set of logical, reasonable criteria that is applied to all material items appearing in the financial statements.

1.2 Report on Special Purpose Frameworks

1.2.1 Report Elements

- Use non-GAAP titles for financial statements.
- Add an emphasis-of-matter paragraph that indicates that the financial statements are prepared using a special purpose framework, states that the basis of presentation is different than GAAP, and refers the reader to the related footnote.
- Add an other-matter paragraph that restricts the use of the report if the financial statements are prepared using a contractual or regulatory basis, or another basis of accounting that uses a definite set of logical, reasonable criteria, unless the financial statements are regulatory basis financial statements intended for general use.
- If the special purpose financial statements are prepared in accordance with a regulatory basis and intended for general use, the auditor should express an opinion about whether the financial statements are:
  - fairly presented, in all material respects, in accordance with GAAP.
  - prepared in accordance with the special purpose framework.

1.2.2 Sample Auditor's Report on Financial Statements Prepared in Accordance With a Special Purpose Framework (Cash Basis)

Independent Auditor's Report

[*Appropriate Addressee*]

We have audited the accompanying financial statements of ABC Partnership, which comprise the statement of assets and liabilities arising from cash transactions as of December 31, 20X1, and the related statement of revenue collected and expenses paid for the year then ended, and the related notes to the financial statements.

Management's Responsibility for the Financial Statements

Management is responsible for the preparation and fair presentation of these financial statements in accordance with the cash basis of accounting described in Note X; this includes determining that the cash basis of accounting is an acceptable basis for the preparation of the financial statements in the circumstances. Management is also responsible for the design, implementation, and maintenance of internal control relevant to the preparation and fair presentation of financial statements that are free from material misstatement, whether due to fraud or error.

Auditor's Responsibility

Our responsibility is to express an opinion on the financial statements based on our audit. We conducted our audit in accordance with auditing standards generally accepted in the United States of America. Those standards require that we plan and perform the audit to obtain reasonable assurance about whether the financial statements are free from material misstatement.

An audit involves performing procedures to obtain audit evidence about the amounts and disclosures in the financial statements. The procedures selected depend on the auditor's judgment, including the assessment of the risks of material misstatement of the financial statements, whether due to fraud or error. In making those risk assessments, the auditor considers internal control relevant to the partnership's preparation and fair presentation of the financial statements in order to design audit procedures that are appropriate in the circumstances, but not for the purpose of expressing an opinion on the effectiveness of the partnership's internal control. Accordingly, we express no such opinion. An audit also includes evaluating the appropriateness of accounting policies used and the reasonableness of significant accounting estimates made by management, as well as evaluating the overall presentation of the financial statements.

We believe that the audit evidence we have obtained is sufficient and appropriate to provide a basis for our opinion.

Opinion

In our opinion, the financial statements referred to above present fairly, in all material respects, the assets and liabilities arising from cash transactions of ABC Partnership as of December 31, 20X1, and its revenues collected and expenses paid during the year then ended in accordance with the cash basis of accounting described in Note X.

Basis of Accounting

We draw attention to Note X of the financial statements, which describes the basis of accounting. The financial statements are prepared on the cash basis of accounting, which is a basis of accounting other than accounting principles generally accepted in the United States of America. Our opinion is not modified with respect to this matter.

[*Auditor's signature*]

[*Auditor's city and state*]

[*Date of the auditor's report*]

Question 1-1 FR-00875

An auditor's report should include a restricted use paragraph and an alert to readers about the preparation of the financial statements in accordance with a special purpose framework when the financial statements are prepared on the:

1. Cash basis.
2. Contractual basis.
3. IFRS basis.
4. Tax basis.

Related Questions

For related questions, go to the online question bank:

- FR-00058

2 Single Financial Statements and Specified Elements, Accounts, or Items

An audit of a single financial statement or of specific elements, accounts, or items of a financial statement may be performed as a separate engagement or in conjunction with an audit of an entity's complete set of financial statements. An incomplete presentation that is otherwise in accordance with GAAP is a type of single financial statement.

2.1 Audit Procedures

The auditor should perform procedures on any interrelated items, such as sales and receivables or inventory and cost of goods sold.

2.1.1 Stockholders' Equity

When the specific element is, or is based on, stockholders' equity, the auditor should perform procedures necessary to express an opinion about financial position.

2.1.2 Net Income

When the specific element is, or is based on, net income or the equivalent, the auditor should perform procedures necessary to express an opinion about financial position and results of operations.

2.2 Modified Opinion on the Complete Set of Financial Statements

If the auditor issues a modified opinion on the complete set of financial statements that is relevant to the audit of a specific element, the auditor should:

- Express an adverse opinion on the specific element when the modified opinion on the complete set of financial statements is due to a material misstatement.
- Express a disclaimer of opinion on the specific element when the modified opinion on the complete set of financial statements is due to a scope limitation.

2.3 Adverse or Disclaimer of Opinion on the Complete Set of Financial Statements

When the auditor expresses an adverse opinion or a disclaimer of opinion on the complete set of financial statements, an unmodified opinion on a specific element in the same auditor's report would contradict the adverse opinion or disclaimer of opinion and would be the same as expressing a piecemeal opinion.

- In this situation, when the auditor considers it appropriate to express an unmodified opinion on the specific element, the auditor should do so only if:
  - the opinion on the specific element is not published with and does not accompany the auditor's report on the complete set of financial statements; and
- the specific element does not constitute a major portion of the entity's complete set of financial statement or the specific element is not, or is not based on, stockholders' equity or net income.
  - A single financial statement is considered to be a major portion of a complete set of financial statements.

2.4 Auditor's Report on a Single Financial Statement

Independent Auditor's Report

[*Appropriate Addressee*]

We have audited the accompanying balance sheet of ABC Company as of December 31, 20X1, and the related notes to the financial statement.

Management's Responsibility for the Financial Statement

Management is responsible for the preparation and fair presentation of this financial statement in accordance with accounting principles generally accepted in the United States of America; this includes the design, implementation, and maintenance of internal control relevant to the preparation and fair presentation of the financial statement that is free from material misstatement, whether due to fraud or error.

Auditor's Responsibility

Our responsibility is to express an opinion on the financial statement based on our audit. We conducted our audit in accordance with auditing standards generally accepted in the United States of America. Those standards require that we plan and perform the audit to obtain reasonable assurance about whether the financial statement is free from material misstatement.

An audit involves performing procedures to obtain audit evidence about the amounts and disclosures in the financial statement. The procedures selected depend on the auditor's judgment, including the assessment of the risks of material misstatement of the financial statement, whether due to fraud or error. In making those risk assessments, the auditor considers internal control relevant to the entity's preparation and fair presentation of the financial statement in order to design audit procedures that are appropriate in the circumstances, but not for the purpose of expressing an opinion on the effectiveness of the entity's internal control. Accordingly, we express no such opinion. An audit also includes evaluating the appropriateness of accounting policies used and the reasonableness of significant accounting estimates made by management, as well as evaluating the overall presentation of the financial statement.

We believe that the audit evidence we have obtained is sufficient and appropriate to provide a basis for our opinion.

Opinion

In our opinion, the financial statement referred to above presents fairly, in all material respects, the financial position of ABC Company as of December 31, 20X1 in accordance with accounting principles generally accepted in the United States of America.

[*Auditor's signature*]

[*Auditor's city and state*]

[*Date of the auditor's report*]

2.5 Auditor's Report on a Specific Element

Independent Auditor's Report

[*Appropriate Addressee*]

We have audited the accompanying schedule of accounts receivable of ABC Company as of December 31, 20X1, and the related notes to the schedule.

Management's Responsibility for the Schedule

Management is responsible for the preparation and fair presentation of this schedule in accordance with accounting principles generally accepted in the United States of America; this includes the design, implementation, and maintenance of internal control relevant to the preparation and fair presentation of the schedule that is free from material misstatement, whether due to fraud or error.

Auditor's Responsibility

Our responsibility is to express an opinion on the schedule based on our audit. We conducted our audit in accordance with auditing standards generally accepted in the United States of America. Those standards require that we plan and perform the audit to obtain reasonable assurance about whether the schedule is free from material misstatement.

An audit involves performing procedures to obtain audit evidence about the amounts and disclosures in the schedule. The procedures selected depend on the auditor's judgment, including the assessment of the risks of material misstatement of the schedule, whether due to fraud or error. In making those risk assessments, the auditor considers internal control relevant to the entity's preparation and fair presentation of the schedule in order to design audit procedures that are appropriate in the circumstances, but not for the purpose of expressing an opinion on the effectiveness of the entity's internal control. Accordingly, we express no such opinion. An audit also includes evaluating the appropriateness of accounting policies used and the reasonableness of significant accounting estimates made by management, as well as evaluating the overall presentation of the schedule.

We believe that the audit evidence we have obtained is sufficient and appropriate to provide a basis for our opinion.

Opinion

In our opinion, the schedule referred to above presents fairly, in all material respects, the accounts receivable of ABC Company as of December 31, 20X1 in accordance with accounting principles generally accepted in the United States of America.

Other Matter

We have audited, in accordance with auditing standards generally accepted in the United States of America, the financial statements of ABC Company as of and for the year ended December 31, 20X1, and our report thereon, dated March 15, 20X2, expressed an unmodified opinion on those financial statements.

[*Auditor's signature*]

[*Auditor's city and state*]

[*Date of the auditor's report*]

Question 2-1 FR-00881

An auditor is engaged by the client to report on inventory and the complete set of financial statements. The auditor expresses a qualified opinion on the complete set of financial statements due to a material misstatement of inventory and cost of goods sold. Under these circumstances, the CPA should express:

1. A qualified opinion on inventory.
2. An adverse opinion on inventory.
3. A disclaimer of opinion on inventory.
4. An unmodified opinion on inventory in a report that does not accompany the auditor's report on the complete set of financial statements.

Question 2-2 FR-00028

Which of the following is *true* about a report on a specific element of a financial statement?

1. An audit of the complete financial statements is required.
2. An unmodified opinion may not be expressed if an adverse opinion or disclaimer of opinion was expressed on the complete financial statements.
3. There should be a reference to both GAAS and GAAP in the report.
4. A restrictive use paragraph is required.

Related Questions

For related questions, go to the online question bank:

- FR-00876
- FR-00877

3 Compliance With Contractual or Regulatory Requirements Related to Audited Financial Statements

3.1 Negative Assurance

The auditor issues negative assurance on compliance in the form of a statement that nothing came to the auditor's attention that caused the auditor to believe that the entity failed to comply with the specified aspects of the contractual agreement or regulatory requirement.

3.2 Report on Compliance

The report on compliance should be in writing and may either be a separate report or provided in one or more paragraphs in the auditor's report on the financial statements.

3.2.1 Separate Report on Compliance

Independent Auditor's Report

[*Appropriate Addressee*]

We have audited, in accordance with auditing standards generally accepted in the United States of America, the financial statements of XYZ Company, which comprise the balance sheet as of December 31, 20X2, and the related statements of income, changes in stockholders' equity, and cash flows for the year then ended, and the related notes to the financial statements, and have issued our report thereon dated February 16, 20X3.

In connection with our audit, nothing came to our attention that caused us to believe that XYZ Company failed to comply with the terms, covenants, provisions, or conditions of sections XX to YY inclusive, of the Indenture dated July 21, 20X0, with ABC Bank, insofar as they relate to accounting matters. However, our audit was not directed primarily toward obtaining knowledge of such noncompliance. Accordingly, had we performed additional procedures, other matters may have come to our attention regarding the Company's noncompliance with the above-referenced terms, covenants, provisions, or conditions of the Indenture, insofar as they relate to accounting matters.

This report is intended solely for the information and use of the boards of directors and management of XYZ Company and ABC Bank and is not intended to be and should not be used by anyone other than these specified parties.

[*Auditor's signature*]

[*Auditor's city and state*]

[*Date of the auditor's report*]

Question 3-1 FR-00878

Which of the following reports requires restricted use language in the report?

1. A report on financial statements prepared on the tax basis of accounting.
2. A report on a client's compliance with a contractual agreement, assuming the report is prepared in connection with a financial statement audit of the complete financial statements.
3. A report on the balance sheet only.
4. A report on an examination of a financial forecast.

? Related Questions

For related questions, go to the online question bank:

- FR-00077
- FR-00879

Class Question Explanations

Topic A

QUESTION 2-1 FR-00891

Choice "4" is correct.

Intentional manipulation of accounting records indicates that management lacks integrity, and as a result, the auditor most likely would conclude that a financial statement audit cannot be performed.

Choice "1" is incorrect. The auditor can accept the engagement even if the auditor does not have experience in the particular industry. However, the auditor should obtain an understanding of the client's business and industry (e.g., by reading appropriate publications) after acceptance of the engagement.

Choice "2" is incorrect. A restriction imposed by circumstances beyond the control of management, such as a hurricane, does not prevent an auditor from accepting an engagement. Additionally, the auditor may be able to perform alternative procedures.

Choice "3" is incorrect. A management-imposed restriction that the auditor believes will result in a qualified opinion does not prevent an auditor from accepting an engagement. However, if the auditor believed the management imposed scope limitation would result in a disclaimer of opinion, then the auditor might conclude that a financial statement audit cannot be performed.

Topic B

QUESTION 2-1 FR-00892

Choice "3" is correct.

A successor auditor's inquiries of the predecessor auditor should include questions regarding communications to management and those charged with governance regarding significant deficiencies (and material weaknesses) in internal control.

Choice "1" is incorrect. The successor auditor generally would not inquire about the number of personnel assigned to the predecessor's engagement.

Choice "2" is incorrect. The successor auditor is responsible for making his or her own judgments regarding the audit, and would not typically inquire regarding the predecessor auditor's judgments with respect to the internal audit function.

Choice "4" is incorrect. The successor auditor generally would not specifically inquire about the response rate for confirmations of accounts receivable. However, the successor auditor would be able to obtain this information when reviewing the predecessor's workpapers.

Auditing I

Topic C

QUESTION 1-1 FR-00895

Choice "2" is correct.

The engagement letter should include a statement regarding the inherent limitations of the audit. This inherent limitation statement describes the unavoidable risk that some material misstatements may not be detected, even though the audit is properly planned and performed in accordance with GAAS.

Choice "1" is incorrect. The engagement letter generally would not describe the advantages of statistical sampling.

Choice "3" is incorrect. An auditor may not be paid in stock of the entity because this would impair the auditor's independence.

Choice "4" is incorrect. The assessment of risk of material misstatement is not included in the engagement letter. The risk of material misstatement is part of the planning process that occurs after engagement acceptance.

Topic D

QUESTION 2-1 FR-00907

Choice "4" is correct.

According to PCAOB standards, audit documentation must be retained for seven years.

Choices "1", "2", and "3" are incorrect, per the above explanation.

QUESTION 3-1 FR-00940

Choice "3" is correct.

Audit documentation should show who performed the work and the date the work was completed.

Choice "1" is incorrect. Audit documentation should be prepared in enough detail so that an experienced auditor, not necessarily a new staff auditor, who has no previous connection with the audit can understand the conclusions reached and any significant judgments made to reach those conclusions.

Choice "2" is incorrect. Audit documentation should enable quality performance reviews and inspections to be performed on the specific audit but does not necessarily by itself "monitor" the effectiveness of the CPA firm's quality control activities. Monitoring is performed at the firm level, not at the individual audit engagement level.

Choice "4" is incorrect. The auditor's understanding of internal control can be documented in a variety of different ways. There is no requirement in professional standards that the design and implementation of internal control must include a flowchart depicting the internal control process.

Topic E

QUESTION 2-1 FR-00108

Choice "2" is correct.

The communication must include material misstatements discovered, even if corrected by management.

Choice "1" is incorrect because while communication to management is allowed, it is not required.

Choice "3" is incorrect because disagreements with management, as well as the other required disclosures, should be communicated in writing when in the auditor's professional judgment, oral communication would be inadequate. Therefore, oral communication of such matters is not entirely precluded.

Choice "4" is incorrect because frequently recurring immaterial misstatements may be communicated if they indicate a particular bias in the preparation of the financial statement.

QUESTION 3-1 FR-00100

Choice "1" is correct.

The auditor must describe his or her responsibility under generally accepted auditing standards in the communication to those charged with governance, but this description is not included in the management representation letter. The representation letter (and not the communication to those charged with governance) would include management's responsibility for fair presentation of the financial statements in conformity with generally accepted accounting principles. Both communications should include uncorrected, nontrivial misstatements identified by the auditor.

Choices "2", "3", and "4" are incorrect, based on the above explanation.

Topic F

QUESTION 1-1 FR-00107

Choice "2" is correct.

Significant deficiencies and material weaknesses must be communicated in writing to management and those charged with governance. The auditor is required to define and separately identify significant deficiencies and material weaknesses.

Choice "1" is incorrect. Significant deficiencies and material weaknesses must be communicated in writing to management and those charged with governance.

Choice "3" is incorrect. The auditor is not required to obtain a management response to significant deficiencies or material weaknesses.

Choice "4" is incorrect. The auditor is required to define and separately identify significant deficiencies and material weaknesses.

Auditing I

Topic G

QUESTION 1-1 FR-00664

Choice "3" is correct.

Independence is impaired when a close family member of a covered person is employed by the client in an accounting or financial reporting role. Employment in the customer service department is not an accounting or financial reporting role and therefore the wife's employment at Warehouse Company would not impair independence.

Choice "1" is incorrect. Independence is impaired if any covered person, including the lead partner, serves on the client's board of directors.

Choice "2" is incorrect. Independence is impaired if the accounting firm employs a former employee of the audit client and the individual participates in an audit related to the period in which the individual was employed by the client. In this case, the former controller worked for Warehouse during Year 10 and therefore should not participate in the audit of Warehouse's Year 10 financial statements.

Choice "4" is incorrect. Independence is impaired when a former member of the audit engagement team is employed by an issuer client in a financial oversight role during the one-year preceding the commencement of audit procedures. In this case, Smith and Company cannot audit Warehouse's Year 10 financial statements because the former engagement manager was employed by Warehouse as the CFO during Year 10.

QUESTION 1-2 FR-00525

Choice "3" is correct.

Under the Independence Rule of the Code of Conduct, independence is impaired if there is a direct financial interest in an audit client regardless of materiality.

Choices "1", "2", and "4" are incorrect because materiality would be important in considering their effects.

QUESTION 3-1 FR-00637

Choice "2" is correct.

The Sarbanes-Oxley Act of 2002 requires registered firms to maintain audit documentation for seven years, not five years.

Choice "1" is incorrect. The Sarbanes-Oxley Act prohibits auditors from performing certain non-audit services, including internal control outsourcing, for audit clients who are issuers.

Choice "3" is incorrect. The Sarbanes-Oxley Act requires the lead and reviewing partners to rotate off the audit engagement after five years.

Choice "4" is incorrect. The Sarbanes-Oxley Act requires the preapproval of tax services to be provided to audit clients.

QUESTION 6-1 FR-00651

Choice "1" is correct.

Under Department of Labor (DOL) rules, independence is not impaired when an actuary associated with the audit firm provides services to the benefit plan.

Choice "2" is incorrect. Under DOL rules, auditor independence is impaired by direct or material indirect interests in the benefit plan or the plan sponsor.

Choice "3" is incorrect. Under DOL rules, independence is impaired if a member of the audit firm maintains the financial records of the benefit plan.

Choice "4" is incorrect. Under DOL rules, independence is impaired if a member of the engagement team serves on the board of directors of the plan sponsor.

Topic H

QUESTION 1-1 FR-00101

Choice "2" is correct.

A system of quality control should include human resource policies and practices, such as recruitment and hiring, determining capabilities and competencies, assigning personnel to engagements, professional development, and performance evaluation, compensation and advancement.

Choice "1" is incorrect. A CPA firm is required to adopt a system of quality control for its auditing, attestation, and accounting and review services.

Choice "3" is incorrect. A system of quality control should be designed, implemented, and maintained to improve the overall conduct of the firm's professional practice; however, this does not necessarily improve audit efficiency.

Choice "4" is incorrect. While an effective system of quality control is conducive to complying with generally accepted auditing standards, it does not necessarily ensure that such standards are followed on every individual audit engagement.

Topic A

QUESTION 1-1 FR-00900

Choice "3" is correct.

Performing inquiries of outside legal counsel regarding pending litigation would not be performed during the planning stage.

Choice "1" is incorrect. Audit planning includes determining the timing of testing.

Choice "2" is incorrect. During the planning stage, the auditor engages in several information gathering activities to obtain knowledge of the client's business, which may include touring the client's facilities.

Choice "4" is incorrect. During the planning stage, the auditor will determine the effect of information technology on the audit because this will help determine the extent of testing.

QUESTION 2-1 FR-00118

Choice "2" is correct.

In an audit conducted in accordance with GAAS, the auditor must document the audit plan, setting forth in detail the procedures necessary to complete the engagement's objectives.

Choices "1" and "4" are incorrect. Documentation of the auditor's understanding of the client's internal control is required, but may take different forms: a narrative, an internal control questionnaire, a flowchart, or simply a memorandum (for a small client) may be sufficient.

Choice "3" is incorrect. A planning memo, while recommended, is not required under GAAS.

Topic B

QUESTION 1-1 FR-00117

Choice "2" is correct.

A lack of physical controls over the safeguarding of assets implies that internal controls are inadequate. Inherent limitations do not relate to controls that are missing or nonexistent, but rather to reasons why internal controls cannot provide absolute assurance.

Choice "1" is incorrect. A programming error in the design of an automated control is a human error. The fact that we cannot completely eliminate human error is one of the inherent limitations of internal control.

Choice "3" is incorrect. Management override of internal control is an inherent limitation of internal control.

Choice "4" is incorrect. Deliberate circumvention of controls by collusion among two or more people is an inherent limitation of internal control.

Auditing II

QUESTION 3-1 FR-00099

Choice "1" is correct.

While obtaining an understanding of internal control, the auditor is required to obtain an understanding of the design of controls and determine whether they have been implemented. The auditor is not required to evaluate the operating effectiveness of controls, but may choose to do so if it is efficient.

Choice "2" is incorrect. The auditor is not required to evaluate the operating effectiveness of controls while obtaining an understanding of internal control.

Choice "3" is incorrect. The auditor may choose to evaluate the operating effectiveness of controls while obtaining an understanding of internal control, if it is efficient to do so.

Choice "4" is incorrect. While obtaining an understanding of internal control, the auditor is required to obtain an understanding of the design of controls and determine whether they have been implemented.

QUESTION 4-1 FR-00020

Choice "1" is correct.

There are two types of reports on the processing of transactions by service organizations: "reports on controls placed in operation" and "reports on controls placed in operation and tests of operating effectiveness." The former do not include tests of operating effectiveness and, therefore, are not intended to provide the user auditor with a basis for reducing the assessment of control risk below the maximum. Accordingly, such reports should include a disclaimer of opinion regarding the operating effectiveness of the controls.

Choice "2" is incorrect because the report should contain an indication that the controls were suitably designed to achieve specified control objectives, but it does not provide any assurance regarding the achievement of the user organization's (in this case, the retailer's) objectives.

Choice "3" is incorrect because the service auditor (Cook) is not required to identify the service organization's (i.e., PDC's) controls relevant to specific financial statement assertions, because this is not a financial statement audit.

Choice "4" is incorrect because the service auditor (Cook) is not required to disclose the assessed level of control risk for the service organization (PDC).

QUESTION 5-1 FR-00005

Choice "3" is correct.

Test data allows the auditor to determine whether adequate controls exist over data processing. Test data consists of fictitious entries or inputs that are processed through the client's computer system under the control of the auditor. The client's computerized payroll system should have adequate controls to prevent input of invalid employee I.D. numbers.

Choices "1", "2", and "4" are incorrect because these controls do not involve the client's computer system and therefore cannot be tested using test data.

QUESTION 5-2 FR-00035

Choice "2" is correct.

Test data consists of "dummy" data run through the client's computer system. The data should be processed under the auditor's control.

Choice "1" is incorrect because only transactions that the auditor wishes to test must be used.

Choice "3" is incorrect because while the auditor will frequently use many valid and invalid conditions, it is not feasible to test every possible valid and invalid condition using a test data approach.

Choice "4" is incorrect because the objective of the test data approach is to test programs that the client uses to process data. Using different programs defeats the primary purpose of the test.

Topic C

QUESTION 1-1 FR-00072

Choice "3" is correct.

The auditor must obtain reasonable assurance about whether the financial statements are free of material misstatements, whether caused by error or fraud.

Choices "1", "2", and "4" are incorrect, based on the above explanation.

QUESTION 4-1 FR-00081

Choice "2" is correct.

Although the risk of material misstatement due to fraud may be greatest when all three fraud risk factors are observed, the inability to observe any or all of these conditions does not imply that there is no fraud risk.

Choice "1" is incorrect. Fraud risk factors include incentives/pressures, opportunity, and rationalization.

Choice "3" is incorrect. Although the risk of material misstatement due to fraud may be greatest when all three fraud risk factors are observed, the existence of all three risk factors is not an absolute indication of fraud.

Choice "4" is incorrect. It is true that fraud risk factors are often present in circumstances where fraud has occurred.

QUESTION 5-1 FR-00914

Choice "1" is correct.

The auditor provides reasonable, not absolute, assurance that the material misstatements are free from error, whether due to error or fraud.

Choice "2", "3", and "4" are all required documentation regarding the required fraud brainstorming session.

Auditing II

Topic D

QUESTION 1-1 FR-00062

Choice "1" is correct.

The auditor would initially have planned the audit to achieve a low level of audit risk. If the risk of material misstatement increased, the auditor would need to reduce detection risk to achieve the same low level of audit risk as initially planned.

Choice "2" is incorrect. The increase in the risk of material misstatement results in an increase in overall audit risk. Increasing detection risk would only exacerbate this problem by increasing audit risk even further.

Choice "3" is incorrect. If the auditor does not modify the desired level of detection risk, it is true that the overall level of audit risk will increase, but this is not the most likely situation. An auditor who discovers a higher risk than initially anticipated would need to develop an appropriate response to offset this increase in risk, so that an overall low level of audit risk could still be attained.

Choice "4" is incorrect. Assuming that the auditor had already planned the audit to achieve an appropriately low level of audit risk, the auditor would most likely revise audit procedures in an attempt to achieve the same low level of audit risk as initially planned. Although it is possible that the auditor would reduce detection risk enough to actually lower overall audit risk, this is not the most likely response to the scenario described.

QUESTION 1-2 FR-00911

Choice "4" is correct.

As the acceptable level of detection risk increases, the assurance that must be provided by substantive tests can decrease. Therefore, the auditor may reduce the sample size.

Choice "1" is incorrect. As the acceptable level of detection risk increases, the level of assurance required from substantive tests decreases. Changing the nature of substantive tests from a less effective to a more effective procedure provides more assurance and is more likely to result from a decrease (not increase) in detection risk.

Choice "2" is incorrect. As the acceptable level of detection risk increases, the assurance that must be provided by substantive tests can decrease. Changing the timing of substantive tests from interim to year-end provides more assurance and is more likely to result from a decrease (not increase) in detection risk.

Choice "3" is incorrect. Although inherent risk affects the level of detection risk, detection risk does not affect the level of inherent risk. Inherent risk exists independently of the audit.

QUESTION 2-1 FR-00071

Choice "3" is correct.

Analytical procedures used in planning the audit should focus on enhancing the auditor's understanding of the client's business and the transactions and events that have occurred since the last audit date.

Choice "1" is incorrect. Analytical procedures used in planning do not reduce tests of controls or substantive tests.

Choice "2" is incorrect. Analytical procedures used in planning are not designed to identify material misstatements.

Choice "4" is incorrect. Audit evidence has not yet been gathered during the planning process, so its adequacy cannot be assessed.

QUESTION 2-2 FR-00913

Choice "3" is correct.

The required risk assessment discussion should include consideration of the risk of management override of controls.

Choice "1" is incorrect. The discussion about the susceptibility of the entity's financial statements to material misstatement may be held concurrently from the discussion about the susceptibility of the entity's financial statements to fraud.

Choice "2" is incorrect. The discussion must involve all "key" members who participate on the audit team, including the engagement partner.

Choice "4" is incorrect. The risk assessment discussion is required to occur at the start of the audit, during the planning phase.

Topic E

QUESTION 1-1 FR-00032

Choice "2" is correct.

The occurrence assertion addresses whether recorded entries are valid. The direction of this test is from the recorded entry in the voucher register to the supporting documents.

Choice "1" is incorrect. Completeness addresses whether all transactions and events are included, and would involve tracing from support for purchases to the recorded entry.

Choices "3" and "4" are incorrect. Tracing from the voucher register to supporting documents provides only limited evidence about allocation and valuation, or about rights and obligations.

QUESTION 1-2 FR-00112

Choice "1" is correct.

Tracing from source documents (evidence of shipments) to the accounting records (sales journal) provides evidence of completeness. If the auditor finds a shipment that was not recorded, this would indicate a lack of completeness of sales.

Choice "2" is incorrect. Accounts receivable turnover may vary from year to year based on changes in the level of credit sales and receivables. With more than one factor affecting this ratio, however, it is not the most likely means of detecting an understatement in sales.

Choice "3" is incorrect. Using common size analysis, total revenue is set at 100 percent for each company. Comparison of common size financial statements would not be useful in trying to identify understatements in credit sales.

Choice "4" is incorrect. If an audit test starts with a selection of *recorded* sales, unrecorded sales will not be discovered by this test.

Auditing II

QUESTION 2-1 FR-00902

Choice "2" is correct.

The auditor is not required to evaluate operating effectiveness as part of understanding internal control, and therefore, need not document the basis for this decision.

Choice "1" is incorrect. A written audit plan setting forth the procedures necessary to accomplish the audit objectives is required to be documented.

Choice "3" is incorrect. An auditor should document key elements of the understanding of the entity and its environment, including each of the five components of internal control. The five components include the entity's control activities.

Choice "4" is incorrect. The assessment of the risks of material misstatement at both the financial statement and relevant assertion levels are required to be documented.

Topic F

QUESTION 1-1 FR-00961

Choice "4" is correct.

An increase in level of supervision represents an appropriate overall response to an increase in financial statement level risk.

Choice "1" is incorrect. An appropriate overall response to an increase in financial statement level risk is to incorporate a greater level of unpredictability into the audit. Informing management of the specific details of substantive procedures would make the audit more predictable.

Choice "2" is incorrect. Testing of controls in a financial statement audit is performed when the auditor's risk assessment is based on the assumption that the controls are operating effectively or when substantive procedures alone are insufficient.

Choice "3" is incorrect. An auditor most likely would perform tests at period end, rather than interim, because it provides greater assurance.

QUESTION 3-1 FR-00052

Choice "4" is correct.

Using a combined approach involves identifying specific internal controls relevant to specific assertions that are likely to prevent or detect material misstatements in those assertions. If those controls are found to be operating effectively, substantive testing can be reduced.

Choice "1" is incorrect. Using a combined approach would most likely lead to less extensive substantive tests with smaller sample sizes.

Choice "2" is incorrect. A combined approach is based on the relationship between the operating effectiveness of controls and the required level of substantive testing. The level of inherent risk is not part of this evaluation.

Choice "3" is incorrect. Substantive tests performed at year-end would be more consistent with a substantive approach, which would require more competent substantive testing to be performed.

Topic G

QUESTION 1-1 FR-00896

Choice "3" is correct.

The client's release of quarterly results before the SEC-prescribed deadline would not result in the auditor reevaluating established materiality levels.

Choice "1" is incorrect. If the materiality level was established initially based on preliminary financial statement amounts and those amounts differ significantly from actual amounts, then this would be a circumstance that would require the auditor to reevaluate the established materiality levels.

Choice "2" is incorrect. A situation that would require reevaluation of established materiality levels include changes in circumstance, such as a major disposition of the entity's business.

Choice "4" is incorrect. A circumstance that would require reevaluation of established materiality levels include significant new contractual arrangements that draw attention to a particular aspect of a client's business that is separately disclosed in the financial statements.

Topic H

QUESTION 1-1 FR-00051

Choice "4" is correct.

Analytical procedures do not ordinarily provide information about the internal auditor.

Choices "1", "2", and "3" are incorrect. Discussions with management personnel, reviews of the internal auditor's work, and previous experience could all provide information relevant to the evaluation of competence and objectivity.

QUESTION 2-1 FR-00898

Choice "2" is correct.

An auditor may not divide responsibility with an auditor's specialist. If the auditor decides to express a modified opinion as a result of the work performed by the specialist, then the auditor may refer to the specialist and should indicate that the reference to the specialist does not reduce the auditor's responsibility for the audit opinion.

Choice "1" is incorrect. When an auditor decides to use the work of an auditor's specialist as audit evidence, the auditor should evaluate the competence, capabilities, and objectivity of the specialist. Evaluation of this may be acquired by obtaining knowledge of the specialist's qualifications.

Choice "3" is incorrect. When an auditor decides to use the work of an auditor's specialist as audit evidence, the auditor should evaluate the competence, capabilities, and objectivity of the specialist. Evaluation of this may be acquired by inquiring of the entity and the auditor's specialist about any known interests that the entity has with the auditor's external specialist that may affect that specialist's objectivity.

Choice "4" is incorrect. The external auditor should verify the adequacy of the work of the auditor's specialist. This may include reviewing the working papers of the auditor's specialist.

Auditing II

Topic I

QUESTION 1-1 FR-00120

Choice "3" is correct.

Reviewing confirmations of loans receivable and payable is useful for determining the existence of related party transactions because guarantees are commonly provided by or for related parties.

Choice "1" is incorrect because detection of unreported contingent liabilities is not a procedure that would assist the auditor in identifying related party transactions.

Choice "2" is incorrect because recurring transactions after year-end are a usual business occurrence. Related party transactions would most likely be nonrecurring.

Choice "4" is incorrect because while financial difficulties may be associated with related party transactions, it is unlikely that analytical procedures would assist the auditor in identifying such transactions.

QUESTION 2-1 FR-00918

Choice "4" is correct.

An illegal payment to a foreign official would most likely raise a question concerning possible noncompliance with laws and regulations.

Choice "1" is incorrect. Failure to retire a piece of obsolete equipment is not likely to raise a question about noncompliance with laws and regulations.

Choice "2" is incorrect. Failure to correct material internal control weaknesses may represent a conscious decision by management to accept the degree of risk because of cost or other considerations.

Choice "3" is incorrect. Receipt of governmental financial assistance most likely would not cause the auditor to raise a question about possible noncompliance with laws and regulations.

Topic J

QUESTION 2-1 FR-00030

Choice "3" is correct.

The auditor's overall responsibility is to obtain sufficient competent audit evidence to provide reasonable assurance that fair value measurements and disclosures are in conformity with GAAP.

Choice "1" is incorrect because while it is true that the auditor should determine whether management has the intent and ability to carry out courses of action that may affect fair values, this is just one part of evaluating fair value measurements and not the best description of the auditor's overall responsibility.

Choice "2" is incorrect because while it is true that the auditor should assess the risk of material misstatement of fair value measurements, this is done to determine the nature, timing, and extent of audit procedures. It is not the best representation of the auditor's overall responsibility.

Choice "4" is incorrect because *management* (and not the auditor) should make fair value measurements and disclosures in accordance with GAAP and should identify and support any significant assumptions used.

QUESTION 2-2 FR-00111

Choice "2" is correct.

The auditor should verify that all material estimates required by GAAP have been developed.

Choice "1" is incorrect. The auditor is responsible for auditing estimated amounts included in the financial statements, to determine that they are reasonable and properly presented and disclosed.

Choice "3" is incorrect. The auditor should focus on assumptions that are *subjective* (not objective), *sensitive* (not insensitive) to variation, and *deviate* from historical patterns, as these types of assumptions are more likely to result in unreasonable estimates.

Choice "4" is incorrect. Management (and not the auditor) bears responsibility for making reasonable estimates and including them in the financial statements.

Auditing III

Topic A

QUESTION 1-1 FR-00954

Choice "4" is correct.

A misstatement may not be an isolated occurrence. Identification of a misstatement that resulted from an inappropriate valuation method that has been widely applied by the entity may indicate that additional misstatements exist.

Choice "1" is incorrect. Management's enforcement of integrity and ethical values implies a stronger control environment, which may result in fewer misstatements, especially due to fraud.

Choice "2" is incorrect. The inclusion of several large, outstanding checks in the monthly bank reconciliation may be a normal occurrence and is not necessarily indicative of material misstatement.

Choice "3" is incorrect. Sometimes companies will outsource the internal audit function to another CPA firm. The CPA firm hired will perform the internal audit procedures and then report the results to management. Evidence of an internal audit function (outsourced or not) typically results in a reduction of misstatements.

Topic B

QUESTION 2-1 FR-00046

Choice "4" is correct.

By using statistical sampling, the auditor can quantify sampling risk to assist in limiting it to a level considered acceptable.

Choice "1" is incorrect because statistical sampling does not provide any advantage with respect to converting the test into a dual-purpose test.

Choice "2" is incorrect because statistical sampling still requires judgment to determine sample sizes. The tolerable rate of deviation, the likely rate of deviation, and the allowable risk of assessing control risk too low are all determined by the auditor's professional judgment.

Choice "3" is incorrect because statistical sampling does not afford greater assurance than a nonstatistical sample of the same size. It only provides the auditor with a better measure of the sufficiency of the evidence found, and helps to evaluate the results found.

QUESTION 2-2 FR-00066

Choice "2" is correct.

Attribute sampling is primarily used to test controls, such as proper approval of purchase orders.

Choice "1" is incorrect. Variables sampling is typically used in substantive testing, such as confirming accounts receivable balances.

Choice "3" is incorrect. Variables sampling is typically used in substantive testing, such as verifying proper extensions and footings of invoices.

Choice "4" is incorrect. Variables sampling is typically used in substantive testing, such as testing that cash receipts are appropriately credited to customer accounts.

Auditing III

QUESTION 3-1 FR-00006

Choice "1" is correct.

The risk of incorrect rejection and the risk of assessing control risk too high relate to the efficiency of the audit. These two errors generally result in an auditor performing unnecessary additional procedures.

Choice "2" is incorrect because the application of additional procedures will ordinarily still lead the auditor to the appropriate conclusion.

Choice "3" is incorrect because these risks do not relate directly to selection of the items included in the sample.

Choice "4" is incorrect because these risks do not relate directly to quality controls.

QUESTION 4-1 FR-00026

Choice "4" is correct.

All else being equal, the sample size required to achieve the auditor's objective increases as the auditor's assessment of tolerable misstatement for the balance or class decreases.

Choice "1" is incorrect because a greater reliance on internal control will lead to a smaller sample size in a substantive test of details.

Choice "2" is incorrect because greater reliance upon analytical procedures will reduce the need for reliance on substantive tests of details, which in turn will result in a smaller sample size.

Choice "3" is incorrect because as fewer errors are expected, a smaller sample size would be used.

QUESTION 5-1 FR-00036

Choice "4" is correct.

The auditor will reduce reliance on a control if the upper deviation rate exceeds the tolerable rate. The upper deviation rate consists of the sample deviation rate plus an allowance for sampling risk. Therefore, if the sample deviation rate plus the allowance for sampling risk exceeds the tolerable rate, that is equivalent to the upper deviation rate exceeding the tolerable rate.

Choice "1" is incorrect because if the sample deviation rate plus the allowance for sampling risk equals the tolerable rate, the auditor may still place the planned amount of reliance on the control.

Choice "2" is incorrect because whether the actual sample deviation rate is less than the expected deviation rate is irrelevant for making decisions about planned reliance levels.

Choice "3" is incorrect because if the tolerable rate less the allowance for sampling risk exceeds the sample rate of deviation, then the upper deviation rate is less than the tolerable rate. This situation supports the planned reliance, and no reduction in planned reliance would be necessary.

Topic C

QUESTION 4-1 FR-00022

Choice "3" is correct.

Confirmation of accounts receivable is a substantive test, not a test of controls.

Choice "1" is incorrect. Records documenting the usage of computer programs may indicate whether access is appropriately controlled.

Choice "2" is incorrect. Examination of canceled supporting documents helps the auditor determine whether this control is being appropriately applied.

Choice "4" is incorrect. Signatures on authorization forms help the auditor determine whether or not required authorizations are received.

Topic D

QUESTION 1-1 FR-00952

Choice "2" is correct.

Interest costs related to construction of a fixed asset by a company may be capitalized to the asset being constructed. This bests explains the reason for the increase in debt outstanding (acquisition of new debt) and interest expense staying approximately the same (the additional interest expense from the construction loan is being capitalized to the construction of the building).

Choice "1" is incorrect. If the company paid off a significant portion of debt, then the overall debt outstanding probably would decrease, not increase.

Choice "3" is incorrect. The company only invests in debt that has a fixed interest rate; therefore, a decrease in the Federal Reserve rate probably would not affect their interest expense.

Choice "4" is incorrect. Acquiring a new loan at midyear would increase the debt outstanding, but would not explain why interest expense stayed approximately the same.

QUESTION 2-1 FR-00115

Choice "4" is correct.

Accounts receivable turnover is calculated as net sales divided by average receivables. Allowing a grace period for customer payments is likely to increase the average receivable balance, thus decreasing accounts receivable turnover.

Choice "1" is incorrect. Accounts receivable turnover is calculated as net sales divided by average receivables. Early payment incentives are likely to reduce average receivables, thus increasing accounts receivable turnover.

Choice "2" is incorrect. Accounts receivable turnover is calculated as net sales divided by average receivables. If credit policy is tightened, there are less likely to be delinquent customers and the average receivable balance should decline, thus increasing accounts receivable turnover.

Choice "3" is incorrect. Accounts receivable turnover is calculated as net sales divided by average receivables. Implementation of more aggressive collection policies will tend to result in a decrease in average receivables, thus increasing accounts receivable turnover.

Auditing III

Topic E

QUESTION 4-1 FR-00021

Choice "3" is correct.

Expenses for the current year are not complete if an expense occurring in one year is not recorded until the following year.

Choice "1" is incorrect. Accuracy relates to recording at an appropriate amount.

Choice "2" is incorrect. Classification relates to recording in the proper accounts.

Choice "4" is incorrect. Occurrence relates to recording only events that have occurred during the given year.

QUESTION 5-1 FR-00935

Choice "4" is correct.

Examining open vouchers as part of the search for *unrecorded liabilities* is a substantive procedure.

Choice "1" is incorrect. Verifying that the vouchers payable package is properly approved is a test of controls, not a substantive procedure.

Choice "2" is incorrect. Observation of the payroll distribution on an unannounced basis is a test of controls, which involves verifying that all personnel being paid are actually employed by the company.

Choice "3" is incorrect. Observing the preparation of the accounts receivable aging schedule is a test of controls, not a substantive procedure.

Topic F

QUESTION 1-1 FR-00929

Choice "3" is correct.

An acceptable alternative procedure is to examine the applicable sales order, shipping document, and subsequent cash receipts.

Choice "1" is incorrect. Generally, an auditor would not visit the client's customer and review documents in their possession. An appropriate alternative procedure is to review the specific subsequent cash receipts, shipping documentation, and invoice to verify the existence of the receivable.

Choice "2" is incorrect. Obtaining an aging of accounts receivable and tracing it to the general ledger control account would provide evidence about the completeness, not existence, assertion.

Choice "4" is incorrect. Examining subsequent cash disbursements and related receiving reports would be an appropriate alternative procedure when testing accounts payable for completeness when the accounts payable confirmations are not received.

QUESTION 2-1 FR-00931

Choice "2" is correct.

Lapping best describes the employee fraud scheme. Lapping occurs when current receipts of cash are withheld and not recorded. Subsequent receipts are applied to prior accounts.

Choice "1" is incorrect. This scheme does not describe kiting. Kiting occurs when a check drawn on one bank is deposited in another bank and no record is made of the disbursement.

Choice "3" is incorrect. This scheme most likely is not identity theft. Identity theft occurs when someone uses a person's personal information for financial gain (e.g., makes purchases).

Choice "4" is incorrect. Fraudulent financial reporting involves intentional misstatements or omissions of amounts designed to deceive financial statement users. It does not appear that the employee is trying to deceive financial statement users. Lapping is more likely to be categorized as a misappropriation of assets, which involves theft of an entity's financial assets.

Topic G

QUESTION 1-1 FR-00003

Choice "1" is correct.

The daily sales summary will include all "billed" sales for a particular day. Comparing this summary to the postings to the accounts receivable ledger will provide evidence regarding whether billed sales are correctly posted.

Choice "2" is incorrect. Comparing sales invoices to shipping documents provides evidence that invoiced sales have been shipped.

Choice "3" is incorrect. Reconciling the accounts receivable ledger to the control account will not provide assurance that all billed sales were posted. The receivable ledger and the control account may both have omitted the sales.

Choice "4" is incorrect. Comparing shipments with sales invoices provides evidence regarding whether all shipments have been invoiced, not whether billed sales are correctly posted to accounts receivable.

QUESTION 1-2 FR-00943

Choice "2" is correct.

Tracing shipments to sales invoices would provide evidence that shipments to customers were properly invoiced.

Choice "1" is incorrect. Tracing from invoices to shipping documents would provide evidence that sales billed to customers were actually shipped.

Choice "3" is incorrect. Tracing from invoices to shipping documents would provide evidence that shipments to customers were invoiced, but does not necessarily indicate that invoices were recorded as sales.

Choice "4" is incorrect. The auditor would compare the signed purchase order to shipping documents to determine if all goods ordered by the customer were shipped.

Auditing III

QUESTION 2-1 FR-00945

Choice "4" is correct.

An auditor most likely would compare subsequent bank statements (specifically looking for cash payments made after the balance sheet date) with the accounts payable listing in searching for unrecorded payables. The auditor is looking for payables that should have been recorded as of the balance sheet date, but were not.

Choice "1" is incorrect. Obtaining a sample of vendor statements and recalculating the invoice amount would provide evidence about the accuracy of the invoice amount.

Choice "2" is incorrect. Obtaining the accounts payable listing and agreeing to subsequent cash payments provides evidence about existence, not completeness.

Choice "3" is incorrect. Comparing cash disbursements made before year-end with vendor invoices would not help the auditor search for unrecorded payables. Cash payments made before year-end for vendor invoices should result in the payable being eliminated.

QUESTION 3-1 FR-00053

Choice "4" is correct.

Companies sometimes erroneously expense property and equipment acquisitions rather than capitalizing them as assets. An analysis of repair and maintenance accounts may reveal such errors.

Choice "1" is incorrect because while auditors will want to determine that noncapitalizable expenses for repairs and maintenance have been recorded in the proper period, analyzing only the recorded entries is an incomplete test. The auditor would also need to look at payments that were not recorded in the current period, in case they should have been.

Choice "2" is incorrect because expenditures for property and equipment would not be included in repair and maintenance accounts.

Choice "3" is incorrect because analyzing items already included in the repair and maintenance account would not identify noncapitalizable expenditures that have been erroneously capitalized.

QUESTION 4-1 FR-00033

Choice "1" is correct.

Payroll is generally determined in a fairly objective manner and is easily tested by the auditor. As such, specific representations with respect to payroll are not often requested.

Choice "2" is incorrect. Segregation of duties is a key control within the payroll cycle. The auditor should verify that the functions of authorization, record keeping, and custody are appropriately segregated.

Choice "3" is incorrect. Year-end payroll accruals are fairly easy to recalculate, and such recalculation provides good audit evidence supporting financial statement amounts.

Choice "4" is incorrect. Payroll is fairly predictable and thus is often compared with standards and budgets.

QUESTION 6-1 FR-00063

Choice "3" is correct.

The legality of a dividend depends in part on whether it has been properly authorized. Thus, the auditor must determine that proper authorization exists, as both cash and stock dividends affect retained earnings.

Choice "1" is incorrect because only a memo entry is required for a stock split.

Choice "2" is incorrect because the write-down of an account receivable will not, in general, be recorded in retained earnings.

Choice "4" is incorrect because gains from the disposition of treasury shares are recorded in paid-in capital accounts.

Topic H

QUESTION 1-1 FR-00926

Choice "3" is correct.

During a tour of the manufacturing plant or production facility, the auditor should be alert for items that appear to be old, obsolete, or defective.

Choice "1" is incorrect. Testing the mathematical accuracy of the inventory report would determine that the numerical amounts are computed correctly, but would not provide evidence about whether the inventory is slow-moving, defective, or obsolete after manufacture.

Choice "2" is incorrect. Inquiry of management about pledged or assigned inventory would provide evidence about the rights and obligation of the inventory, but would not inform the auditor about slow-moving, defective, or obsolete inventory.

Choice "4" is incorrect. Testing the computation of standard overhead rates relates to the accumulation of costs during the manufacturing process, and not to whether the inventory is slow-moving, defective, or obsolete after manufacture.

QUESTION 2-1 FR-00064

Choice "1" is correct.

A custodial statement provides valid and relevant external evidence regarding the existence of securities.

Choice "2" is incorrect. The client's securities ledger is internal evidence, and as such it is not as valid as a custodial statement.

Choice "3" is incorrect. Broker's advices regarding purchases and sales provide valid external evidence about transactions occurring during the year, but a custodial statement provides more direct evidence about the existence of securities as of the year-end date.

Choice "4" is incorrect. A year-end listing of market prices is not relevant to the existence of marketable securities, although it would provide evidence about the valuation of such securities.

Auditing III

Topic I

QUESTION 1-1 FR-00947

Choice "2" is correct.

The attorney's refusal to respond when the attorney has given substantial attention to the matter would represent a scope limitation. Depending on materiality, this may result in a qualified opinion or disclaimer of opinion.

Choice "1" is incorrect. A refusal to permit inquiry will generally result in a disclaimer of opinion or withdrawal from the audit.

Choice "3" is incorrect. If the auditor is satisfied that financial statement disclosure is adequate, no modification to the opinion would be required.

Choice "4" is incorrect. Lawyers may limit their replies to matters to which they have given substantial attention.

QUESTION 1-2 FR-00091

Choice "3" is correct.

The primary purpose of an external inquiry of the client's attorney is to obtain corroboration of information provided by management regarding litigation, claims, and assessments.

Choices "1" and "2" are incorrect. The auditor's external inquiry of the client's attorney provides information about litigation, claims, and assessments, such as the nature of the matter, the progress of the case, the degree of likelihood of an unfavorable outcome, and an estimate of potential loss. It does not provide information about the client's controls with respect to recognizing the financial statement impact of such matters.

Choice "4" is incorrect. The client's attorney provides information such as the nature of the matter, the progress of the case, the degree of likelihood of an unfavorable outcome, and an estimate of potential loss, but does not comment or provide advice regarding the fair presentation of such matters in the financial statements.

Topic J

QUESTION 2-1 FR-00057

Choice "3" is correct.

Calibro should issue an unmodified opinion with an emphasis-of-matter paragraph describing the situation.

Choice "1" is incorrect. In situations where there is substantial doubt about the entity's ability to continue as a going concern, the auditor generally should add an emphasis-of-matter paragraph (not other-matter paragraph) to the unmodified opinion.

Choice "2" is incorrect. In situations where there is substantial doubt about the entity's ability to continue as a going concern, the auditor generally should add an emphasis-of-matter paragraph to the unmodified opinion. There is no need to qualify the opinion.

Choice "4" is incorrect. In situations where there is substantial doubt about the entity's ability to continue as a going concern, the auditor generally should add an emphasis-of-matter paragraph to the unmodified opinion. As long as the auditor adds the appropriate explanatory language, there would be no need to withdraw from the engagement.

QUESTION 3-1 FR-00037

Choice "4" is correct.

Management's ability to negotiate reductions of required dividends will decrease required cash outflows, and thereby increase the likelihood that the entity will be able to continue as a going concern.

Choices "1", "2", and "3" are incorrect because they involve spending cash, rather than reducing outflows of cash.

Topic K

QUESTION 3-1 FR-00803

Choice "3" is correct.

Significant deficiencies in the design or operation of internal control are control weaknesses that are important enough to merit attention by those charged with governance.

Choice "1" is incorrect because information that significantly contradicts the auditor's going concern assumption is not considered a significant deficiency.

Choice "2" is incorrect because fraud perpetrated by high-level managers should be reported to the audit committee (i.e. those charged with governance). However, it does not necessarily represent a significant deficiency in internal control.

Choice "4" is incorrect because fraud should be reported to an appropriate level of management, and sometimes to the audit committee (i.e. those charged with governance). However, it does not necessarily represent a significant deficiency in internal control.

Topic L

QUESTION 1-1 FR-00930

Choice "2" is correct.

U.S. GAAS require the date of the written representations to be the date of the auditor's report.

Choice "1" is incorrect. According to ISAs, not U.S. GAAS, the management representation letter should be dated as near as possible to, but not after, the date of the auditor's report.

Choice "3" is incorrect. U.S. GAAS require the date of the written representations to be the date of the auditor's report. The auditor will complete the audit after the date of the financial statements.

Choice "4" is incorrect. U.S. GAAS require the date of the written representations to be the date of the auditor's report. The auditor will complete the audit after the date of the financial statements.

Auditing III

Topic M

QUESTION 1-1 FR-00027

Choice "3" is correct.

The acquisition provided evidence of a condition which came into existence after year-end [a "Type 2" (nonrecognized) subsequent event] and therefore the proper accounting approach would be note disclosure rather than adjustment.

Choice "1" is incorrect because adjustments are only appropriate for subsequent events which provide evidence that the condition was in existence at year-end ["Type 1" (recognized) events].

Choice "2" is incorrect because the auditor does not issue financial statements for the client.

Choice "4" is incorrect because the opinion paragraph of the report need not be modified. The auditor might choose to add an explanatory paragraph emphasizing the matter, but is not required to do so.

QUESTION 3-1 FR-00094

Choice "3" is correct.

The auditor has an active responsibility to investigate subsequent events between the date of the financial statements and the date of the auditor's report, and must also consider the effect of any events occurring after the date of the auditor's report that come to his/her attention.

Choice "1" is incorrect. The auditor has no active responsibility to investigate events occurring after the date of the auditor's report, unless such events come to his or her attention.

Choice "2" is incorrect. The auditor has an active responsibility to investigate the 2/1/Year 2 event, but also may have some level of responsibility with respect to the 3/1/Year 2 event. Despite the fact that it occurred after the date of the auditor's report, if the event comes to the auditor's attention, it cannot be ignored.

Choice "4" is incorrect. The auditor has an active responsibility to investigate subsequent events between the date of the financial statements and the date of the auditor's report, and must also consider the effect of any events occurring after the date of the auditor's report that come to his/her attention.

Topic N

QUESTION 2-1 FR-00871

Choice "4" is correct.

The question addresses subsequent discovery of facts that may have existed at the balance sheet date that the auditor should have known about during the audit. Discovery of information related to a material *unrecorded* expense that occurred during the year under audit most likely would result in the auditor making further inquiries about the previously issued financial statements.

Choice "1" is incorrect. The issuance of a bond for a material amount is an example of a subsequent event occurring after the date of the auditor's report that the auditor has no obligation to investigate. The issuance of the bond does not provide additional information about the previously issued financial statements, nor did the issuance exist at the date of the audit report.

Choice "2" is incorrect. The loss of a plant is an example of a subsequent event occurring after the date of the auditor's report that the auditor has no obligation to investigate. The loss of the plant does not provide additional information about the previously issued financial statements, nor did the loss of the plant exist at the date of the audit report.

Choice "3" is incorrect. The purchase of a business is an example of a subsequent event occurring after the date of the auditor's report that the auditor has no obligation to investigate. The purchase of the business does not provide additional information about the previously issued financial statements audit. In addition, the purchase of the business occurred after the date of the auditor's report.

Topic A

QUESTION 3-1 FR-00865

Choice "4" is correct.

Determining the type of work to be performed on the components is not required when the group auditor decides to make reference to the component auditor. The group auditor should determine the type of work to be performed on the financial information of the components when assuming responsibility for the work of the component auditor.

Choice "1" is incorrect. The group auditor should be satisfied with the independence of the component auditor even when the group auditor references the component auditor in the report.

Choice "2" is incorrect. One of the requirements to reference the component auditor in the group auditor's report is that the component auditor's report is not restricted.

Choice "3" is incorrect. The group auditor should be satisfied with the competence of the component auditor even when the group auditor references the component auditor in the report.

QUESTION 4-1 FR-00864

Choice "3" is correct.

Financial statements that are prepared in accordance with a special purpose framework require the use of an emphasis-of-matter paragraph in the auditor's report.

Choice "1" is incorrect. An other-matter paragraph is required when there is an alert in the audit report that restricts the use of the audit report.

Choice "2" is incorrect. An other-matter paragraph is required when prior to the audit report date, the auditor identifies a material inconsistency in other information that is included in the document containing audited financial statements that management refuses to revise.

Choice "4" is incorrect. An other-matter paragraph is required when the auditor chooses to report on supplementary information presented with the financial statements in the auditor's report, rather than in a separate report.

QUESTION 6-1 FR-00860

Choice "4" is correct.

Inadequate disclosure of a material item or event results in a qualified or adverse opinion.

Choice "1" is incorrect. Although the general rule in adequately disclosed going concern cases is to add an emphasis-of-matter paragraph to an unmodified opinion, the auditor is not prohibited from choosing to disclaim an opinion due to a going concern uncertainty

Choice "2" is incorrect. Management's refusal to permit inquiry of the attorneys generally will result in a disclaimer of opinion or withdrawal from the audit.

Choice "3" is incorrect. When the auditor is not independent but is required by law or regulation to report on the financial statements, the auditor should disclaim an opinion and should specifically state that the auditor is not independent.

Auditing IV

QUESTION 7-1 FR-00085

Choice "2" is correct.

Randall may revise the prior opinion, but must include an emphasis-of-matter or other-matter paragraph describing the situation and including the date and type of the previous opinion, the reason for the previous opinion, the changes that have occurred, and a statement that the new opinion differs from the old.

Choice "1" is incorrect. Randall may revise the prior opinion if the situation warrants such revision.

Choice "3" is incorrect. Randall may revise the prior opinion if the situation warrants such revision, and is not prohibited from issuing a report on the comparative financial statements.

Choice "4" is incorrect. Randall may revise the prior opinion, but must include an emphasis-of-matter or other-matter paragraph describing the situation and including the date and type of the previous opinion, the reason for the previous opinion, the changes that have occurred, and a statement that the new opinion differs from the old.

Topic B

QUESTION 3-1 FR-00960

Choice "2" is correct.

Entity-level controls are high-level controls that have a pervasive effect on the company's internal control. Entity-level controls include controls related to the period-end financial reporting process, such as management's procedures used to initiate, authorize, and record journal entries into the general ledger.

Choice "1" is incorrect. An entity-level control exists at the client and is independent of the audit. Therefore, the auditor's adherence to a system of quality control would not be considered an entity-level control.

Choice "3" is incorrect. Entity-level controls are high-level controls that have a pervasive effect on the company's internal control. Examples of entity-level controls include controls related to control environment, monitoring the results of operations, centralized processing, period-end financial reporting process and the company's risk assessment process. Preparation of an aging schedule relates to the revenue cycle and is a control at the assertion level.

Choice "4" is incorrect. Entity-level controls are high-level controls that that have a pervasive effect on the company's internal control. Creating a duplicate listing of checks after receipt of a customer check by mail is a control related to the revenue cycle and is a control at the assertion level.

Topic C

QUESTION 1-1 FR-00110

Choice "1" is correct.

The auditor of a nonissuer may be engaged to express an opinion on the design and/or operating effectiveness of the entity's internal control. This is considered an audit engagement. Note that an audit of internal control should be integrated with an audit of the financial statements.

Choice "2" is incorrect. The auditor of a nonissuer may not express an opinion as a result of a financial statement audit, but may report on significant deficiencies or material weaknesses noted during the audit. The report on control deficiencies noted should specifically state that the auditor is not expressing an opinion on the effectiveness of internal control.

Choice "3" is incorrect. A financial statement audit includes consideration of internal control as a basis for designing audit procedures, not as a basis for expressing an opinion. An auditor of a nonissuer may report on significant deficiencies or material weaknesses noted during the audit, but is prohibited from expressing an opinion based solely on the audit.

Choice "4" is incorrect. While an auditor of a nonissuer is required to communicate significant deficiencies or material weaknesses to management and those charged with governance, this type of report does not provide an opinion on the operating effectiveness of the entity's internal control.

QUESTION 2-1 FR-00957

Choice "3" is correct.

A material weakness in internal control, which is a control deficiency, or a combination of control deficiencies in internal control such that there is a reasonable possibility that a material misstatement of the entity's financial statements will not be prevented, or detected and corrected on a timely basis, requires the auditor to issue an adverse opinion.

Choice "1" is incorrect. A material weakness would result in an adverse, not unmodified, opinion.

Choice "2" is incorrect. A material weakness would result in an adverse, not qualified, opinion.

Choice "4" is incorrect. A disclaimer of opinion is rendered when there is a scope limitation.

Auditing IV

Topic D

QUESTION 2-1 FR-00888

Choice "2" is correct.

An engagement for agreed-upon procedures provides no assurance, which means that a disclaimer of opinion is rendered on the subject matter. Specifically, the report should state that "We do not express an opinion," which is a disclaimer of opinion.

Choice "1" is incorrect. The procedures do not need to be comparable to those performed in a compilation. The procedures that the practitioner and specified parties agree upon may be as limited or as extensive as the specified parties desire.

Choice "3" is incorrect. The report includes a listing of procedures performed and the related findings, but does not provide any assurance on these items.

Choice "4" is incorrect. The sufficiency of procedures is solely the responsibility of the specified parties, not the practitioner.

QUESTION 3-1 FR-00038

Choice "4" is correct.

Financial forecasts are considered prospective financial statements, and they are appropriate for general use.

Choice "1" is incorrect because financial projections are only appropriate for the party responsible for preparing them or for third parties with whom the responsible party is negotiating directly.

Choices "2" and "3" are incorrect because partial presentations and pro forma financial statements are not considered prospective financial statements.

Topic E

QUESTION 1-1 FR-00008

Choice "3" is correct.

Statements on Standards for Accounting and Review Services do not apply to preparing a working trial balance or to preparing standard monthly journal entries. Accordingly, no compilation or review report needs to be issued when these services are provided.

Choices "1", "2", and "4" are incorrect, based on the above explanation.

QUESTION 1-2 FR-00095

Choice "1" is correct.

Before issuing a compilation report, an accountant should read the compiled financial statements and consider whether they are appropriate in form and free from obvious material errors.

Choice "2" is incorrect. Inquiry and analytical review procedures are performed as part of a review engagement, not as part of a compilation engagement.

Choice "3" is incorrect. A representation letter is obtained in audit and review engagements, but is not required for compilation engagements.

Choice "4" is incorrect. Accounts receivable confirmations would be sent during an audit, but not during a compilation engagement.

QUESTION 1-3 FR-00885

Choice "3" is correct.

A change in client requirements represents an acceptable reason for a change in engagement.

Choice "1" is incorrect. Generally, refusal to provide a signed representation letter is considered an unacceptable reason for the change. In addition, the auditor would not be able to issue a review report without a representation letter.

Choice "2" is incorrect. The client's refusal to allow correspondence with legal counsel is not an acceptable reason for the change.

Choice "4" is incorrect. The client's attempt to create deceptive financial statements is not an acceptable reason for the change.

QUESTION 1-4 FR-00884

Choice "2" is correct.

The predecessor accountant is not required to obtain a letter of representation from management before reissuing a compilation report. This procedure is required when an audit, not compilation, report is reissued.

Choice "1" is incorrect. The predecessor accountant is required to read the financial statements and the report of the current period before reissuing a compilation report.

Choice "3" is incorrect. The predecessor accountant is required to compare the prior period financial statements with those issued previously and currently before reissuing a compilation report.

Choice "4" is incorrect. The predecessor accountant is required to obtain a letter from the successor accountants before reissuing a compilation report.

Auditing IV

QUESTION 3-1 FR-00886

Choice "3" is correct.

When issuing letters for underwriters, an accountant typically provides positive assurance concerning the compliance of the audited financial statements with the requirements of the SEC Act.

Choice "1" is incorrect. The auditor may provide negative, not positive assurance, for financial statements that have been reviewed.

Choice "2" is incorrect. In a comfort letter, no comment should be made regarding the compliance of MD&A with SEC rules and regulations.

Choice "4" is incorrect. The auditor should not comment or provide any assurance on qualitative disclosures and market-sensitive instruments in a comfort letter.

Topic F

QUESTION 1-1 FR-00048

Choice "3" is correct.

A review report states that a review includes primarily applying analytical procedures to management's financial data and making inquiries of company management.

Choice "1" is incorrect because the review report does not state that limited assurance is provided. The report simply states that the accountant is not aware of any material modifications that should be made to the financial statement.

Choice "2" is incorrect because an audit report, not a review report, refers to "examining on a test basis." A compilation report, not a review report, refers to "information that is the representation of management."

Choice "4" is incorrect because although a review does not contemplate obtaining corroborating evidential matter or applying certain other procedures ordinarily performed during an audit, this is not stated in the report. The review report simply states that a review is substantially less in scope than an audit.

Topic G

QUESTION 1-1 FR-00870

Choice "4" is correct.

The auditor should read the letter to the shareholders (considered other information) and verify the information is materially consistent with the information presented in the audited financial statements.

Choice "1" is incorrect. The audited financial statements may be contained in a document that contains additional financial information that is outside the audited financial statements. In addition, the auditor's opinion is on the basic financial statements, not the entire document that the financial statements may accompany.

Choice "2" is incorrect. The auditor is not required to reference the other information in the audit report. However, the auditor *may* choose to include an other-matter paragraph disclaiming an opinion on the other information.

Choice "3" is incorrect. The auditor should inquire of management regarding the purpose of the supplementary information and the criteria used to prepare the information when engaged to report on the supplementary information. The auditor is not engaged to examine this information, so the auditor is not required to perform those inquiries.

Auditing IV

QUESTION 3-1 FR-00088

Choice "4" is correct.

With respect to the supplementary information, Jorge should perform limited procedures in order to determine whether required supplementary information is included and is presented in conformity with GAAP requirements.

Choice "1" is incorrect. Jorge may accept this engagement, but must perform limited procedures in order to determine whether required supplementary information is included and is presented in conformity with GAAP requirements.

Choice "2" is incorrect. Jorge must perform limited procedures in order to determine whether required supplementary information is included and is presented in conformity with GAAP requirements.

Choice "3" is incorrect. Jorge may accept this engagement and should perform limited procedures with respect to the required supplementary information. There is no requirement that an attest engagement be performed.

QUESTION 5-1 FR-00097

Choice "3" is correct.

The appropriate form of audit report is dependent upon the expected distribution of the financial statements. If distribution is to occur outside the United States only, the auditor may use either the other country's audit report, the report set out in the ISAs, or a U.S. form with reference to the other country's standards. If there is to be distribution within the U.S., a U.S. form report with an emphasis-of-matter paragraph is required.

Choice "1" is incorrect. The other country's auditing standards do not determine the appropriate form of audit report for financial statements prepared in accordance with a financial reporting framework generally accepted in another country.

Choice "2" is incorrect. The geographic location of the company does not determine the appropriate form of audit report for financial statements prepared in accordance with a financial reporting framework generally accepted in another country.

Choice "4" is incorrect. Countries generally do not have reciprocity agreements with respect to the appropriate form of audit report.

Topic H

QUESTION 3-1 FR-00059

Choice "2" is correct.

Audits performed in accordance with government auditing standards require a written communication regarding the auditor's work on internal control. Generally accepted auditing standards only require written communication about internal control when significant deficiencies are noted.

Choice "1" is incorrect. Both GAAS and GAGAS require an opinion on the financial statements taken as a whole.

Choice "3" is incorrect. Neither GAAS nor GAGAS audits require an opinion on internal control over financial reporting.

Choice "4" is incorrect. An opinion on the financial statements taken as a whole *is* required by both GAAS and GAGAS.

Auditing IV

QUESTION 4-1 FR-00069

Choice "4" is correct.

The provisions of the Single Audit Act apply to entities that receive and expend federal financial awards equal to or in excess of $750,000.

Choice "1" is incorrect. Pure receipt of federal financial assistance does not mandate application of the provisions of the Single Audit Act to an entity's financial statements. Federal financial assistance must be expended by an entity in an amount equal to or in excess of $750,000 to result in an audit subject to 2 CFR 200 single audit requirements.

Choice "2" is incorrect. Pure receipt of federal financial assistance does not mandate application of the provisions of the Single Audit Act to an entity's financial statements. Federal financial assistance must be expended by an entity in an amount equal to or in excess of $750,000 to result in an audit subject to 2 CFR 200 single audit requirements.

Choice "3" is incorrect. The provisions of the Single Audit Act apply to entities that receive and expend federal financial awards equal to or in excess of $750,000.

QUESTION 5-1 FR-00009

Choice "2" is correct.

The requirement is to determine the proper scope of a government audit. The Government Accountability Office's Yellow Book suggests that in addition to financial statements, such an audit may include consideration of (1) program results; (2) compliance with laws and regulations; and (3) economy and efficiency.

Choice "1" is incorrect because government audits may involve expression of an opinion on economy and efficiency.

Choice "3" is incorrect because government audits may involve expression of an opinion on program results.

Choice "4" is incorrect because government audits may involve expression of an opinion on compliance.

Topic I

QUESTION 1-1 FR-00875

Choice "2" is correct.

An auditor's report should include a restricted use paragraph and an alert to readers about the preparation of the financial statements in accordance with a special purpose framework when the financial statements are prepared on the contractual basis of accounting.

Choice "1" is incorrect. An auditor's report should include an alert to readers about the preparation of the financial statements in accordance with a special purpose framework when the financial statements are prepared on the cash basis of accounting. There is no requirement that the auditor's report must be restricted for this type of framework.

Choice "3" is incorrect. Financial statements prepared using IFRS do not require a restricted use paragraph in the auditor's report. In addition, IFRS is not considered a special purpose framework.

Choice "4" is incorrect. An auditor's report should include an alert to readers about the preparation of the financial statements in accordance with a special purpose framework when the financial statements are prepared on the tax basis of accounting. There is no requirement that the auditor's report must be restricted for this type of framework.

QUESTION 2-1 FR-00881

Choice "2" is correct.

The auditor modified the opinion on the complete financial statements due to a material misstatement of inventory and cost of goods sold. Because the modification is relevant to the audit opinion on inventory, the auditor should express an adverse opinion on inventory.

Choice "1" is incorrect. Qualified opinions are not permitted on an audit of a specific element when the modification of the opinion on the complete financial statements was due to the specific element.

Choice "3" is incorrect. The auditor would render a disclaimer of opinion on inventory if the opinion on the complete financial statements were modified due to a scope limitation related to inventory.

Choice "4" is incorrect. The auditor may not issue an unmodified opinion on inventory because the auditor modified the opinion on the complete financial statements due to a material misstatement of inventory. Because the modification is relevant to the audit opinion on inventory, the auditor should express an adverse opinion on inventory.

QUESTION 2-2 FR-00028

Choice "3" is correct.

The report on a specific element of a financial statement follows the standard auditor's report very closely, referring to GAAS in the auditor's responsibility paragraph and GAAP in the opinion paragraph.

Choice "1" is incorrect because an audit of the complete financial statements is not required, although the audit of a specific element of the financial statements may be done in conjunction with an audit of the complete set of financial statements.

Choice "2" is incorrect because an unmodified opinion on a specific element may be expressed as long as 1) the opinion on the specific element is not published with and does not accompany the auditor's report on the complete set of financial statements and 2) the element does not encompass a major portion of the financial statements and is not, or is not based on, stockholder's equity or net income. Note that if the modified opinion on the complete set of financial statements is relevant to the audit of the specific element of the financial statements, then the auditor should:

- Express an adverse opinion on the specific element when an adverse opinion is expressed on the complete set of financial statements
- Express a disclaimer of opinion on the specific element when a disclaimer of opinion is expressed on the complete set of financial statements

Choice "4" is incorrect because a restrictive use paragraph is only required if the element was prepared to comply with a contract or agreement rather than in accordance with GAAP.

Auditing IV

QUESTION 3-1 FR-00878

Choice "2" is correct.

A report on a client's compliance with a contractual agreement, assuming the report is prepared in connection with a financial statement audit of the complete financial statements should include a restriction as to the use of the report.

Choice "1" is incorrect. A report on financial statements prepared on the tax basis of accounting does not require a restriction as to the use of the report.

Choice "3" is incorrect. Reports on a single financial statement do not require restriction as to the use of the report.

Choice "4" is incorrect. A report on the examination of a financial forecast does not require a restriction on the use of the report.